THEMES FOR INFANT ASSEMBLY

Lynne Burgess

and a whole lot more...

Hodder & Stoughton

LONDON SYDNEY AUCKLAND TORONTO

British Library Cataloguing in Publication Data
Burgess, Lynne
  Themes for infant assembly : and a whole lot more.
  1. Great Britain. Schools. Morning assembly
  I. Title
  377.14

ISBN 0–340–53185–1

First published 1991

Typeset by Wearside Tradespools, Fulwell, Sunderland.
Printed in Great Britain for the educational publishing division of Hodder
and Stoughton Ltd, Mill Road, Dunton Green, Sevenoaks, Kent by
St Edmundsbury Press.

CONTENTS

Acknowledgments

The author would like to express her thanks to the pupils at the following schools for the realia which appears in the book: Burwash C.E. Primary School, Maynards Green Primary School and Punnetts Town County Primary School.

The author and publishers would like to thank the following for permission to reproduce material in this book:

A & C Black for the song *Think of a world without any flowers* by Doreen Newport from *Someone's Singing Lord* and the poem 'I'm a parrot' by Grace Nichols from *Come on into my Tropical Garden*; The BBC for the poem 'Sharing' by Elizabeth Lindsay from *Something to Think About*; Oxford University Press for the poems 'The dustbin men' by Gregory Harrison from *A First Poetry Book*, 'Don't spray the fly, dad' by John Kitching from *A Second Poetry Book*, 'Under the stairs' by Daphne Lister from *A Very First Poetry Book* and for the story *The Lazy Bear* by Brian Wildsmith; Mammoth for the poem 'Plants in the classroom' by Irene Rownsley from *Ask a Silly Question*; Young Puffin for the poems 'Never a dull moment', 'Special things', 'Everything will be all right', 'My mum's a dinner lady' and 'Helper', all by Tony Bradman from *Smile Please* and for the poem 'Be nice to a new baby' by Fay Maschler from *The Mad Family*, the extract from the story *The owl who was afraid of the dark* by J. Tomlinson, and for the story *Anyone can make mistakes* by Margaret Joy from *Allotment Lane School Again*; Blackie for the poems 'The flowers in town', 'Ladybirds' and 'In the garden in winter' by Stanley Cook from *The Squirrel in Town*; Scholfield and Sims for the poems 'The pines' by Margaret Mahy from *Poetry Plus – Green Earth and Silver Stars*,

'Hedgehog' by Jean Kenward from *Poetry Plus – Creatures Real and Make Believe*, 'Houses' by Rachel Field and 'Demolition of a crescent' by Marian Lines both from *Poetry Plus – The World We Have Made*; Louis Miller for the story *The little fir tree* adapted by Moira Miller for *Playtime*, BBC Schools Radio; Beaver Books for the poems 'Caterpillar' by D. Evans from *Fingers, Feet and Fun*, 'I'm alone in the evening' by Michael Rosen from *Rhyme Time*, and 'The Policeman' by Christopher Rowe from *Over and Over Again*; Tressell Publications for the poems 'Inside my cage' from *Pets Project Pack* and 'The fireman' from *Fire and Heat Project* both by Lynne Burgess; BBC Radio for the poem 'The chain' by Elizabeth Lindsay from *Something to Think About*; Heinemann for the untitled poem by Tony Bradman from *A Kiss on the Nose*; Ward Lock Educational for the songs 'When I am happy' and 'People we see' both from *Sing as You Grow*; Andre Deutsch for the poem 'Deep down' by Michael Rosen from *The Hypnotiser*; Magnet for the extract from the story *Play with me?* by Angela Pickering from *Story Time*; Scripture Union for the poem 'What are friends like?' from *Sing, Say and Move*; Bodley Head for the poems 'Lollipoplady' from *I Din Do Nuttin*, 'One finger can't catch flea' and 'If you don't have horse, then ride cow' both from *Say it Again Granny*, and all by John Agard; Macmillan for allowing the author to adapt a story taken from *Anasai and the Spiderman*; and Picture Puffin for the untitled poem by Fay Maschler from *A Child's Book of Manners*.

INTRODUCTION

This book is primarily aimed at teachers of infant children although much of the contents could also prove useful to junior teachers. It contains a wide range of assembly material which is divided into two parts; Part 1 – Living with the Earth and Part 2 – Living with People. The aims of each half of the book are as follows:

Part 1   Living with the Earth aims to:

- Encourage curiosity, care and concern about the environment

- Foster a sense of wonder of the natural world

- Develop an appreciation of the interdependence between man and the environment

- Show the pupils what contribution they can make to their own environment.

Part 2   Living with People aims to:

- Examine pupils' thoughts and feelings and thereby further their understanding of their own emotions

- Develop pupils' self esteem, drawing attention to their individual value as a member of a home, school and community

- Explore pupils' relationships with others and encourage empathy with them

- Show pupils ways of improving their relationships with others.

These two areas have been selected because they help to build the essential foundations needed to deal with the complex and profound issues contained in many religions. In the majority of the agreed syllabuses adopted by LEAs, the themes of nature, self and relationships with others feature prominently as acceptable areas for exploration by young children, and the Education Reform Act 1988 does nothing to refute their validity. Both areas are also of concern to all pupils, irrespective of age, gender, culture or faith. They apply equally to children living in inner cities and rural areas. Therefore, it is expected that all teachers will find material in this book which they will be able to use with their pupils.

Obviously, as no two schools are identical, the content and presentation of assemblies will be equally diverse. This is surely a positive indication that teachers are attempting to provide for the individual needs of their pupils. This need to ensure that assembly material is educationally appropriate is emphasised by the Education Reform Act 1988 which stresses the importance of considering the age, aptitude and family background of the children. Consequently, it is hoped that teachers will approach this book with a flexible attitude, modifying and expanding the material to suit their pupils' circumstances.

Some items have been included for the busy teacher to use with little preparation whilst other activities demand much greater preparation. This reflects the common practice in many schools of sometimes having assemblies presented solely by the teacher, whilst on other occasions the pupils may make a contribution or even lead the entire assembly. Teachers will no doubt find that a great deal of suitable assembly material arises naturally from the work which pupils are already engaged upon in the classroom.

There is a strong emphasis on pupil involvement in many of the suggestions because most infant teachers acknowledge that children learn most effectively by 'doing'. If pupils are responsible for presenting part of the assembly and if audience participation is actively encouraged, the assembly will be more enjoyable, interesting and thought provoking.

Teachers will also need to be conscious of their own role when presenting an assembly. Occasionally, it will be necessary to discuss or explain the content of a story, poem, dance, piece of music etc. but on other occasions a more open approach may be required with the teacher raising questions and encouraging pupils to develop interpretative skills and to respond at their own level. There will also be instances where it is most effective to allow the story, poem, etc. to stand alone without any follow-up discussion. Although indications are given for follow-up discussions/questions for many of the activities, only the teacher can decide whether this is appropriate. Teachers tread a delicate balance between directing pupils' thinking and over-talking/over-moralising.

The Education Reform Act 1988 stipulates that all pupils shall 'on each school day take part in an act of collective worship'. This is a phrase which is fraught with difficulties as there is no one clear definition of what constitutes an 'act of worship'. Some may feel it can only be achieved by mentioning God in a hymn or prayer, some may require no explicit religious words (e.g. Buddhists and Quakers), whilst others may prefer a time of quiet for reflection. If a school recognises that the majority of its' pupils do not belong to a faith community, their definition of 'worship' may well be to focus on things of worth or value i.e. exploring shared values, raising ethical questions, reflecting on spiritual values, etc. As there will obviously be many interpretations of this phrase, it would be impossible, and rather presumptuous, to prescribe more explicit aspects of 'worship' in this book. Such a delicate question is best decided by individual schools. However, in whatever context teachers will still be able to use the ideas and activities in this book as a basis for an assembly.

Another specification of the Education Reform Act 1988 is that the collective worship in a school 'shall be wholly or mainly of a broadly Christian character'. The word 'mainly' appears to imply that only three out of five assemblies have to be 'of a broadly Christian character' thus leaving two days where schools may choose to explore multi-faith or more secular themes. The Act also says that the collective worship must 'reflect the broad traditions of Christian belief without being distinctive of any particular Christian denomination'. Once again, this appears to infer that each assembly does not necessarily have to consist entirely of 'Christian' material but could, in fact, include a wide range of material. It can be argued that the majority of the themes explored in this book 'reflect the broad traditions of Christian belief' because they deal with issues which are not only central to Christianity i.e. encouraging a responsible attitude towards the Earth and concern for our fellow person, but are equally relevant to many other faiths.

As with many subjects, religious education is naturally cross-curricula in nature and especially so with young children. Studying the life-cycle of a butterfly may be fulfilling Attainment Target 3 (Processes of life) of the Science National Curriculum, but it can also be used to help develop a spiritual appreciation of nature. Similarly, sharing a box of bricks equally can be viewed as a mathematical skill (AT3) or as fostering a sense of fairness and concern for the rights of others. Other creative areas of the curriculum such as poetry, dance, music and art can also promote an atmosphere which encourages a spiritual or emotional response.

Brief details are outlined below to show which of the Attainment Targets contained in the National Curriculum documents for Science, English and Mathematics can be explored through the activities suggested in this book.

Science Attainment Targets

1 Exploration of science

2 The variety of life

3 Processes of life

4 Genetics and evolution

5 Human influences on the earth

6 Types and uses of materials

14 Sound and music

English Attainment Targets

1 Speaking and listening

2 Reading

3 Writing

5 Handwriting

Mathematics Attainment Targets

1 Using and applying mathematics

2 Number

3 Number

5 Number/Algebra

7 Algebra

8 Measures

10 Shape and space

11 Shape and space

12 Handling data

13 Handling data

Young children are undeniably egocentric and view the world from the standpoint of 'me'. Assembly should be a special time of the day, a pause for thought, a time when everyone is encouraged to look outside themselves and consider life reflectively. It is hoped that by exploring the themes suggested in Part 1, pupils will begin to appreciate not only their own interaction with the environment but also move towards an understanding of the environment in which others live. By examining their own emotions and relationships with others via the themes in Part 2, it may be possible to heighten their awareness of not only the people immediately surrounding them but also of people worldwide. Surely, the foundations for any religious education must include care and concern for our planet and our fellow mankind?

STRUCTURE OF THE BOOK

The book is divided into two sections; Part 1 is called Living with the Earth and Part 2 is called Living with People. Each part deals with 15 themes, all of which follow a similar structure.

Starting Point

For each theme, one starting point is offered as a means of securing the audience's attention. However, this is a suggestion only and teachers may wish to use other equally acceptable starting points; an activity from the Core activities section, a poem, song, story, or an idea of their own.

Core Activities

The activities outlined in this section will form the main part of the assembly. Although several activities are provided, it is not intended that they would all be used in one assembly. Depending upon the time available, teachers may wish to select one or two of the activities. Symbols are used to guide the teacher as to the amount of preparation required before the assembly.

◎ indicates that the activity could be undertaken by the teacher alone

▣ denotes an activity which involves the pupils and thus requires preparation in the classroom beforehand.

As the activities suggested also cover a wide range of ability, teachers will need to choose those best suited to their pupils.

Alternative Activities

This section contains a similar range of activities which could be chosen instead of those listed in the Core Activities. Once again, teachers would probably not wish to use all the suggestions in one assembly but rather select one or two appropriate to their pupils. Likewise, the same symbols are used to indicate whether the teacher presents the activity alone or with the assistance of pupils prepared beforehand.

Conclusion—What Can We Do?

A brief summary is given of the positive contribution which we can all make in relation to each theme. Again, it is not proposed that all the points will be relevant to all assemblies. Teachers will obviously choose those which best sum up the content of their assembly or add their own conclusions.

Poems

The poems included have been selected to reflect a wide variety of style and level of difficulty. Some poems, especially when used with the youngest pupils, may well require further explanation and discussion. On other occasions, a poem could be offered purely as something to reflect upon without further discussion or comment. Hopefully, teachers will find the poems explore one particular aspect of a theme in a thought provoking way and can be used to initiate or conclude a discussion.

Additional Information

The content of this section varies for each theme. It may include an extract or a complete story which relates to the theme. Alternatively, it may incorporate further material which expands on one of the activities such as factual information, examples of plays, movement suggestions, etc. Both plays and movement ideas are included to act as catalysts for teachers' own ideas and are not intended to be prescriptive. It is hoped that teachers will extract one or two ideas from these examples and develop them with their pupils, encouraging their contributions so that the end product relates specifically to them.

Resources

The list of resources at the end of each theme includes poems, songs and stories. These can all be used to supplement the other material contained in the theme. Many of the resources could be used before, during or after the assembly, in that some may be suitable for introducing the theme during classwork, used during the assembly or to initiate follow-up work. Again, the poems, songs and stories range from simple to more demanding and the teacher will have to assess whether they match the needs of her/his pupils.

CONSERVATION

AIM

*To introduce the idea of conservation in general terms.
To convey a sense of wonder at the beauty of the natural
world and the need to look after it.*

STARTING POINT

◎ Sing a song with a 'conservation' theme e.g. *Think of a
world without any flowers.* (See page 10 for details.)

Discuss Introduce the word 'conservation' and help
the audience define it e.g. protecting things from damage
or change. In what context do we use the word? E.g. it
can be applied to land, buildings, animals, plants, air, soil,
water etc. Can the children name any plants, animals etc.
which need conserving and say why they are under
threat?

CORE ACTIVITIES

◎ Ask the audience to help make an acrostic
'poem' for the word conservation. (See page 9 for
details.) Display the finished version of the poem in
a prominent place within the school once the
assembly has finished. Challenge the children to add
their own versions to the display.

◎ Devise an activity to show whether we take our
surroundings for granted and no longer bother to
look properly. For example, ask volunteers from
the audience to describe an oak leaf or a daisy in
detail. Then show them a picture (or the real thing)
and compare their description to see how
observant they are.

◎ Arrange for a representative from a local (or
national) conservation organisation to give a talk
during the assembly. Alternatively, find out if it is
possible to borrow a film/video which explains
some of the work undertaken by one of the
organisations.

◎ Play a game to develop the children's awareness
of the diversity of life on Earth. Make a large spinner
divided into six segments each coloured with a
different colour. Each of the six colours could
represent one category of life e.g.

red	animals	green	trees
blue	insects	white	plants
yellow	birds	black	fish

The above colour key would need to be displayed
for the children to read. Ask members of the
audience to take turns to spin the spinner and name
a member belonging to that set. For example, if the
spinner stops on yellow and yellow represents
birds, the child might suggest a robin, sparrow, owl
or woodpecker. Alternatively, children could be
asked to select one picture from a collection of
different pictures which depict a creature, plant,
etc. belonging to the correct category.

CONCLUSION—WHAT CAN WE DO?

• Be eager to find out more about 'conservation'.
Watch television programmes and read books which
deal with the subject. Write to national organisations
for leaflets and information. Some of them have special
groups which children can join.

• Find out about local conservation groups. What are
they trying to achieve? Can children join or help in any
way?

• Help look after the local environment even if only in a
small way e.g. by picking up litter, feeding birds,
planting trees and wild flowers etc.

• Avoid wasting the resources we have: save energy by
closing doors, turning off lights; recycle as much as
possible by reusing envelopes etc.; reduce the waste of
paper; limit the use of disposable items such as paper
plates.

• Use all of our senses more often so as to be more
aware of the beauty of the natural world.

Conservation

C aring for the world means
O tters tumbling in untainted rivers
N esting birds left undisturbed
S aving the whale, badger and frog
E lephants with their tusks unharmed
R hinos running for joy not fear
V iolets carpeting the woodland floor
A nimals never becoming extinct
T adpoles wriggling in pond water pure
I nsects humming, untouched by sprays
O ak trees thriving for hundreds of years
N o sadness for man's time on the Earth.

ALTERNATIVE ACTIVITIES

◎ Organise a fund-raising event for a charity concerned with conservation such as the World Wide Fund for Nature or the Royal Society for the Protection of Birds.

◎ Design a treasure hunt in the assembly hall. Ask the audience what sort of treasure they would normally hope to find on a treasure hunt e.g. gold and diamonds. Explain that this treasure hunt is to find something equally important to all of us—the various forms of life on Earth. Ask several volunteers from the audience to look carefully round the room for pictures or objects which have been hidden. If some children in the audience have noticed where these pictures are, perhaps they could offer clues to help those searching.

Once all the pictures have been found and identified, ask the audience to allocate each picture to an appropriate label. These labels might include

trees, plants, insects, reptiles, birds, fish or people. How many pictures were found for each category? Point out the diversity for each category. For example, in the animal category have pictures of mice, elephants, dogs and hedgehogs to illustrate just how different animals can be. Which creatures can be seen in this country?

Help the children to appreciate that all these 'treasures' add richness to our lives and should be guarded vigilantly because, in each category, there are many species under threat.

◎ Demonstrate the delicate balance of nature using a bucket balance or scales. Label six bricks (of equal weight) to represent air, water, soil, plants, animals and trees. Show the bricks to the audience and explain what they represent. Put the bricks labelled air, water and soil into one bucket and those labelled plants, animals and trees into the other. Hopefully, these should balance to illustrate nature 'in harmony'.

Show the audience that if we take out a brick from either side, we affect the balance of nature. For example, if the brick labelled 'trees' is taken out to represent deforestation, the balance is upset. Likewise, if a brick is taken out to represent the reduction of water e.g. draining marshes, the balance is also disturbed. Similarly, if an extra brick, labelled pollution, is added to either side, the balance is once again altered.

▣ Compose a class poem which could be read and illustrated by some children. Use the phrase 'Conservation is . . .' as a starter for the poem. Encourage the children to consider all areas of conservation, including buildings, air, water and noise as well as the more familiar areas such as animals, plants and trees.

▣ Ask a group of children to prepare a nature trail round the school (or neighbourhood) focusing on natural features which may be constantly overlooked. Design a map of the trail and ask a child(ren) to talk through the route pointing out the interesting features. For example, these could include daisies in the grass, various seed heads on long grass, birds singing on telegraph wires, the brilliant colours of leaves on a shrub etc. Encourage the audience to use their play/dinner time to follow the trail and perhaps report back in another assembly. Provide hand lenses/binoculars for children wishing to follow the trail.

■ Arrange for a small group of children to draw pictures of a house, animals, birds, trees, water, flowers, etc. which can be fixed with Blu-tack to a large sheet of grey paper. Ask each child to remove her/his picture giving reasons for the items' disappearance. For example, people chopped down the trees for firewood, people put rubbish in the water, etc. Discuss how the picture has changed. Has it improved or deteriorated? Do the audience realise that people are often the cause of detrimental changes to the environment?

■ Invite a small group of children to design posters to inform people about the various threats to our world. Display these and discuss them with the audience. What particular threat does each one deal with? Which poster has the most impact and why? Look at posters designed by conservation organisations. (These are available from some of the organisations whose addresses are listed on page 12.) What messages are they trying to convey and how successful are they?

■ Some people regard Noah as the first 'conservationist'. Read or tell the story of Noah's Ark. Although there are many versions of this story, the one by Sophie Windham (see page 12 for details) contains some splendid illustrations and concludes with some particularly appropriate thoughts:

I did not realise how beautiful the flowers are—even the smallest of them—until they disappeared,' said Noah. 'The world is a beautiful place,' said Mrs. Noah, 'and the animals and plants make it so. We must never risk losing it again.'

If possible, ask a group of children to prepare a long frieze showing the animals queuing in pairs to enter the ark. Gradually unroll the frieze to reveal each pair of animals and ask the audience to identify them. Are there any modern Noahs? E.g. people, such as David Bellamy and Gerald Durrell, who are particularly concerned with protecting the environment.

Glossary

biodegradable   Something which breaks down/rots naturally e.g. leaves.

conservation   Protecting areas of land/buildings/animals/plants/air/water etc. from harm or adverse changes.

ecosystem   The plants, animals and physical environment of a particular area.

endangered species   Animals and plants which could become extinct as there are now so few left.

environment   The surroundings of a plant or animal.

extinct   A plant or animal which has died out completely.

food chain   The way in which each of a series of organisms is the food for the next.

pollution   When water, air, etc. is made impure by harmful/poisonous substances.

Think of a world without any flowers

Words by Doreen Newport; music by G. C. Westcott (the full text of this hymn may be found in *New Songs for the Church*), from *Someone's Singing, Lord*, A & C Black.

1   Think of a world without any flowers,
Think of a world without any trees,
Think of a sky without any sunshine,
Think of the air without any breeze.
We thank you, Lord,
    for flowers and trees and sunshine,
We thank you, Lord,
    and praise your holy name.

2.   Think of the world without any animals,
Think of a field without any herd,
Think of a stream without any fishes,
Think of a dawn without any bird.
We thank you, Lord,
    for all your living creatures,
We thank you, Lord,
    and praise your holy name.

3   Think of a world without any people,
Think of a street with no-one living there,
Think of a town without any houses,
No-one to love and nobody to care.
We thank you, Lord,
    for families and friendships,
We thank you, Lord,
    and praise your holy name.

Sharing

by Elizabeth Lindsay from *Something to Think About*, BBC Summer 1982

I am walking on the ground
My head turns to look around
The leaves are green
The trees grow tall
Which makes me seem
So very small.

I am looking at the soil
The ants are running at their toil
They march in line
To the hole they dig
Which makes me seem so very big.

I am looking at a mole
Who's poked his nose from out his hole
He blinks his eyes
The light is bright
Then turns and scurries
Out of sight.

I am looking at a fish
I'm keeping still to watch him swish
Swish your tail
Please let me see
But I'm so still
You can't see me.

I am looking at a bird
His jolly song is what I heard
Stand little bird
On the apple tree bough
Your song is long
And joyously loud.

I am sitting to think of me
And when I grow up of what I will be
I won't forget
All the creatures I see
I'll remember the earth
Is not just for me.

Can the audience name the various forms of life which the poet refers to in this poem? What does she/he notice particularly about each one? How do people hurt the Earth and the creatures who live on it? What should we do to make sure the Earth is fit for all forms of life and not just humans?

USEFUL ADDRESSES

Conservation Trust
George Palmer Site
Northumberland Avenue
READING RG2 7PW

Council for Environmental
   Education
School of Education
University of Reading
London Road
READING RG1 5AQ

Nature Conservancy
   Council
Northminster House
PETERBOROUGH
   PE1 1UA

Department of the
   Environment
2 Marsham Street
LONDON SW1P 3EB

Friends of the Earth
26–28 Underwood Street
LONDON N1 7JQ

Greenpeace
30–31 Islington Green
LONDON N1 8XE

Royal Society for the
   Protection of Birds
The Lodge
Sandy
BEDFORDSHIRE
   SG19 2DL

World Wide Fund for
   Nature
Panda House
Weyside Park
Catteshall Lane
Godalming
SURREY GU7 1WR

RESOURCES

Poems

Sharing Something to Think About (BBC)
Hurt No Living Thing Young Puffin Book of Verse (Young Puffin)
Wasteland Poetry Plus—The World We Have Made (Schofield and Sims)
New Road Corn growing (Hodder and Stoughton)

Songs

Stand up Clap Hands Someone's Singing, Lord (A and C Black)
Over the Earth is a Mat of Green Someone's Singing, Lord (A and C Black)
This is a Lovely World Someone's Singing, Lord (A and C Black)
The World is such a Lovely Place Every Colour Under the Sun (Ward Lock Educational)
Use your Eyes Every Colour Under the Sun (Ward Lock Educational)
Pollution Calypso Every Colour Under the Sun (Ward Lock Educational)
Pollution The Jolly Herring (A and C Black)
Air The Jolly Herring (A and C Black)
The Wildlife King Trig Trog (OUP)

Stories

Noah's Ark S. Windham (Macmillan)
Our Planet M. B. Goffstein (Canongate)
Oi! Get off our Train J. Burningham (Cape)
Giant J. and C. Snape (Julia MacRae)
The Goose that Laid the Golden Eggs (in Fables of Aesop*)* V. Biro (Ginn)
Michael Bird-Boy T. de Paola (Collins)
Green is Beautiful M. Rogers (Andersen)

THE COUNTRYSIDE CODE

AIM

To introduce the children to the Countryside Code.
To make them aware that it is important to have rules in certain circumstances.

STARTING POINT

◎ Show some slides which portray the beauty of the countryside. Discuss each slide with the audience. What do they find particularly attractive in each scene?

Discuss What would the audience expect to see if they went for a trip to the nearby countryside? What would they do there? E.g. walk, have a picnic, go riding, etc. If they live in the town or city, where is their nearest countryside and what is it like? How often do they visit the countryside and do they prefer it to the town? What facilities do you find in a town but not necessarily in the countryside?

CORE ACTIVITIES

◎ Ask the audience if they can name any of the important points which make up the Countryside Code. Can they specify the reason behind each 'rule'? It might be useful to have each rule written on a separate piece of paper which could then be stuck onto a board as individual rules were suggested by the audience.

◎ Discuss whether there should be codes for other public places. What about the park, the school playground, the seaside? Can the children suggest rules to include in such codes. How would the children suggest the general public could be informed about such 'codes'?

The Countryside Code

Fasten all gates.
Take litter home.
Keep dogs under close control.
Keep to public footpaths across farmland.
Guard against fire.
Leave livestock/crops/machinery alone.
Make no unnecessary noise.
Keep water clean and free from dangers e.g. glass.
Use gates/stiles to cross hedges/fences/walls.
Take care when driving on country roads.

◎ Invite the audience to make suggestions for a Town Code. What 'rules' would they include and why? They might like to consider whether the following should be included in the Code.

- No graffiti.
- No skateboarding on busy pavements.
- Hold doors open for people entering or leaving shops.
- Avoid bumping into people on crowded pavements.
- Queue at bus stops etc. in an orderly manner.

◎ Reinforce the importance of observing the Countryside Code by asking the audience to participate in a missing word/phrases exercise. The teacher could read a short passage in which some of the words or phrases have been omitted. When the teacher reaches such a place in the passage, the audience could be given two alternatives (written on separate cards) to choose between in order to complete the sentence so as to follow the Countryside Code. The following passage is an example which teachers will, no doubt, wish to adapt to suit their own pupils.

Jane had finished her picnic in the field so she gathered up the empty juice carton, the biscuit wrappers and her sandwich box and put them all in a . . . . . . ditch/bag. She picked up the bag and set off back across the field, calling to her dog, Sam. He was a disobedient dog and ignored her calls because he was enjoying himself, chasing the sheep in the next field. Jane whistled and he reluctantly came back so she . . . . . . put him on a lead/let him run ahead. They headed towards the gate, ... walking through the corn/keeping to the footpath. Near the gate a large blue tractor was parked. Jane had always wanted to ride in the cab of a tractor and the door wasn't locked. She hesitated and then . . . . . . climbed into the cab/ decided it might be dangerous. She continued walking until she reached the gate. Sam slipped underneath and waited whilst Jane opened the heavy wooden gate. Before she walked home along the road, she remembered the open gate and . . . . . . closed it/ignored it.

▣ Help a small group of children to write and act out a short play which illustrates the importance of a 'sensitive' approach to the countryside. An example is included (see page 16 for details) but teachers would obviously wish to devise situations appropriate to their particular pupils. After the play has been performed, discuss the message which it contains with the audience.

▣ Play a cumulative memory game with members of the audience. 'I went to the countryside and I saw . . .' Each child repeats the list of previous items and adds another. The list could include good things e.g. beautiful flowers, interesting animals, etc. and bad things e.g. broken bottles, open gates, children playing on machinery etc. Suggest each child who is adding to the list, stands in a line in front of the

Walking along a footpath

audience, so that at the end of the game, the children could be sorted into sets according to whether they suggested good or bad things.

▣ Organise a group of children to draw or paint a large frieze showing a typical countryside scene. Encourage them to include some deliberate mistakes which relate to the Countryside Code. For example, they could show a gate left open with some livestock escaping, an unsupervised dog chasing some chickens, some picnickers leaving litter behind, etc. Display the frieze during the assembly and ask members of the audience to spot the deliberate mistakes. The children could stick on warning symbols such as exclamation marks in red triangles.

CONCLUSION—WHAT CAN WE DO?

● Always follow the Countryside Code and remind others if they forget.

● Apply similar principles to the whole environment e.g. town or city, seaside, park, school etc.

● Don't dismiss 'rules' without thinking carefully about the underlying reason for them.

Poor Dan!

What a pity young Dan didn't know
all about the Countryside Code
when he went to seek green fields
far away from traffic jammed roads.

He strayed from the path, missed the stile
and crawled through the hedge on his knees.
He soon got stuck on a bramble
and was surrounded by angry bees.

He decided to make a fire
to warm his hands before.
He tripped over a log, dropped the match
and set light to a bale of straw.

Screaming, he ran to the gate.
In his panic he left it undone.
Alarmed by the noise, a bull gave chase!
Poor Dan could do nothing but run!

The bull was gaining behind him
so Dan leapt into the river.
With slime on his hair, litter bobbing around him,
the filth and the cold made him shiver.

In dismay, he hauled himself out
and dripped all the way back.
'The countryside's full of disasters' he grumbled
'Give me cities with endless tarmac!'

ALTERNATIVE ACTIVITIES

◎ Farm machinery is very dangerous but it is extremely tempting for children to play on it when they come across it in the country. As well as discussing the importance of not touching other people's property, point out that although tractors, trailers and other farm implements may look attractive, children can easily get hurt by playing on them. Display some toy farm machinery and discuss each one in general terms—its name, colour, function, special features, time of the year when it would be used, etc. Then ask the audience to suggest how each piece of equipment could prove dangerous e.g. sharp edges and spokes which could cut, and moving parts where fingers or limbs could be trapped.

The same approach could be taken with machinery found in towns such as road mending apparatus or equipment on building sites. These often look equally inviting to children but similar principles apply.

◎ Litter can be extremely dangerous to livestock so it is important not to leave it in the countryside. Display some familiar examples of litter and explain why these are harmful to both farm animals and wildlife. (See examples suggested in the Litter theme on page 19.)

▣ Help a small group of children to devise signs or symbols (similar to road signs) to illustrate the Countryside Code. For example, the following sign could mean 'Don't drop lighted matches'.

Display the signs during assembly and ask the audience if they can guess what message each sign or symbol is attempting to convey.

▣ Use a toy telephone to act out conversations following the violation of one of the 'rules' of the Country Code. For example, someone might be phoning for the fire brigade as a result of a carelessly dropped match, a farmer might be phoning the police about some vandalised machinery, and a neighbour might be phoning a farmer about some escaped livestock.

▣ Ask a small group of children to develop strip cartoons showing a local beauty spot being invaded by hordes of day trippers. What damage is caused? This could include footpaths being eroded by too many people, litter being dropped, cars parked in unsuitable situations, damage to wildlife etc. Why is it no longer a beauty spot? The children could read and display their cartoons during the assembly. Discuss the important points contained within each cartoon with the audience.

▣ Organise a group of children to find out about public footpaths. Who can or cannot use them?

Where is the nearest one? Where does it go to and from? If feasible, arrange a walk along part or all of it. What did the children see? How old is the footpath and why was it originally developed? The children could present their findings in the assembly in the form of pictures or writing.

▣ Arrange for a group of children to write a short story which they could read out during assembly time. Ask them to base their stories around a dog who causes damage whilst unsupervised. In a country setting, the damage could be to crops or livestock whilst in an urban setting the damage might be to property. The story *Fireman Sam* and *The Lost Lamb* by Diane Wilmer (see page 17 for details) could be helpful in introducing this theme.

▣ Read a mock newspaper article about animals straying onto a road because field gates were left open. An example is given on page 17 but teachers may wish to create their own article in order to make it more relevant to their pupils. Discuss the article with the audience and emphasise the possible serious consequences of leaving gates open.

The Picnic

The following play aims to encourage a sensitive approach to the countryside. It was devised by a group of middle infants. It is included to stimulate ideas which a teacher could adapt to relate to her/his own pupils.

Characters   Narrator
Mum
Dad
Boy
Girl
Superman

Narrator   It was such a lovely day that the Smith family decided to go for a picnic in the countryside. As they were driving along, they looked for somewhere to stop.

Mum   That looks like a good place for a picnic. Let's stop there.

Narrator   They parked the car and sat down on the grass.

Mum   Here's the food. Help yourselves everybody.

Children   Good, we're starving!

Narrator   Everybody ate until they had finished all the picnic food.

Mum   Give me all the rubbish and I'll throw it away in the bushes.

Superman   (Leaping out from behind a tree.) Here, you can't do that, you'll make the countryside all messy. You take your rubbish home or find a proper bin. (Superman disappears behind a tree again.)

Narrator   Mum thought about what Superman had said and decided to take the rubbish home with her.

Dad   I'll just light a fire to keep us warm. It's getting a bit chilly now. (Dad lights a fire and throws the match into the bushes.)

Superman   (Leaping out from behind a tree.) What are you doing? You'll set the whole forest on fire. Put that fire out and watch where you throw matches. (Superman disappears behind a tree again.)

Narrator   Dad stamped on the match and put soil on the fire to put it out. Then he read his newspaper.

Children   Can we go and play?

Mum   Yes, but not too far. (The children walk a little way off.)

Boy   Look, there's a bird's nest with some eggs in it. Let's take the eggs home. (He reaches for the eggs.)

Superman   (Leaping from behind a tree.) Stop! You're not allowed to do that. If you take the eggs, there won't be any chicks to grow into birds. (Superman disappears again.)

Narrator   The boy decided not to take the eggs and went on walking with his sister.

Girl   Just look at all these lovely flowers. Let's pick them.

Narrator   The children started to pick the flowers.

Superman   (Leaping out from behind a tree.) Not you two again! If you pick all the flowers, there won't be any left for other people to see and there won't be any seeds for next year. I'll be glad when you've gone home. I just settle down for a nap when someone silly disturbs the countryside.

Mum (Shouting.) Time to go home children.

Superman (Sighing loudly.) Good. Now perhaps I'll get some sleep!

The Express

Motorway Traffic Brought to a Standstill!

Last Wednesday afternoon, the traffic on the M4 motorway was completely stopped by a herd of cows who had wandered onto the road. Fortunately, nobody was hurt as all the motorists managed to avoid the terrified animals. A policeman who attended the incident, said 'We were very lucky that no one was killed. There could easily have been a very nasty accident'.

On the whole, most of the drivers very sensibly slowed down but some blew their car horns causing the frightened cows to scatter all over one half of the motorway. Eventually, all the traffic had to stop until the farmer managed to herd the cows back into their field. Mr Briggs, the farmer, told our reporter 'I expect it was holidaymakers looking for somewhere to picnic. They always seem to come off the motorway at this spot, pull up at the edge of the road and then set off across the fields in search of a good place to eat. Several times before they have left the gate open but the cows have never strayed this far. It was lucky that none of them were killed or injured'.

Fortunately, Mrs Ada Jones, who was out walking her dog, noticed the parked car and gave the police a good description of it together with the registration number. After being interviewed by the police, the family admitted to leaving the gate to the field open. 'I'm very sorry,' said Mr. Green, 'I'm afraid I just didn't think'.

Shopping in Town

Suffocated by crowds of people.
Doors slamming snappily in my face.
Struggling to keep my feet on the ground.
Carried along at a speedy pace.

Umbrellas attacking from above.
Impatient pushchairs catching my heels.
Squeezed off the pavement, squawking with fear,
By skateboarders on bright flashing wheels.

Breathlessly swimming into the store.
People jostling, elbows in my back.
Bright new trousers catch my eye.
Waves of people, I can't reach the rack.

Grabbing the nearest thing on a hanger.
Zigzagging to the desk where you pay.
Pushed and shoved to the back of the queue.
Robot at the till, nothing to say.

Fighting against the tide to the door.
Voices nagging 'Hey, get out of my way!'
Wounded and limp, I want to go home.
Shopping in town's a battle today!

Does the poet enjoy shopping in town? Why not? What do other people do to make shopping extremely uncomfortable? Does the audience believe people behave in this manner on purpose or merely without thinking? Sometimes shopping can be even more uncomfortable for children because they are smaller and easily overlooked by adults.

Can anyone in the audience describe their feelings about shopping in a crowded store? Does anyone enjoy the bustle of a crowded shop? What rules would the audience suggest that both children and adults should follow in order to make shopping more pleasant for everyone? Do elderly or handicapped people need particular consideration?

RESOURCES

Poems

Up on the Downs A Very First Poetry Book (OUP)
Over the Fields Seeing and Doing New Anthology (Thames/Methuen)

Songs

Keep the Countryside Tidy Every Colour Under the Sun (Ward Lock Educational)

Come Let us Remember the Joys of the Town Someone's Singing, Lord (A and C Black)

Stories

Fireman Sam and the Lost Lamb D. Wilmer (Heinemann)
Postman Pat's Tractor Express (in My Postman Pat Storytime Book) J. Cunliffe (Andre Deutsch)
Timmo in the Forest (in Bad Boys) E. Colwell (Young Puffin)
Wilberforce Goes on a Picnic M. Gordon (Picture Puffin)
The Picnic C. Baines (Frances Lincoln)

LITTER

AIM

To develop an awareness of the problems caused by litter in the environment.
To show the children ways in which the amount of litter/waste materials can be reduced.

STARTING POINT

◎ Display a large picture depicting a beach scene with litter, broken bottles, tins, fishing line etc. but with no people. Real litter could be stuck onto a polythene overlay on top of a beach scene poster.

Discuss   Why are there no people on the beach? Would the audience like to play on such a beach? Why not? What are the dangers to people? Their reasons could include health hazards caused by rats and flies attracted to rotting food, dangerous litter such as tins and broken glass etc. Are there any dangers to animals? If any of the children have visited a beach recently, what litter, if any, did they see? Where do they think it came from? Can they think of any local litter 'black spots'?

CORE ACTIVITIES

◎ Ask the audience for a definition of litter i.e. rubbish in the wrong place.

◎ Which sorts of litter are biodegradable (rot and return to the soil)? Demonstrate this by putting different kinds of litter outside for a month or longer, if feasible. These could include a banana skin, a newspaper, a yoghurt pot, a plastic bag, a drink can, a lolly stick. Show the audience the results and discuss what effect the weather has had on each item. How long does it take for the print to disappear? Which types of litter are indestructable? Ask the audience to help sort a set of rubbish into biodegradable and non-biodegradable.
   Note: Children should only handle litter under supervision. They should *always* wear gloves and be reminded to wash their hands thoroughly afterwards.

◎ Display items which are 'over-packaged' in that they use more paper, plastic or metal than is necessary. Cosmetics and confectionary are often good examples. Ask the audience for arguments for and against packaging. The following reasons may be put forward.

For

● It makes the items look more attractive.

● It keeps them in good condition.

● It prevents them from becoming contaminated. This is especially important with regard to food which must be kept germ free.

● To a limited degree, it may reduce theft if the goods are well sealed.

Against

● Unnecessary layers of packaging use up a lot of resources such as paper and plastic.

● More packaging means more litter to be disposed of.

● It adds extra cost to the item.

● It often makes it more difficult to open the item.

◎ Show the audience how to recycle kitchen waste by using a compost heap. (See page 20 for details.)

▣ Ask a small number of children to read their own stories, written from the point of view of a household appliance which has been dumped in a hedgerow e.g. I am a vacuum cleaner and my owner didn't want me anymore . . . Emphasise the fact that children can become trapped in abandoned fridges or cars and they should not play in or near them.

▣ Organise a small group of children to show the journey of the contents of the classroom waste bin. What different stages does it go through and where does it end up? The children could draw pictures to illustrate this accompanied by one or two brief sentences. Each stage of the journey could then be mounted on a large dustbin shape cut out of newspaper.

▣ Organise a display which demonstrates how

waste materials can be put to good use. Here are some ideas.

• Make litter bug monsters from cereal packets and boxes. Decorate them with old wrapping paper and sweet papers.

• Make musical mobiles or wind chimes from junk materials. Tie foil, nails, ring tops or other metallic refuse on to fine string and hang them in a group so that they produce an interesting sound when gently knocked together. However, warn the children to be careful of sharp edges on any metal objects used.

• Make skittles from old plastic bottles. Fill them with water to make them more stable and decorate them with secondhand paper. Invite members of the audience to try the skittles out.

▣ Ask a small group of children to make a large map of the school to show where litter is to be found. Indicate where there is the most/least litter. (This could be extended to a map of the neighbourhood if appropriate.) Ask the group to present their map during assembly, explaining where litter was found.

CONCLUSION—WHAT CAN WE DO?

• Always put litter in the correct place. Can the children suggest where they would put litter in the classroom, in the playground, during school dinners, outside the school gate, on the bus home, etc? Make sure that dustbin lids are firmly closed against the wind, flies and animals.

• Politely refuse bags in shops when they are not absolutely necessary.

• Whenever possible, recycle litter e.g. use bottle banks.

• Take the opportunity to organise a school recycling scheme for paper, glass or metal. Alternatively, collect for a charity—stamps, Christmas cards, milk bottle tops etc.

• Recycle kitchen waste on a compost heap both at home and at school.

• Put waste materials to good use e.g. return egg boxes, reuse envelopes, put food scraps out for birds, give magazines to old people's homes.

The Playground?

5 glass bottles smashed against a tree.
Take care, or you'll cut your knee.

4 crushed coke cans with round metal rings.
Birds' beaks get stuck in these vicious things.

3 plastic bags that dance on a windy day.
They are here forever, they don't rot away.

2 mouldy sandwiches, buzzing with flies,
Attracting rats with beady eyes.

1 old car with door hinges snapped.
A place where a child could easily be trapped.

I come to this playground every day,
But with all this rubbish, where can I play?

ALTERNATIVE ACTIVITIES

◎ Display various items of litter which are hazardous to animals, such as a fishing line (birds can become entangled in it), lead weights (poisonous if swallowed by swans), plastic bags (can choke and suffocate animals if they try to eat them), ring pulls on cans (birds' beaks get caught in them), glass bottles (voles and other small mammals get trapped in them). Can the audience suggest why they are dangerous to animals? How can these dangers be avoided?

◎ Discuss recycling with the children. Do they know what it means and what sort of materials can be recycled? Why is this a useful thing to do? For example, aluminium cans can be recycled by melting them down to make more cans. This process uses less energy than making brand new cans from the raw material. (Information on recycling aluminium can be obtained from the Aluminium Can Recycling

Association, Freepost, BM 4239, Birmingham
B1 1BR.)

Focus on one particular form of recycling. For example, bottle banks may be the most familiar. If possible, show a picture of a bottle bank and discuss its function. Where is the nearest bottle bank and do any of the children's parents use them? Go through the Bottle Bank Code with them.

1 Remove all tops and caps and thoroughly clean the bottles.

2 Put all the bottles in the correct colour compartment.

3 Don't use bottle banks at night as they can cause noise.

4 Don't throw away returnable bottles.

Do the children know of any returnable bottles e.g. milk. Can they suggest other commodities where bottles could be refilled and reused e.g. perfumes, washing up liquids, etc.

Similar banks exist for collecting cans and tins but these are more unusual.

◎ Guess the weight of a bag of litter. Ask members of the audience to volunteer to pick up a bag of litter and compare it with a bag of sugar. Which is heavier or lighter? Bearing this in mind, can they estimate the weight of the litter in kilogrammes.

◎ Display a collection of rubbish (such as food waste, tins, paper, glass, plastic etc.) and discuss each item as it is placed in a bin. Ask questions such as—What is it made out of? What was inside? How many layers of packaging are there? etc. Use fairly bulky items so that the bin is full. Empty the bin out and repeat the process but this time ask the audience whether it is possible to recycle each item and how. If it is possible to recycle it, don't put it into the bin. Compare how full the bin is this time.

Note: Make sure that you use gloves and emphasise to the children that handling rubbish can be dangerous to their health.

◎ Take a small packet of wrapped sweets. Flatten each individual wrapper and stick them onto squared paper. Ask the audience how many squares one packet covers. Can they predict how many squares two packets would cover? Relate this to the amount of paper needed to wrap sweets and to be disposed of afterwards.

▣ Make a chart to show the quantity of litter dropped during a week. Collect the litter each day. Weigh and record it. Discuss the chart with the audience. Can they identify which is the worst day and suggest why this should be so?

▣ Set a Design and Technology project for a group of children involving the design of packaging, bearing in mind the need for minimal use of resources. Ask one or two children to explain the project and show their solutions. (See page 21 for more details.)

CONSTRUCTING A COMPOST HEAP

Show the children examples of kitchen waste such as cabbage leaves, carrot tops and potato peelings, and ask them what they would do with it? If most of them suggest putting it in the dustbin or burning it, explain that it could all be recycled into useful compost. If possible have some compost available in various stages of decay to compare and contrast with the kitchen refuse. Perhaps one or two members of the audience would like to handle the final product and describe the feel, colour, smell etc. Discuss the importance of compost and how it can be used to nourish new plants. Use simple diagrams to explain how to construct a compost heap and how it works. Here is one method.

1 Find a suitable site in a shady spot away from buildings.

2 Build the compost container on bare soil. Construct a box using wooden planks or stakes with wire netting. You could use a dustbin with holes in the side for ventilation.

3 Put in a layer of brushwood or prunings to create ventilation at the bottom.

4 Continue making 20 cm layers of mixed kitchen waste and garden refuse.

5 Water the layers if they are dry.

6 When the heap reaches the top of the container, cover it with polythene with holes punctured in for ventilation.

7 Insulate the heap by putting old carpet or straw on the top.

8 Leave the heap to rot. This can take anything from three months to a year.

Heat is generated as the refuse gradually rots with the aid of bacteria, worms, slugs, beetles and centipedes. Because of all these minibeasts, the heap also provides food for many animals e.g. toads, hedgehogs, slow worms, grass snakes etc. If possible, have pictures (or even the real thing) of all the creatures living in the compost heap together with those who visit to use it as a food supply.

Take this opportunity to build a compost heap somewhere in the school grounds so that the children can witness the cycle of life and decay at first hand. Regular reports on the progress of the compost heap could be made during assembly by interested pupils.

Design and Technology Project

The following is an example of the type of 'design' project which could be proposed to the children. Obviously, teachers will devise activities which suit the age, ability and experience of their pupils.

Project   Design suitable packaging for some sweets (alternatives could include a bar of soap, biscuits, etc.).

Before the children embark on their own designs, it might prove profitable to look in detail at various methods used to package a range of sweets. It would probably be helpful to focus the children's attention on some of the following points:

- What materials are used? Are they biodegradable?

- How is the packaging constructed?

- What shape and size is the packaging? Dismantle a variety of boxes and tubes to investigate the nets used.

- How many sweets are contained in the packaging?

- How many layers of packaging are there? Identify, in particular, any unnecessary packaging.

Formulate proposals

Discuss with the children precisely what sorts of sweets they are going to design packaging for e.g. boiled sweets, chocolates, mints. Teachers may decide to set identical projects or allow individuals some choice. If possible, use real sweets but if this is not practical, agree upon a substitute e.g. beads, Unifix bricks, plastic buttons. The following considerations may well arise during discussion.

Structure of the packaging

Size—How many sweets will it need to contain? What shape are they? Do they tessellate? Does it matter if they don't?

Strength—Is it important to make the packaging heavy/ light? Will it need to be strong enough for stacking on a shelf in a shop?

Suitability—Do the sweets need to be kept separate? What sort of opening will the packaging have? Will there be adequate space for all the necessary information to go on the inside/outside?

Environmental constraints—Is it possible to use all biodegradable materials? Will the design use a minimum of resources? Is it possible to use recycled waste materials? Will there be a reminder on the outside to put litter into a bin?

Attractiveness—How will the children ensure the packaging is pleasing visually? Can they invent a suitable name and logo for the sweets?

Construction materials

Joining—What methods will be used to join the various parts of the packaging?

Cost—Is the design cost effective?

Availability—Are the materials to be used easily obtainable?

Toxicity—Are all the materials being used 'safe' for containing food?

Hygiene—Does the design ensure that the sweets cannot be contaminated in any way?

Water/air proof—Will special attention need to be given to preventing the sweets from becoming stale?

Encourage the children to offer their own solutions to the above points. They can then draw a plan of their packaging designs, giving details of the construction and listing the tools and materials required. The next stage is to implement the design and then test out its effectiveness. Finally, the children can suggest improvements to the original design and modify their packaging accordingly. Obviously, the sophistication of the solutions offered by the children will vary tremendously from a simple sealed bag to more sophisticated boxes.

Putting litter in a bin

The Dustbin Men

by Gregory Harrison from *A First Poetry Book* by John Foster, OUP

The older ones have gone to school,
My breakfast's on the plate,
But I can't leave the window-pane,
I might be just too late.

I've heard the clatter down the street,
I know they're creeping near,
The team of gruff-voiced, burly men
Who keep our dustbins clear.

And I must watch and see them clang
The dustbins on the road,
And stand in pairs to heave up high
The double-handled load.

Yes, there they come, the lorry growls
And grinds in bottom gear;
The dustman knees the garden gate
As, high up by his ear,
Firmly he balances the bin,
Head tilted to one side;
The great mouth of the rubbish cart
Is yawning very wide;
To me the mouth looks like a beast's,
A dragon's hungry jaws
That snap the refuse out of sight
Behind those sliding doors.

The lorry-dragon every day
Is in a ravenous mood,
And cardboard boxes, bottles, jars
Are all part of his food.
He gobbles up old magazines,
Saucepans and broken jugs,
Pieces of red linoleum,
And dirty, tufted rugs.

He crunches shattered pictures,
Old bicycles and tyres,
A bird-cage with its seed-tray,
Its bell and rusty wires;

And fractured clocks and mirrors,
A rocking-chair and broom,
A mattress and an iron bed;
Where does he find the room?

And like a dragon sated,
His great maw crammed quite tight,
He lifts his head and swallows
His breakfast out of sight.

What would the careless people
Who clutter up the street
Do without hungry dragons
To keep our houses neat?

How many of the children have seen the dustmen collecting rubbish? What day do they come? Can they describe the lorry, the clothes the dustmen wear and what happens? Do they think the poet's description of the lorry as a 'hungry dragon' is a good one and why? Can they suggest alternative descriptions? What does the dragon in the poem eat? Would the local dustmen take away old bicycles and rocking chairs or would a special collection be required? What would happen if no one collected the dustbins? Where do the lorries take the refuse?

RESOURCES

Poems

The Dustbin Men A First Poetry Book (OUP)
Carbreakers A First Poetry Book (OUP)
The Litter Bug Tinderbox Assembly Book (A and C Black)
Sarah Cynthia Sylvia Stout All the Day Through (Evans Bros. Ltd)
Litter Playtime Activity Book (BBC)
The Dustman Gently into Music (Longmans)

Songs

The Litter Bin Song Songs from Playschool (BBC/A and C Black)
The Sluberdegullion's Song Something to Think About (BBC)
The Tidy Song Tinderbox Song Book (A and C Black)
The Wombling Song Apusskidu (A and C Black)
Litter Song Mrs Macaroni (Macmillan Ed.)
Milk Bottle Tops and Paper Bags Someone's Singing, Lord (A and C Black)
The Tidy Song The Music Box Song Book (BBC)

Stories

Dinosaurs and all that Rubbish M. Foreman (Hamish Hamilton)
Joachim the Dustman K. Bauman and D. McKee (A and C Black)
The Scrapyard Monster L. Arnelli (Macdonald)
The Sluberdegullion (in Something to Think About) A. Hewett (BBC)

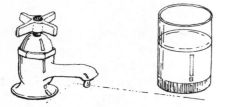

AIM

To develop an understanding of how crucial water is for life and the need to care for it.

STARTING POINT

◎ Place a glass of water inside a box decorated to look like a treasure chest. Can the audience guess what precious object is inside? After a while, give them some clues.

Discuss   Why should water be treasured? What would happen to us if we didn't have any? What effect would it have on plants and wildlife? Do all people have easy access to water? What does 'pollution' mean? Can the children name any causes of water pollution? Take the opportunity to warn children against drinking water from any sources which might be polluted e.g. streams, rivers, ponds.

CORE ACTIVITIES

◎ Play a memory game with the audience – 'I use water for . . .' Each volunteer repeats the uses suggested by previous children and adds another one of their own. How many different uses of water can the audience suggest? They could include washing clothes, baths and showers, making drinks, growing food, putting out fires, producing electricity and water sports.

◎ List the causes of water pollution with the help of the audience. These could include sewers, rubbish, dumping (such as chemicals), factory waste, oil tanker accidents or deliberate washing out of tanks, run off from fields (fertilizers and pesticides). How do these forms of pollution affect humans? They make it unpleasant for swimming and water sports, and are sometimes harmful to health. How do they affect birds? Oil sticks to their feathers and feet making them unable to swim or fly and sometimes their food supply is destroyed or poisoned. How do they affect fish and plant life? Seaweed and other water plants die, fish and seals become sick and sometimes die.

◎ Read a simple passage to the audience and ask them to put up their hands whenever the use of water is involved.

◎ Ask the audience to suggest words to describe water—the colour, the sound it makes in various circumstances, the movement under different conditions, the feel of it as rain, in the bath, and as ice cubes. Extend this activity by asking volunteers to choose two words to put together e.g. slippery drips, transparent coldness. Can these pairs of words be used to form a poem with two words to each line? Write the six best 'two word' suggestions on individual cards.

▣ Prepare a small number of children to mime various uses of water such as washing up dishes, drinking, watering flowers. Can the audience guess what they are? Is a volunteer from the audience willing to mime a different use of water? This activity could be developed further by asking one child to pretend to pass an object to a second who continues the mime e.g. brushing their teeth, cleaning windows, wiping up dishes.

▣ Arrange for a group of children to present a water dance. See the example on page 25.

CONCLUSION—WHAT CAN WE DO?

● Try not to waste water by leaving taps running etc.

● Reduce the amount of water used by taking a shower rather than a bath, keeping clothes clean so that washing machines are used less etc.

● Never pollute water by throwing rubbish into ponds, rivers or the sea.

● Don't use excessive amounts of washing up liquid, soaps and bleaches. Try to buy products which will cause the minimum amount of pollution.

● Avoid putting waste other than water into the drains such as food and chemicals etc.

● Find out about the work of charities, such as Oxfam, who organise projects to help people living in areas of drought. What can we do to support such organisations?

Water

I am water.
I bubble and sing in streams.
My salty waves splash toes.
I drip from leaky taps
And squirt noisily from a hose.

I am water.
I quench the horse's thirst
And cool fiery flames leaping high.
Without me boats would be grounded
And fish would surely die.

I am water.
But green slime covers my skin.
Brown foam oozes from every pore.
Oil seeps into my veins
So I cannot breathe any more.

I am water.
I give precious life to this earth.
I'm important, can't you see?
I give life to you
So why pollute me?

ALTERNATIVE ACTIVITIES

◎ Conduct some water pollution experiments during the assembly. Have a transparent plastic tank full of water together with various types of rubbish. Ask the audience to predict whether each piece of rubbish will sink or float on the water. Test them and see. Can they suggest whether the water will cause any changes in the items of rubbish? For example, paper will eventually break down in the water but plastic bottles are not biodegradable. Also repeat the experiment with oil. Will it float or sink? Can the audience suggest ways of getting rid of the oil? They might suggest skimming it off, using paper towels to absorb it, using detergents to disperse it, etc. Link these activities with pollution in rivers and the sea and the problems of dealing with it.

◎ Show examples of how much water is used in daily activities. For instance, fill a container with 1 litre water. Ask the children to estimate how much water is in it. Have several other containers with 1 litre water in each. If one flush of a toilet uses 10 litres, how many containers would it use? Other examples could be shown using 10 litre containers e.g. a shower uses 30 litres, a bath uses 80 litres, a washing machine uses 100 litres. Can they predict how many containers will be needed for each activity?

◎ Ask the audience if they have any idea where the waste water from their sink goes to when they pull out the plug. Draw simple poster sized diagrams of each stage of the journey of waste water from sink to sea. Explain each stage in simple terms, using a diagram as an aid. The final outcome should be a series of diagrams in a sequence. Ask the audience to close their eyes whilst the position of one diagram is changed. Can they indicate which diagram has been moved and where its correct place is.

◎ Demonstrate how water can be cleaned. Show the audience samples of water which you have collected from various sources—a puddle, ditch, pond, stream or swimming pool. Compare and contrast them with a sample of tap water. Can the audience identify similarities or differences. Which water sample is the dirtiest? Use this one to show it is possible to clean water. Do the children already know of methods to clean water? Filter the dirty water through a coffee filter paper and then compare it with the tap water. Would it be safe to drink now? Explain that at a water treatment works, once the water had been filtered (probably through beds of sand), chemicals would be added to kill any germs and make it safe to drink.

◎ Focus on an area of the world which is experiencing drought conditions. Explain the causes of the drought and the effect it has on the population. Try to relate the experiences of the children in the drought conditions to the children in the audience by comparing their daily lives. Use posters or magazine pictures as a visual aid. Discuss ways in which the school could help, perhaps by supporting a charity, such as Oxfam, who are trying to improve the supply of water in these areas. For further information about the work of Oxfam, contact Education Department, 274 Banbury Road, Oxford.

◎ Devise an activity to demonstrate that water can be a source of fun as well as being essential for life. For example, make sounds using water in bottles. Display a number of glass bottles (the same size) which contain water in increasing amounts. Tap one with different kinds of beaters. Which do the audience think make the most pleasing sounds? Ask the audience to close their eyes whilst the bottle is tapped with one of the beaters. Can they indicate which beater was being used? Tap each bottle in turn using the same beater. Does more water in the bottle produce a low or high note? Tap a sequence of sounds and ask volunteers from the audience to see if they can imitate your sequence. Can the audience suggest other ways in which water can be fun? They might suggest swimming, water play toys, etc.

▣ Discuss the rain cycle in simple terms and ask the children to write a story based on the journey of a raindrop from cloud to tap. Ask one or two of the children to read their stories during assembly.

▣ Organise a group of children to draw a picture of themselves in the rain. Ask them to decide whether they enjoy the rain or not and to think up one or two sentences which reflect their response. For example, I like drizzle because it tickles my face, I hate rain when I can't go out to play. During the assembly, the children could hold up their pictures and read their sentences. Volunteers from the audience could then help partition the set of children (using a rope) into a subset of those liking the rain and a subset of those disliking it.

▣ Ask a small group of children to make up their own poems beginning 'If no water came out of my tap . . .' Perhaps the children could read their poems to the audience.

Water Pollution Dance

The purpose of the following activity is to interpret water pollution as a series of movements. Whilst it is important to encourage the children to develop their own ideas, teachers may find it helpful to consider the suggestions outlined below as a starting point.

Divide the children into two groups—one to represent rain/water and the other to represent pollution. In the activities below, the former will be referred to as the Blue group and the latter as the Black group.

Ideas	Possible Movements	Percussion
Blue group		
Raindrops falling softly.	Fluttering hands from high to low on the spot.	Gentle tapping of xylophone, triangle, Indian bells etc.
Raindrops becoming heavier and faster.	Jumping and bouncing with feet together on the spot and then repeat whilst travelling in different directions.	Continuing above but becoming faster and louder.
Raindrops gather together to form bubbling streams.	Two children act as leaders. When they touch others, they form a line behind, running quickly, rising and sinking, making a meandering pathway.	Continuing above.
Black group		
Pollution seeping into river.	Black group creep slowly and stealthily from all directions to surround blue group who are squeezed into a circle in the middle, whirling and spiralling on the spot.	Add slow regular beats on drum or tambourine.

Pollution gradually killing river.

Black group form high menacing shapes, arms stretched, fists and elbows punching the air. One by one, Blue group cease quick bubbly movements and slowly sink to floor in the middle of the circle.

As above but becoming louder.

The river is dead.

Blue group continue to make small, upward grasping gestures whilst black group surround and cover them with outstretched arms. All movement ceases abruptly at a given signal.

One final sharp beat on a cymbal.

Elaborate costumes would not be necessary but some differentiation between the groups would be helpful. Black group could wear black leotards or trousers whilst blue group could wear white shirts or blouses with white shorts. Additional distinctions such as blue or black crepe streamers could be stapled onto a headband, pinned onto clothing or waved in hands.

Plants in the classroom

by Irene Rawnsley from *Ask a Silly Question*, Mammoth

Plants in the classroom seem to say,
'We've not been watered today.'

What must they think,
Standing above the sink,
When they hear how the water gushes,
And you're only washing the brushes?

It's a daily habit,
Giving fresh water
To the rabbit.

Even the fish
Have their wish,
Every Friday when the tank is scrubbed.
Plants must think that they've been snubbed;

Not a drop of water
Comes their way.
They see you carefully watering the clay

But to them
Not a dribble.
They'd climb out of their pots
If they were able,
Step down from their ledges,
Balance on the edges of the water trough,
Drink and drink till they'd had enough.

But they can't.
So they stay where they've been put,
Quietly withering away.

What is wrong with the plants in the classroom? What will happen if they don't get enough water? Can the audience remember which things in the poem are having water? Are there any plants wilting in the school? Whose responsibility is it to water them? What sort of plants can survive with little water? Are there plants which like lots of water?

RESOURCES

Poems

The River A Very First Poetry Book (OUP)
Pollution Tinderbox Assembly Book (A and C Black)
Water when you're Thirsty Is a caterpillar ticklish? (Young Puffin)
The Sound of Water Singing in the Sun (Young Puffin)
Jetsam Another First Poetry Book (OUP)

Songs

What have they Done to the Rain? Alleluya (A and C Black)
Raindrops Child Education Infant Projects 51 (Scholastic)
Water in the Rain New Horizons (Stainer and Bell)
Glass of Water Sing for your Life (A and C Black)
Glug, glug, glug Mrs Macaroni (Macmillan)
Water Playtime Activity Book (BBC)

Stories

Tiddalick, the Frog who Caused a Flood R. Roennfeldt (Picture Puffin)
Bringing the Rain to Kapiti Plain V. Aardema (Macmillan)
Thank You for a Glass of Water P. and V. Smeltzer (Lion)
Bertha Gets into Trouble (in More Stories to Tell*)* E. Colwell (Young Puffin)
Ming Ming and the Lantern Dragon J. E. Edwards (Methuen)
The Little Man with Big Feet (in Topsy Turvy Tales*)* L. Berg (Magnet)

NOISE POLLUTION

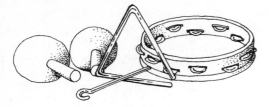

AIM

To introduce the concept of noise pollution.
To increase the children's awareness of the noise they produce and to develop sensitivity to others.

STARTING POINT

◎ Listen to a tape recording of everyday sounds e.g. traffic, washing machine, laughter, food processor, children singing, vacuum cleaner, someone snoring. Ask the audience to identify the sounds.

Discuss Which sounds do the audience like/dislike? E.g. aeroplanes, building work, babies crying, streams, cats purring. How do they feel when listening to sounds they like/dislike? What ill effects do they think loud, unwanted noises could cause? E.g. headaches, deafness, damage to the eardrum which results in a permanent ringing or buzzing in the head, difficulty concentrating, stress. What action do they take if someone is being noisy and disturbing them?

CORE ACTIVITIES

◎ Show the audience a pair of ear defenders. Ask a volunteer to test them out by making loud noises behind him/her. Which people wear them and why? E.g. people who work on building sites, in noisy factories, drivers of noisy vehicles such as tractors.

◎ Noise pollution can be very subjective. What is a horrible noise to one person can be a pleasant one to another. Demonstrate this by playing two contrasting pieces of music—one loud noisy record followed by a soft soothing one. How many of the audience prefer the first piece of music? Which would they find a nuisance if played loudly?

◎ People making unnecessary noise can be doing so without thinking. Read *Mr Noisy* by Roger Hargreaves (see page 30 for details) as an example of this. If possible, use a flannel graph (similar to a Fuzzy Felt board) as an aid to tell the story.

◎ Ask volunteers from the audience to play a 'match the sound' game. Have at least six identical opaque containers such as small yoghurt pots plus lids. Fill two with pebbles, two with dried peas and two with sand. Obviously, a wide variety of other objects such as drawing pins, wooden beads or nails would be equally good. Encourage the children to take turns to shake the containers and match the pairs with the same sound.

◎ Play a silent 'pass the parcel' game. Ask four or five volunteers to pass a noisy toy such as a rattle or a noisy musical instrument such as a tambourine or maracas, from one to the other as quietly as possible. Suggest that the audience raise their hands if they hear the slightest sound. Repeat this activity several times with various objects. Does practice improve the children's ability to pass the object quietly? Are some objects more difficult to pass quietly than others?

▣ Relate noise pollution to the school environment. Ask a small number of children to draw a picture of Mr Noisy and say when they behave like him during school hours e.g. I am Mr Noisy when . . . . . . ! slam the door/scrape my chair on the floor/bang my cup on the table/shout when moving round the school.

CONCLUSION—WHAT CAN WE DO?

● Listen to silence. Is there such a thing as total silence? Ask the audience to say what they can still hear.

● Practise getting quieter e.g. clap/stamp loudly at first and then gradually become quieter until silent (without fidgeting or rustling noises!). Agree on a signal to indicate when the audience should get quieter e.g. a raised arm for noisy which is slowly lowered to show getting quieter.

● Have a large picture of Mr Quiet. Write on suggestions from the audience on how to be more like Mr Quiet and less like Mr Noisy, e.g. close doors carefully, be sensitive to others working, avoid banging into furniture unnecessarily.

● Tiptoe back to the classroom!

Nasty Noises!

Motorbikes revving, vroom, vroom, vroom!
Jet planes diving, zoom, zoom, zoom!

Car horns blaring, toot, toot, toot!
Football fans yelling, shoot, shoot, shoot!

Workmen hammering, bang, bang, bang!
Machinery throbbing, clang, clang, clang!

No more room in my head, head, head!
For all this constant noise, NOISE, **NOISE!!**

ALTERNATIVE ACTIVITIES

◎ Tape record noises around the school throughout the day. Can the audience identify these and say which ones are unnecessarily loud? Which sound is the loudest/softest and longest/shortest? Are any of the noises causing a nuisance to other people? What action could be taken to reduce the noise level?

◎ On a blackboard write a list of onomatopoeic words which describe various noises such as clang, splash, sizzle, ring. Can the audience add to the list and then suggest which words describe a noise which would be intrusive or a nuisance.

◎ Have a selection of objects inside a box/bag such as an alarm clock, a rattle, and a bell. Make a sound with each one and ask the audience to guess what the object is. Which one makes the loudest noise?

◎ Select one set of percussion instruments which makes long sounds e.g. cymbals, triangles, gongs, and another set which produces short sounds e.g. tambourine, drum and castanets. Ask a small

number of children from the audience to participate in using these instruments. One child makes a sound with one instrument and the next child continues with his/her instrument only when the first sound has totally died away. Can the audience say which sounds were long/short?

◎ Play the record *The Sound of Silence* by Simon and Garfunkel (on the record *Simon and Garfunkel's Greatest Hits*, Colombia). Does the audience enjoy silence? Are there particular times during the day when they prefer to be quiet? What are the times during the school day when they must be quiet, such as when the teacher is calling the register or when listening to instructions? Are there good reasons for being quiet at these times?

◎ Sing a well known song but ask the audience to leave a gap of silence on certain specified words. For example, if 'Mary had a little lamb' were chosen, a gap of silence could be substituted for 'lamb' throughout the song. A further development of this is the song 'Heads, shoulders, knees and toes' where cumulative gaps of silence are substituted for various parts of the body.

▣ Ask a small group of children to paint patterns which reflect a particular sound. These could include a drum beaten loudly, a reverberating cymbol, feet skipping, typewriter tapping etc. Display these patterns and encourage the audience to predict whether each sound was loud/soft, gentle/forceful, regular/irregular etc. Compare the audience's reactions with the descriptions given by the children.

▣ Prepare a small group of children to mime movements which reflect various sounds e.g. soft, gentle, rippling, swirling movements contrasted with sharp, jerky, strong movements. What feelings or ideas do the movements communicate to the audience?

▣ Invite a small group of children to each draw a large picture of one of the numerous noisy machines which are common features of our daily lives. These could include washing machines, lawn mowers, lorries, motorbikes and electric drills. Can they describe the noise made by the machine they have drawn?

▣ Organise a group of children to devise a 'sound story' which could be used in assembly. An example is given on the next page.

'Sound story'

The short sound story below is given as an example only. It is likely that teachers will want their pupils to devise a story which is relevant to their own particular circumstances. The passage could be read by the teacher or a child. Encourage the children to devise their own sound effects. These could be produced by percussion instruments, children's voices, real objects, junk materials, etc.

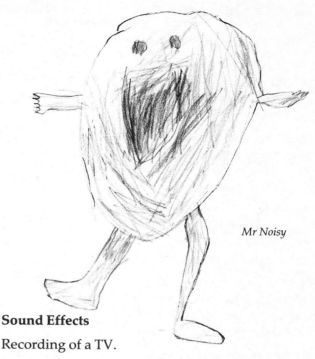

Mr Noisy

A Peaceful Walk?

Text

Ian had a headache. He was fed up with watching the television and mum was nagging him to tidy up his room so he decided to go for a quiet walk down the lane. As he closed the back gate, he could hear Simon and Louise arguing loudly in next door's garden. They were fighting over that bike again! He hurried along the path, glad to be leaving them behind. A car sped past him, hooting angrily at another motorist. Ian turned into the lane only to find workmen were digging up the tarmac. 'Oh no!' he moaned 'Not more noise!' The piercing squeal of the drill made his teeth go on edge so he quickly covered his ears with his hands. An ice cream van added to the din as it drove past playing an awful tinkling tune. Usually, Ian welcomed the sound of the van but not today. He thought he would avoid any more noise by taking the short cut home using the footpath across the field. But still there was no peace to be found! Some picnickers were playing a radio loudly whilst their son was flying a radio controlled model aeroplane. Ian ducked automatically as the plane buzzed low overhead. He ran rapidly across the field which backed onto his garden. As he climbed over the gate, he could hear the children next door still arguing! A door slammed as one of them stormed furiously into the house. Ian let himself into the kitchen and sat down with a sigh. 'Silence!' he muttered softly to himself, clutching at his throbbing head. But not for long . . . .
    Mum's screeching voice pierced the air . . . .

Sound Effects

Recording of a TV.

Nagging mum e.g. 'Ian, tidy up your room now! Hurry up before I really get cross!'

Gate closing.

Two children arguing e.g. 'It's my turn to ride it first! No, it's my turn! Bell ringing.

Voice—beep! beep!

Road work noises e.g. bang a metal biscuit tin or upturned yoghurt pot, run a fingernail along corrugated card, voice.

Tap glass bottles filled with varying amounts of water.

Play tape of loud music.

Voice for buzzing noise.

'It's mine! No, it's not!' Bang two pieces of wood together.

'Ian, haven't you finished your room yet! Get a move on, it's nearly tea time!'

Never a Dull Moment

by Tony Bradman from *Smile Please*, Young Puffin

If you like to keep lively,
If you hate being bored,
Just come down to our house
And knock on the door.

It's the noisiest house
In the whole of our town,
There's doors always slamming
And things falling down.

There's my dad, who keeps shouting,
And my mum, who breaks things,
The baby (who'll bite you!)
And our dog running rings.

There's my sister the screamer
And my brother who roars,
And a grandpa who's stone deaf
(He's the one who slams doors).

So come down to our house,
You won't need the address,
You'll hear it ten miles away
And the outside's a mess.

You won't mind the racket,
You'll just love the din —
For there's never a dull moment
In the house we live in!

Can the audience name some of the noisy people or
activities in this house? Would they like to live next door
to the people in this poem? Do they get annoyed by the
noise their neighbours make? What noises do the children
make which they think might disturb their neighbours?
E.g. shouting when playing, having the television on
loudly, ringing bicycle bells constantly, and stamping up
the stairs noisily. Can the audience suggest ways of
modifying their own noisy behaviour?

RESOURCES

Poems

Never a Dull Moment Smile Please (Young Puffin)
Whispers Is a caterpillar ticklish? (Young Puffin)
What a Noisy House Over and Over Again (Beaver Books)
Noise Over and Over Again (Beaver Books)
I Like Noise Rhyme Time 2 (Beaver Books)
Be Quiet Rhyme Time 2 (Beaver Books)
Night Sounds Rhyme Time 2 (Beaver Books)
The Sounds in the Evening A First Poetry Book (OUP)

Songs

Lord, I love to Stamp and Shout Someone's Singing, Lord (A and C
    Black)
I Like Peace, I Like Quiet Songs from Playschool (BBC/A and C
    Black)
Sound Song Tinderbox Song Book (A and C Black)
Talking Tinderbox Song Book (A and C Black)
Clap and Stamp Sing as you Grow (Ward Lock Educational)
O listen to Sounds New Horizons (Stainer and Bell)
Loud and Soft The Music Fun Shop (Hamish Hamilton)

Stories

Mr Noisy R. Hargreaves (Price Stern Sloan)
Noisy S. Hughes (Walker Books)
Noisy Nora R. Wells (Fontana)
Too Much Noise J. Ash (Hippo)
Goodnight Owl P. Hutchins (Picture Puffin)
Peace at Last J. Murphy (Macmillan)
The Owl and the Woodpecker B. Wildsmith (OUP)
Nights and O.T. (in Joe and Timothy Together) D. Edwards
    (Magnet)
Paul's Quiet Day (in Allotment Lane School Again) M. Joy (Young
    Puffin)
Awkward Aardvark Mwalimu (Hodder and Stoughton)
The Little Yellow Jungle Frogs (in The Anita Hewett Animal Story
    Book) A. Hewett (Young Puffin)

PLANTS

AIM

To develop an appreciation of the importance of plants in our daily lives.

STARTING POINT

◎ Display items which are linked because plants are their original source e.g. food (bread, lettuce), drink (orange squash), beauty products (perfume, shampoo, soap with plant extracts), medicines (witchhazel), etc.

Discuss Can the children identify the plant source? Can they name others in each category? Plants are also a source of food for other animals. Can the audience name any animals together with one of the plant foods they eat such as cow and grass? Discuss the visual contribution plants make to our world. Can the children describe what our environment would look like without any plants? If feasible, look out of the nearest window and ask them to describe what would be left if all the plants were suddenly taken away.

CORE ACTIVITIES

◎ Prepare a simple salad with help from the audience. Volunteers could read instructions, cut, chop and mix the ingredients, eat and describe the results. Why are plant foods important in a healthy diet? (They are high in vitamins and fibre.) Example of a suitable recipe is given on page 33.

◎ Display pictures of rare wild flowers e.g. cowslip, corncockle, snakeshead fritillary. Discuss why they are becoming rare—people dig them up or pick the flowers so that they cannot seed, some are sprayed with weedkillers whilst others only grow in certain conditions and if those places are replaced by roads or houses, they are unable to grow elsewhere. Can the audience suggest why it is important to protect them. E.g. many medicines originate from plants and no one can tell which plants may provide cures for the future.

◎ Explain how picking flowers interrupts the self perpetuation of the species. For example, illustrate the life cycle of a plant from seed to flower to seed on separate cards. Ask members of the audience to put the cards in order correctly. Remove the appropriate cards to show what would happen if someone picked a flower or dug up a plant.

◎ Ask volunteers from the audience to smell distinctive plants e.g. lavender, mint, sweet peas, etc. Blindfold them to see if they can guess which plant it is from the perfume alone. Help the children to realise that most flowers have a sweet smell to signal to visitors such as bees and butterflies, that there is food nearby. Honeysuckle, for instance, has a strong smell at night so it attracts moths. These visitors all help to pollinate the plants in return for their nectar. Discuss how plants add beauty to our world with their perfume as well as their colour.

▣ Exhibit fabric which has been dyed using extracts from plants (preferably done by a group of children). Explain the process of dying the material to the audience. Can the audience suggest what alternatives could be used if there were no more plants.

CONCLUSION—WHAT CAN WE DO?

● Never pick or dig up wild flowers.

● Respect plants wherever they may be.

● Grow as many plants as possible both at home and at school.

● Avoid using weedkillers whenever possible. Not only do they kill wild flowers but some may also kill beneficial minibeasts such as worms.

● Avoid wasting food, especially bearing in mind that many people in the world have none.

Poppies

One red poppy nodding in the sun.
Paper petals faded.
Seeds grew ripe.
Breezes helped the scattering.
Tiny seedlings sprouted.
So—
Four more poppies were nodding in the sun.

Five red poppies nodding in the sun.
Paper petals faded.
Seeds grew ripe.
Breezes helped the scattering.
Tiny seedlings sprouted.
But—
Some were trampled by horses hooves.
Some eaten by slugs.
Some were sprayed with weedkiller.
Some thoughtlessly picked.
Until—
No red poppies were nodding in the sun.

ALTERNATIVE ACTIVITIES

◎ Discuss how certain plants were important in the past. Show the audience some of the following and ask if they can guess how they were used. For instance, nettles (eaten cooked like cabbage), gorse (used for fuel), lady's bedstraw (used as stuffing for pillows), dandelions (leaves eaten as a salad), elderberries (made into wine), fleabane (used for driving away fleas). These are just a few of the numerous examples which could be shown. Emphasise that no one knows which plants may become vital to us in the future.

◎ Ask the audience to help sort pictures of plants into flowers/weeds. Which ones would the audience grow in a garden? Try to define a 'weed' (a plant growing in the wrong place). Some 'weeds' are extremely important to other creatures e.g. Lady's Smock is an essential food source for the orange tip butterflies. Many 'weeds' are also extremely beautiful and more people are increasingly keen to grow them in their gardens to attract wildlife.

◎ Devise a demonstration to show how plant roots prevent soil erosion. For example, take two plastic seed trays. Fill one with soil and the other with a grass turf. Tilt both slightly and water with a small watering can. In which case is the most movement of soil noticed? What part of the plant is helping to hold the soil in place? Why is it important to prevent soil erosion? What would happen to the soil if there were no plants in the world?

◎ Invite members of the audience to help plant some fast growing seeds. Cress is obviously ideal but other food plants such as alphalpha or mung beans would make an interesting alternative. For example, mung beans (Chinese bean sprouts) should be grown indoors in a warm even temperature. Wash the beans and soak them overnight in cold water. Wash them again before spreading them evenly over a damp cloth or cotton wool in a flat dish. Keep them damp but not too wet otherwise they will go mouldy. Put the dish into a polythene bag and cover with newspaper to exclude the light. The beans should be ready to eat in 6 to 9 days when they are roughly 25 to 40 mm long. The progress of the plants could be monitored at regular intervals and a report made in another assembly. Alternatively, if sufficient time allows, examples of the mature plant could be grown beforehand. Discuss the conditions needed for the plants to thrive. Do they differ from those required by plants outside in the garden? Can the children predict what would happen to plants growing outside if the soil, air or water were polluted?

◎ Show the audience a range of plants which grow in diverse habitats. These could include those requiring little or no water such as cacti and succulents, those demanding lots of water such as bog or pond water plants (e.g. marsh marigolds like damp ditches whilst water crowsfoot floats on top of the water), climbing plants relying on the support of others such as honeysuckle, plants depending upon a host such as mistletoe. Discuss how each plant is particularly adapted for each situation. Help the audience to realise that if man changes the conditions for any of the plants by draining ponds or marshes, or pulling up hedgerows, each plant will have difficulty in surviving.

▣ Prepare a small group of children to act out *The King's Flower* by M. Anno (see page 34 for details). The story tells of a king who had to have everything bigger than anyone else; he needed a ladder to climb into his bed, two servants to carry his enormous toothbrush and a gigantic pair of pincers to pull out his tooth. He commanded his servants to fill a huge flower pot with soil and plant one tulip bulb. When spring came, one small but very beautiful tulip flower grew and the King realised that biggest is not always best after all. After the performance, show the audience pictures of small wild flowers e.g. violets, celandine, speedwell, etc. Help them to appreciate the beauty which is encapsulated in such tiny flowers.

▣ Prepare a small group of children to develop a movement sequence to show the growth of a plant. The following is an example of the movements and ideas which could be explored. Percussion instruments could be used to accompany the sequence.

Idea	Movement Suggestions
Seed	Whole body curled up low to the ground.
Germination	Finger or hand slowly moving upwards to indicate the growth of the shoot. Fingers, hands and arms spreading downwards and outwards to indicate growth of roots.
Stem	Whole body growing upwards, curving and bending slightly.
Leaves	Arms, elbows, hands and fingers making leaf shapes. Encourage a diversity of shapes e.g. rounded, long and thin, sharp and spiky.
Buds and flowers	Hands and fingers forming bud shapes which open slowly. Final flower position held still for a few moments.

Salad Recipes

Obviously, a wide range of vegetable or fruit salads would be suitable and the recipe given below is just one example. Teachers will, no doubt, wish to choose recipes which relate particularly to their own pupils. In a multi-cultural situation, parents could be encouraged to demonstrate a favourite recipe from their own culture or one associated with a particular religious festival.

Useful points

1 Thorough preparation is needed to ensure that all the relevant equipment and ingredients are immediately to hand.

2 Try to arrange the seating of the audience to allow for the maximum number of children to see clearly.

3 Make safety a high priority. Whilst the recipe recommended below does not involve any hot substances, knives and tin openers can be dangerous if mishandled.

Tabbouleh

Equipment

Tablespoon	Knife (plastic?)	2 bowls
Teaspoon	Sieve	Spoon

Containers and spoons for the finished tabbouleh

Ingredients

4 tablespoons burghul
2 spring onions, chopped
quarter of cucumber, chopped
1 tablespoon fresh mint, chopped
6 tablespoons parsley, chopped
2 tablespoons fresh coriander, chopped
2 teaspoons olive oil
juice of 1 lemon
salt and pepper

Method

1 Soak the burghul for 15 minutes in a bowl full of water.
2 Sieve the burghul to remove the water, squeezing the excess moisture out.
3 Put the burghul in a bowl, add the vegetables and herbs and mix well.
4 Add the salt and pepper and lemon juice. Mix well. Add the oil and mix thoroughly.

Points to discuss with the audience

Have any of the children eaten tabbouleh before? Do they realise the recipe originated from another part of the world (the Middle East)? Many of the common dishes which now appear in our supermarkets come from other countries, adding richness to our own culture. Can the children name any of these dishes and say which is the country of origin? Have any of them eaten unusual dishes when they have been on holiday abroad? Do any of the audience know what burghul is? (Cracked wheat). Do they realise that it is the seeds of a plant? If possible, show them an ear of wheat and discuss ways in which wheat is an important ingredient in many of our foods e.g. in cornflakes, as flour in bread, cakes, biscuits etc. Have the children eaten any herbs before? Which part of the herbs in the recipe are going to be used? Why do we use herbs? It might be easier to have some burghul which has already been soaking for 15 minutes before the assembly. Compare the feel of the burghul before and after soaking. Does the burghul float or sink in the water? Can the children name other ingredients which need to be soaked before using? Can the children think of another occasion when a solid is separated from a liquid by using a sieve? Can they name another piece of kitchen equipment which performs a similar task? (E.g. tea strainer, colander, filter paper, etc.) Make a set of green ingredients. Smell these ingredients individually and then ask the children to name them using smell only with their eyes shut. Ask some of the children to taste the finished tabbouleh and say which is the dominant flavour. Do they like or dislike it?

Take the opportunity to remind the children that not everyone in the world has the same luxurious range of fruit and vegetables available to them. Many children in other countries have a monotonous diet, often consisting of rice only. The lack of fresh fruit and vegetables also means that many of them suffer a wide range of diseases. Of course, some of them simply have no food at all.

The Flowers in Town

by Stanley Cook from *The Squirrel in Town*, Blackie

Among the busy streets
In the middle of the town
Is a flowery field
Where houses have been knocked down.

Men with cranes and bulldozers
Left the ground brown and bare
Except for the broken bricks
Scattered everywhere.

The ground was rough and bumpy
And there the old bricks lay
Like a construction set
That hadn't been put away.

But the seeds of flowers
That were looking for a home
Travelled there on the wind
And made the place their own.

Ragweed that seems to be knitted
Out of yellow wool
And poppies like red crêpe paper
Have filled the hollows full.

High in the air, the willow herb
Raises its pointed towers
And daisies and butterfingers
Pattern the grass with flowers.

Where the people used to live
In the houses the men knocked down
All kinds of flowers and insects
Have come to town.

Where is the flowery field? What had happened on the site before? How had the seeds got there? What kinds of flowers were growing there? Have the children ever seen flowers growing in strange places e.g. on the walls of buildings, in cracks between pavements, even on the roofs of buildings?

RESOURCES

Poems

The Flowers in Town The Squirrel in Town (Blackie)
Dandelions The Squirrel in Town (Blackie)
Yellow Weed Rhyme Time (Beaver Books)
Seed Song Rhyme Time (Beaver Books)

Songs

Leave them a Flower Jolly Herring (A and C Black)
We are going to Plant a Bean This Little Puffin (Young Puffin)

Let it be Tinderbox Song Book (A and C Black)
Where have all the Flowers Gone? Alleluya (A and C Black)
Little Seed Sing a Song 1 (Nelson)
Song of the Seed Songs from Playschool (BBC)

Stories

The King's Flower M. Anno (Bodley Head)
The Tiny Seed E. Carle (Hodder and Stoughton)
Farmer John D. Bruna (Methuen)
One Watermelon Seed C. Baker Lottridge (OUP)
The Flower C. Baines (Frances Lincoln)

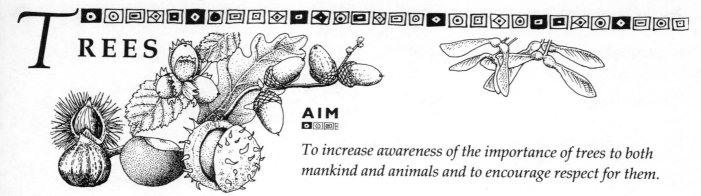

TREES

AIM

To increase awareness of the importance of trees to both mankind and animals and to encourage respect for them.

STARTING POINT

◎ Display a poster of a landscape with lots of trees. Ask members of the audience to suggest reasons for the disappearance of trees. For each reason cover up a tree with sugar paper.

Discuss   Encourage the audience to describe the landscape with and without trees. Why are trees important to mankind? They provide wood, food (in the form of fruit and nuts), oxygen, absorb sound (muffling traffic noise in cities) and add beauty to our surroundings.

Why are trees important to animals? They provide food (berries and nuts) and shelter for many creatures. Why are there fewer trees now than in the past? They may have been affected by natural diseases (Dutch Elm disease) and disasters (hurricanes and storms), interference by man (when they are cut down and replaced by houses and roads), and acid rain. There has also been very limited replacement planting.

Do the children realise trees are the Earth's largest living plants?

CORE ACTIVITIES

◎ Place several items which originate from trees into a 'feely box' and ask members of the audience to guess what each item is purely by touching. Reveal each item to see if they are correct and when this activity is completed, ask the audience to suggest how the items are linked—they all come from trees. The items could include paper, fruit, pencil and nuts. Extend this activity by playing an 'odd one out' game. Show four or five items to the audience, all of them linked to trees apart from one. Can they spot which item is not a member of the set?

◎ Collect a variety of leaves and sort them with the help of the audience in different ways—by colour, size, smooth/jagged edges, etc. Find out how dirty or dusty the leaves are by placing them between white tissue paper and rubbing with a spoon. Any dirt or dust should adhere to the paper.

Compare leaves from several situations—on the tree, on the ground, near a busy road etc. Which ones are the dirtiest? What would happen to the tree if all of its leaves were dirty?

◎ If seasonally appropriate, collect seeds produced by trees. These could include acorns, conkers, plum stones and sycamore wings. Display these together with large cards, each with the name of one of the parent trees. Ask members of the audience to match the correct card to each seed.

Discuss seed dispersal in relation to trees, highlighting the most common methods such as wind, animals or birds. Can the audience suggest which method(s) might apply to each seed on show?

▣ Help a group of children to devise a play which demonstrates the ecosystem of an oak tree—those plants and animals which use the tree for food and shelter. Children could assume the role of various creatures and explain the importance of the oak tree in their lives. For instance, nuthatches eat acorns, goat moth caterpillars tunnel into the wood, oak gall wasps lay their eggs in the buds of twigs, tawney owls nest in the trunk, grey squirrels eat acorns, woodlice live on decaying leaves, foxes make earths in the roots, etc.

The oak tree could be under some sort of threat such as being cut down to allow for the building of a motorway or houses. Other children could play the part of the workmen felling the trees or constructing the road/houses. They could put forward the opposing view and explain why the new houses and roads are required. (This also links with the story on page 37.)

▣ Organise a group of children to make a dictionary of trees. Can they find one tree whose name begins with each letter of the alphabet? Suggest that for each tree they draw a large picture and add one or two sentences describing its size, shape, leaf, flowers, fruit or habitat. Encourage them to choose examples which illustrate the diversity of trees.

CONCLUSION—WHAT CAN WE DO?

- Buy products made from recycled paper e.g. stationery, toilet roll, kitchen towel.

- Do not waste wood and wood-derived products such as paper. This is particularly relevant in school where children are not always conscious of the amount of paper they are consuming. In 1987, a forest the size of Wales had to be cut down to supply all the paper Britain needed.

- Whenever possible, recycle envelopes by reusing them.

- Respect and care for the trees in our environment e.g. don't vandalise them.

- Beware of the risk of fire in woods during long periods of dry weather.

- Plant as many trees as possible, using native trees which attract the widest range of wildlife.

- Avoid buying tropical hardwood furniture or timber.

Trees

Trees provide shade on a hot summer day.
Trees are a climbing frame for children at play.
Trees give shelter to nesting birds.
Trees, a source of paper, for endless words.
Trees offer food to squirrels and voles.
Tree roots are home for foxes in holes.
Trees whispering softly in a gentle breeze.
Trees with perfumed flowers to entice the bees.
Trees supply kindling and logs for a fire.
Trees with brilliant colours for us to admire.
Trees are a perch for owls hunting mice.
Trees powdered with snow, sparkling with ice.
Trees produce wood for man's ceaseless greed.
Trees disappearing at a frightening speed.

ALTERNATIVE ACTIVITIES

◎ Use the assembly as an occasion to plant a tree in the school grounds. A personal involvement with one particular tree is often a good way of promoting care and respect for trees generally. Discuss why a native species such as an oak, rowan, willow, birch or hawthorn would be preferable to a conifer such as leylandii. For example, about 280 different species of insect live on an oak compared to only 16 on a fir. What are the advantages to wildlife of the species which has been chosen? How will it improve the school environment? Devise a special tree planting ceremony such as inviting someone 'important' to plant it.

◎ Show a picture of a tropical rain forest and explain about deforestation in simple terms. The causes for deforestation vary according to the area of the world involved. Sometimes the native people clear the forests to grow food to eat but often it is done to supply the developed world with goods such as cheap beef (exported from Latin America) and hardwoods such as teak and mahogany (exported from West Africa and South East Asia). A globe may prove useful to show the children exactly where these areas are in the world.

Removing the forests also often causes tragedies for the local inhabitants as floods can result from the soil erosion. Can the audience suggest any reasons for conserving the rain forests? For example, many food products (coffee, sugar, cocoa, peanuts) originated from plants found there; one in four chemicals or medicines found in a chemists have compounds derived from rain forest plants; products such as rubber for car tyres and resins for paints also originated there. Who can tell what future medicines, foods or other products the rain forests may hold?

Obviously, it is difficult for young children to grasp some of the rather abstract concepts involved in this subject and teachers will have to decide how much the children can assimilate. It would probably help to show them some of the products which have links with the rain forest.

◎ Acid rain is another subject which young children may find rather hard to comprehend. However, teachers may feel it appropriate to mention in simple terms. Show pictures of factory chimneys and car exhausts and explain that poisonous gases from these are absorbed by the raindrops in the clouds and then when the rain falls, sometimes hundreds of miles away, the harmful water adversely affects not only trees and plants but also fish and other water creatures. Even though this is an invisible form of pollution, it is no less harmful.

▣ Organise a small group of children to draw a simple map of the school environment to show the position of trees. Can they describe which trees are old or young, deciduous or evergreen, and explain which species are most common and why? Encourage them to look carefully to see if all the trees are healthy. Are any of them diseased, dying from lack of water, being damaged by birds, animals or people, or affected by any forms of pollution? Display the map and ask one or two of the group to explain it and summarise their findings.

▣ Display art and design work created by a group of children based on a tree theme. These could include bark rubbings, leaf prints, collages, textures in clay, etc.

Death of an Oak?

The old oak tree was 20 metres tall. It was taller than all the other trees, taller than the telegraph poles and taller than the old barn. The bark on the trunk was rough, the branches twisted and gnarled. It had sprouted from a tiny acorn over a hundred years ago. Now, fully grown, it stood silently soaking up the summer sun.

For several days a faint droning noise hummed in the air and minute men with machines lumbered lazily in the distance. As the days passed, the noise grew louder and louder — whining and banging, hammering and clanging — until the sky was bursting. The men and machines loomed larger and larger — digging and sawing, cutting and clawing — until the green meadow was brown and bare. The oak tree trembled with the vibrations and shuddered as thick dust clung to its leaves.

Today there was a loud rumbling noise as a large yellow digger trundled towards the oak tree, breathing out clouds of dust. A man wearing a yellow helmet jumped down from the cab with a chain-saw in his hands. For a couple of minutes, he stared at the oak tree deciding how he should tackle felling it. He started up the chain saw which screeched and whined deafeningly. But, before he could use it, an elderly man rushed out from behind the tree waving frantically. As the noise of the chain saw died away, the elderly man shouted 'What are you doing? That terrible noise woke me up. I was having a wonderful doze under this tree.' The workman explained that he had come to fell the tree to make room for the garages which were needed for the new housing estate being built on the site.

'Garages!' exclaimed the old man in amazement. 'Surely, you're not going to replace this beautiful tree with garages?'

'Well, it's in the way and besides, there's plenty more trees around. No one will miss it,' argued the workman.

'But I will miss having my nap in the shade of its cool branches. You can't cut it down!'

The workman was just about to argue further when two legs dangled in front of his eyes. The workman blinked in surprise when he realised it was a young boy hanging from one of the branches. The boy let go and jumped down beside the workman. 'You can't possibly cut this tree down' snapped the boy 'I come here when I'm fed up and need to think. I always feel better once I've sat up in the branches for a while.'

'Well, I'm sorry but only two of you use this tree but there will be lots of people living in these new houses and they will *all* need garages,' said the workman sighing heavily.

'But what about all the creatures who depend upon this tree?' asked the old man.

'Creatures? What creatures? I can't see anything at all!' No sooner had the workman spoken, than several large woolly sheep butted him gently from behind, bleating loudly.

'There you are,' said the old man, 'I've often seen these sheep sheltering here, away from the rain or the hot sun. What will they do?'

The workman opened his mouth to reply but stopped suddenly when the branch above his head began to quiver violently. 'What . . . . . !'

'Don't worry, it's only the squirrel who lives in this tree. He feeds on the acorns. I don't think he's too pleased with you,' added the boy. The squirrel swished his tail in annoyance above the workman's face and scampered swiftly along the overhanging branches, causing the workman to duck nervously. A short, sharp drilling noise just above his head caused the workman to freeze in fear.

'What's that?' he stammered. The old man peered into the overhanging branches and said 'I think it's a woodpecker. He's probably searching for insects to eat under the bark.'

'Oh . . . . . . Still, I've got to get on,' said the workman, shuffling uncomfortably from one foot to another. 'I'm afraid I've still got to cut this tree down even though it will affect a few of you.' As he bent down to pick up his chain saw, a rabbit, startled by all the noise, scuttled terrified out of the nearby ditch and dashed into a large hole amongst the roots of the oak.

'What will happen to that poor rabbit and her family?' asked the boy. 'Why should they lose their home under the tree just because people want garages for cars?'

Before the workman could reply, a van arrived and the foreman of the site got out. 'What's the problem here? Haven't you started felling this tree yet?' he asked slightly annoyed. As the workman explained the situation, the foreman grew more and more irritated. 'We've got a job to do and we're already behind schedule. Houses and garages for people are far more important than one tree. Get it chopped down and be quick about it!'

'But this tree provides food and homes for so many creatures. They depend upon it and without it, they may die,' pleaded the old man. The workman hesitated.

What should he do? Can you help him decide? What would you suggest?

The Pines

by Margaret Mahy from *Poetry Plus—Green Earth and Silver Stars*, Schofield and Sims (acknowledgement to author and J. M. Dent and Sons Ltd. from The first Margaret Mahy Story Book)

Hear the rumble,
Oh, hear the crash.
The great trees tumble
The strong boughs smash.

Men with saws
Are cutting the pines—
That marched like soldiers
In straight green lines.

Seventy years
Have made them tall.
It takes ten minutes
To make them fall.

And breaking free
With never a care,
The pine cones leap
Through the clear, bright air.

What words describe the fall of the trees? Can the children think of some suitable alternative words or phrases? How long does it take for the trees to grow? And how long to be cut down? What are the children's responses to this?

RESOURCES

Poems

The Pines Poetry Plus—Green Earth and Silver Stars (Schofield and Sims)
Trees Is a Caterpillar Ticklish? (Young Puffin)
The Bossy Young Tree Gargling with Jelly (Viking Kestrel)
Trees Fingers, Feet and Fun (Beaver Books)
The Acorn that Grew The Squirrel in Town (Blackie)
Autumn Smile Please (Young Puffin)
Autumn Leaves Pudmuddle Jump In (Magnet)
Ten Tall Oak Trees Another Fifth Poetry Book (OUP)

Songs

Treefella Child Education July 1989 (Scholastic Publications)
The Oak Tree Sing a Song 1 (Nelson)
5 Trees Over and Over Again (Beaver Books)
Life in the Rain Forest Birds and Beasts (A and C Black)

Stories

Flames in the Forest R. Bond (Julia MacRae)
Where the Forest Meets the Sea J. Baker (Julia MacRae)
Out of the Wood G. Underhill (OUP)
Tales of the Magic Tree H. E. Glease (Piccolo)
When Dad Cuts Down the Chestnut Tree P. Ayres (Walker)
The Oak N. Russell (Methuen)
Rain Forest H. Cowcher (Deutsch)
Trees Rule OK S. Limb (Orchard Books)
The Tale of a Hazelnut (in Tell me a story) E. Colwell (Young Puffin)
Shoes and Shoots (in Allotment Lane School Again) M. Joy (Young Puffin)
The Hurricane Tree L. Purves (Bodley Head)

$\mathcal{B}$IRDS

AIM
◻◻◻

To promote a caring approach to wild birds.

STARTING POINT

◉ Display some pictures of common wild birds (calendars are a good source) and ask the audience to identify them. Examples could include robin, blue tit, sparrow and blackbird. Play an attributes game with them e.g. I often live in hedgerows and eat insects, I sometimes make my nest in strange places and I have a red breast. Who am I? Can a member of the audience name the bird being described and point to the appropriate picture?

Discuss What contribution do wild birds make to our lives? Suggestions might include: they are interesting to watch; they keep numbers of certain insects under control; and their songs are pleasant to hear. What do wild birds need to survive e.g. shelter, food, water, nesting sites? What time of the year are birds especially vulnerable? Many birds, such as the lapwing, snipe, barn owl, corncrake and merlin, are seriously threatened. Can the children suggest why these birds should be in danger?

There is a decline in many of their natural habitats because hedgerows are being pulled up, marshes are drained and moorlands developed. Eggs are sometimes stolen from nests and some birds are still hunted. Some also die due to man's thoughtlessness such as pesticides and pollution in both rivers and the sea. According to the Royal Society for the Protection of Birds, 300 different species of bird have vanished from the world over the last 300 years.

CORE ACTIVITIES

◉ *Food.* Birds only need feeding in the harsh winter months (November to March), especially if snow is covering their natural food source or towards the end of winter when natural food supplies begin to dwindle. They should not be fed in the summer and especially not when nesting in case unsuitable nuts are given to baby birds. Can the audience suggest appropriate foods? These could include mixed bird seed, kitchen scraps (e.g. rind, fat, bread soaked in water), fruit, nuts (unsalted), cheese, etc. Remind the children not to put out desiccated coconut or uncooked rice because if a bird drinks water after eating these, they may swell up in its stomach. However, a variety of food will encourage a diversity of bird life.

Obviously, it is best to place food in an open space, away from cats and it is important to remember that not all birds will feed from a bird table. Some, such as wrens, dunnocks, blackbirds, chaffinches and thrushes, prefer feeding on the ground. Emphasise that once started, regular feeding must continue as birds become reliant on humans.

◉ *Water.* Water is important all the year round for drinking and bathing. It is particularly important in winter when many sources may be unobtainable because they are frozen over. Can the children suggest why it is important for birds to bathe? Show the audience examples of appropriate water containers. These should be shallow and gently sloping e.g. an upside down dustbin lid, a shallow hole in the ground lined with polythene and covered with gravel, etc. If possible, put a container in the school grounds and keep a record of which birds drink and bathe in it and how often.

◉ Listen to recorded bird songs e.g. *The sounds of the Countryside* by Johnny Morris. Ask the audience to help compile a list of words to describe the sounds e.g. hoot, twitter, squawk. Does anyone in the audience ever hear birds singing at home, on the way to school or whilst walking to the shops.

◉ Show the audience a redundant bird's nest and discuss its construction—the various materials used, time taken to make, place where found, etc. Display pictures of various types of birds' eggs and encourage the audience to suggest reasons for not touching or taking birds' eggs.

▣ *Shelter.* Use the story *The Little Fir Tree* (see page 42) as a basis for a puppet play. It illustrates the need for birds to have shelter in winter and is an easy story to adapt as a play. After the performance, discuss what happens to birds who are unable to find shelter in the winter. How can we help to provide this shelter?

▣ Prepare two or three children to draw and explain simple diagrams on the construction of a basic bird table. Encourage them to incorporate certain features. For example, a roof offers protection from the elements and a rim helps prevent food being blown away. Deter squirrels by encasing the pole in plastic drainpipe and avoid cats by siting the bird table away from bushes and trees and if possible, surrounded by prickly roses or brambles. If feasible, build a bird table and put it in the school grounds.

▣ Organise one or two children to write a short report about the work of the Royal Society for the Protection of Birds. This could include information about its history, the reserves managed by the organisation, its protection of rare species and the educational role it performs, in particular the Young Ornithologists Club. Children could write to The Royal Society for the Protection of Birds, The Lodge, Sandy, Bedfordshire SG19 2DL, for leaflets and further information, together with lists of films and videos for hire.

Wild Birds

Swallows swoop skilfully
catching insects on the wing.
A wren hides in the hedgerow
but we can hear her sing.

A pair of bright bullfinches
perch boldly in a fruit tree.
Seagulls screeching and wheeling
over the glistening sea.

A bluetit hovers at the birdtable
agile as an acrobat.
Whilst the robin, tame and trusting,
will even nest in a hat.

If we use our eyes and ears
birds are everywhere.
But they won't be here for ever
unless we take great care.

CONCLUSION—WHAT CAN WE DO?

● Help birds survive the winter by putting out regular supplies of food and water.

● Plant and maintain trees, shrubs and hedges to provide shelter for them.

● Plant flowers and shrubs which can provide food for them in the form of seeds or berries. Leave the dead flowers on the plants to develop seeds for the birds to eat.

● Avoid disturbing birds when they are nesting.

● NEVER take birds' eggs. Warn the children that it is illegal to collect the eggs of wild birds in this country.

ALTERNATIVE ACTIVITIES

◎ *Food.* Demonstrate the making of a bird cake with help from members of the audience. Melt some fat and mix in bread or cake crumbs, cooked potato, currants, bird seed, chopped bacon rind, etc. Use approximately 250 g of fat to 500 g of mixture. Press down firmly in a container and leave to set. Once the mixture has set, it can be tipped out onto the bird table. Alternatively, the mixture can be put into small yoghurt pots with string threaded through the base so that they can be hung up.

◎ Show pictures of plants or shrubs which provide food for birds. These might include berry bearing species such as rowan, hawthorn, elder, holly, crab apple, berberis, pyracantha and seed bearing plants such as sunflower, marigold and Michaelmas daisy. Can the audience name any of the plants featured in the pictures and say why they would be attractive to birds? If possible, plant some of these species in the school grounds.

◎ *Nesting.* Display various types of nest boxes and discuss their purpose and construction. Emphasise that correct siting of nest boxes is important. For example, consideration must be given to place the box so that it is above the reach of cats and children and it should be facing north or east to avoid the rain and the midday sun. Also, all nest boxes should be cleaned out at the end of each breeding season to avoid the build up of parasites.

◎ Listen to recordings of classical music which feature birds or bird calls. Can the children name the instruments used to represent the bird or bird call? Is it possible to identify a particular bird? The following is a brief list of music which teachers may find suitable.

Exotic birds	Olivier Messiaen
Pines of Rome	Resphigi
On hearing the first cuckoo in spring	Delius
Siegfried—Song of the birds	Wagner
Song of the birds	Jannequin
Song of the birds	Gombert
Cuckoo and nightingale (organ concerto)	Handel
Nightingale chorus in Solomon	Handel
Fugue with a cock-crow	Bach
Toy Symphony	Michael Hayden
Pastoral symphony Number 6	Beethoven
The swan in Carnival of the Animals	Saint-Saens
The lark ascending	Vaughan-Williams

◎ Display a collection of various bird feathers. Discuss the size, colour, shape and pattern of each one together with its possible origin e.g. wing, tail feather. Why are feathers important to birds and what functions do they perform? What effect does oil pollution have on feathers? If possible, have pictures of the owner of each feather and ask the children to match the correct feather to each bird.

▣ Arrange for a small number of children to experiment with various types of nesting material. For instance, they could put out twigs, straw, string, cotton wool, wood shavings, etc. and record which materials the birds take and their order of preference. The children could explain their findings to the audience.

▣ If feasible, ask one or two children to record bird songs around the school environment which could then be played to the audience. Why do birds have a variety of songs e.g. for singing, contesting territory and alarm calls? Were the children able to see the birds and identify them? How many different kinds were seen and where were they perching? Use the opportunity to remind the audience not to scare birds especially when they are nesting.

▣ Challenge a small group of children to design collars for cats to wear which make a sound to warn the birds of the cat's approach. Display these during the assembly and ask the children to explain how they were made and how they work.

A robin

The Little Fir Tree

adapted by Moira Miller for *Playtime*, BBC School Radio, Autumn 1983

A little bird was looking for a home for the winter. He flew from tree to tree trying to find a place where he could live. First he came to a beech tree, growing in the forest.

'Beautiful beech tree,' said the little bird, 'May I come and live among your golden leaves until the spring?'

'No,' answered the beech tree. 'I have the loveliest leaves in the forest but I must take good care of them. I have no room for a scruffy little bird like you'.

The little bird flew off and came to a tall oak tree that stood alone in the middle of the field.

'Mighty oak tree,' said the little bird. 'May I come and live among your strong branches until the spring?'

'Goodness gracious, no!' said the oak tree, 'I am the King of trees. It would not do to have a scruffy little bird like you among my fine branches'.

Sadly, the little bird flew away. He flew on and on across fields and gardens, woods and farms, until he came to rest on the dark green sweet-smelling branches of a little fir tree, that swayed and tossed in the winter winds.

'Little fir tree,' said the bird, 'May I come and live among your thick green needles? The cold winter is coming and I must find somewhere safe and warm.'

'Of course you may!' said the little fir tree.

So the little bird lived warm and happy through the long cold autumn days into the winter. The wild North Wind and Jack Frost came howling down from their icy palace in the north. They froze the fingers and toes of the children playing in the fields, until they had to run and jump and stamp their feet to keep warm. Then the North Wind and Jack Frost came to the trees of the forest. They saw the little bird warm and happy amongst the green needles of the little fir tree. 'Look,' they said, 'How the little fir tree has helped the bird, when the other trees did not. We will take away all the leaves of the beech tree and the oak tree, but we will leave the warm green needles on the little fir tree, so that the bird will be safe and happy'.

So Jack Frost nipped and pinched and the wild North Wind puffed and blew until all the beautiful golden beech leaves and the mighty oak leaves had been blown away. But they left the thick green needles on the fir tree, and the little bird was warm and happy all through the winter.

Probably the easiest way to adapt the story for a puppet play is to have a narrator who moves the story forward and links all the characters—the bird, the beech tree, the oak tree, the fir tree, Jack Frost and the North Wind. Encourage the children to invent their own dialogue to express the feelings of the characters.

There are many methods for making puppets to represent the above characters, ranging from simple finger bobs to more complex stringed puppets. The following is just one suggestion from the various methods which could prove suitable.

1 Ask the children to draw a large simple picture of their character on a piece of white card.

2 Add colour, preferably using wax crayon, coloured pencils or felt tips. Avoid paint as it tends to make the card curl up.

3 Cut carefully around the outside of the character.

4 Draw round the character on another piece of white card and cut it out.

5 Place the blank piece of card back to back with the coloured version. Draw and colour on the blank card as if it were the back of the character.

6 Staple and/or glue the two halves of the character together with a rod sandwiched in between. The rod could be a cardboard tube, bamboo stick or wooden dowel.

bird   north wind   fir tree

I'm a Parrot

by Grace Nichols from *Come on into my Tropical Garden* A and C Black

I am a parrot
I live in a cage
I'm nearly always
in a vex-up rage

I used to fly
all light and free
in the luscious green
forest canopy

I am a parrot
I live in a cage
I'm nearly always
in a vex-up rage

I miss the wind
against my wing
I miss the nut
and the fruit picking

I am a parrot
I live in a cage
I'm nearly always
in a vex-up rage

I squawk I talk
I curse I swear
I repeat the things
I shouldn't hear

So don't come near me
or put out your hand
because I'll pick you
if I can
pickyou
pickyou
if I can
I want to be Free
Can't you understand?

How does the parrot feel being kept in a cage? Where would it rather be? What does it miss from its previous life? What other types of caged birds have the children seen? Did the birds seem happy? Did the cage appear to be large enough? Do the children think there is any harm in caging wild birds? Are there any benefits for the birds or for us? Would the children think it a good idea to put a robin or a sparrow in a cage? Take the opportunity to remind the children that it is illegal to trap and cage wild birds in this country.

RESOURCES

Poems

Marcus Able Tinderbox Assembly Book (A and C Black)
Feeding the Pigeons The Squirrel in Town (Blackie)
The Bluetit The Squirrel in Town (Blackie)
Robin A Very First Poetry Book (OUP)
Birds Nests Seeing and Doing Anthology of Poetry (Methuen)
The Nest Animals Like Us (Blackie)
The Bird Table A Patter of Poems (Ginn Goes Home series) (Ginn)

Songs

The North Wind Doth Blow Over and Over Again (Beaver Books)
Little Birds in Winter Time Someone's Singing, Lord (A and C Black)
A Little Tiny Bird Someone's Singing, Lord (A and C Black)
Blackbirds Song (Something to Think About) (BBC)
A Little Bird Built a Warm Nest in a Tree The Funny Family (Ward Lock Educational)
Owl Song Songs from Playschool (BBC)
Five Baby Birds Jump into the Ring (Ward Lock Educational)
Don't Forget to Feed the Birds in Winter Playtime Activity Book (BBC)
Little Red Bird The Music Box Song Book (BBC)

Stories

The Bird of Happiness L. Paleckova (Lutterworth Press)
The Singing Bird B. Resch (A and C Black)
Topsy and Tim can help Birds J. and G. Adamson (Blackie)
The Little Lighthouse Keeper M. Joy (Viking Kestrel)
The Nest C. Baines (Frances Lincoln)
The Magpie's Nest (in Play School Stories) M. Rosen (BBC)
Mr and Mrs Ostrich (in The Anita Hewett Animal Story Book) A. Hewett (Young Puffin)
Gran's Bird Cake (in Playtime Activity Book) A. English (BBC)

BUTTERFLIES

AIM
▫◻▣▧

To promote greater understanding of the conditions which butterflies need to survive.

STARTING POINT

◎ Explain the life cycle of a butterfly—from egg, to caterpillar, to chrysalis, to adult. If possible, make use of a visual aid to reinforce the various stages. This could take the form of posters or alternatively, a cardboard circle split into four quarters could be used. Each quarter could contain a simple picture together with the name of each stage. Another cardboard circle with one quarter cut away could be pinned over the first circle with a split pin. Thus, the top circle can be moved round to reveal one quarter at a time. Start with the 'egg' quarter revealed and ask the audience to predict which stage will appear next when the circle is turned.

Discuss Do the audience like butterflies? What do they enjoy about them? Can they describe any which they have seen recently? Where were the butterflies which they observed?

Explain that the survival of butterflies can often depend upon a delicate balance of conditions. For example, the Large Blue butterfly became extinct in England because the larvae depended upon a specific type of ant in conjunction with the plant, wild thyme. Another example is the Large Copper which has also disappeared in this country because the marshes were drained in Cambridgeshire and Huntingdonshire where this particular species lived.

CORE ACTIVITIES

◎ Devise an activity to illustrate the diversity of butterflies. Show pictures or slides of a variety of common species e.g. the Whites, Tortoiseshell, Peacock, Red Admiral, Meadow Brown. Discuss their shapes, colours, patterns, etc. If possible, have cards with pictures of butterflies on them, two of each kind. Ask a member of the audience to hold up one card whilst another child goes through the rest of the pack of cards, holding up each one. Encourage the audience to say 'snap' when two cards are held up showing the same species of butterfly. This activity will improve the children's ability to distinguish between butterflies.

◎ Read *The Very Hungry Caterpillar* by E. Carle (see page 48 for details). This popular children's story shows a caterpillar eating an amazing range of fantastic foods from strawberries and chocolate cake to Swiss cheese and watermelon. After the story, ask the audience if caterpillars really do eat these foods. Do they know what caterpillars usually eat? Give them some examples ideally by showing them a picture of the adult butterfly, the caterpillar and the food plant. For instance, the caterpillars of the Orange Tip butterfly feed on the leaves of honesty, sweet rocket, milkmaids flowers or hedge mustard, the Common Blue feeds on birdsfoot trefoil, clover or black medick whilst the Meadow Brown feeds on the uncut leaves of meadow grasses. Emphasise the fact that if these food sources disappear, then so do the caterpillars and, as a consequence, the adult butterflies.

◎ Display a large clump of stinging nettles. If possible, show the audience the tough yellow rhizomes and extensive root system which enable the nettle to spread rapidly. Explain that both the stem and leaves are covered with stinging hairs, each of which has a reservoir of poison at the base. Ask the audience whether they like stinging nettles or not and to give reasons for their answers. For each reason given for disliking nettles, suggest a child from the audience comes to the front of the hall or room. Repeat the list of reasons, asking each child to say 'I hate nettles because . . . . . .'

Having established that most people dislike nettles, explain that many butterflies and moths depend upon them as food for their caterpillars. Although humans and some grazing animals such as rabbits are stung by nettles, caterpillars and other insects are not. Have cards prepared with one species of butterfly on each e.g. Peacock, Tortoiseshell, etc., and ask members of the audience to hold up one card. Contrast the reasons for people disliking nettles, with the large number of butterflies and moths (over 40 species in all) which rely on them. Is it possible for everyone to leave a small clump of nettles in their garden or a large area in the school grounds?

◎ Discuss how butterflies feed from the nectar of flowering plants. Explain that their tongue (proboscis) is hollow like a drinking straw and it is used to probe deep inside the flower and to suck up the nectar. When the tongue is not being used, it is coiled up under the head. Butterflies are particularly attracted to purple flowers such as buddleia, lavender, honesty, candytuft, ice plants, etc. Explain that whilst feeding from these plants, butterflies are also performing an important function in that they often pollinate them, thus helping in the seed production. Show examples of these plants and encourage the children to grow them at school or at home.

◎ Borrow some butterfly specimens, mounted in cases. The local Schools Museum Service may prove a good source. Show them to the audience and explain how, especially in the past, it was considered an acceptable hobby to collect butterflies. Refer the audience back to the butterfly cycle (see starting point) and help them to appreciate that capturing the adult prevents further eggs from being laid and can, therefore, drastically reduce the population of that species. Although collecting is illegal for a small minority of species, the majority of butterflies have no such protection. Obviously, the nearer a species comes to extinction the more desirable it becomes to a collector. Suggest that keen butterfly watchers could photograph rather than kill butterflies.

▣ It is possible to make artificial nectar. Ask a group of children to make some which could then be placed outside so that they can monitor whether butterflies feed from it and if so, what species are involved. Dissolve one teaspoon of honey and one teaspoon of sugar in 1 litre of water with a pinch of salt. Place it in a shallow dish or a small drinking bottle, similar to those used for pet hamsters. Encourage the group to record their findings and report back during the assembly.

CONCLUSION—WHAT CAN WE DO?

● Never catch or collect butterflies as this prevents more eggs from being laid. Handling adults can damage the scales on their wings and affect their ability to fly.

● Never keep caterpillars in matchboxes away from their plant food. If caterpillars are kept for study purposes, ensure a regular supply of fresh leaves required by that particular species. When the caterpillars are no longer needed for study, always return them (or the adults) to their original habitat.

● Plant flowers and shrubs which provide the food source for the caterpillars e.g. stinging nettles for Tortoiseshells, honesty for Orange Tips.

● Plant flowers and shrubs which attract butterflies to their nectar e.g. Michaelmas daisies and buddleia.

● Avoid spraying pesticides which may kill caterpillars or butterflies.

● Think carefully before destroying a habitat which may be supporting a particular range of butterflies e.g. hedgerows which contain ivy are vitally important for the survival of the Holly Blue which lays its eggs on the flowers in October and for the Brimstone which hibernates amongst the leaves over winter.

I Hate Nettles

I hate nettles!
They sneak up and sting.
The red rash swells up,
Bumpy and itching.

I hate nettles!
Let's cut them all down.
Why don't we spray them?
They'll die and go brown.

I hate nettles!
But—what's this strange leaf?
A butterfly closed,
drab wings underneath.

I hate nettles!
Caterpillars will too!
Surely they won't think
them tasty to chew?

I hate nettles.
But—I suppose they'd better stay.
Butterflies need them
To breed, they say.

ALTERNATIVE ACTIVITIES

◎ Use the butterfly to illustrate symmetry. Draw a large chalk outline of a butterfly shape on the blackboard. Ask a member of the audience to add coloured markings to one half and then ask another member of the audience to repeat the same markings on the other half to form a symmetrical pattern.

◎ Play the song *The Ugly Bug Ball* and prepare a small group of children to devise a caterpillar dance. They could form a line, holding on to each other's waists and develop a follow my leader dance, twisting and turning, rising and sinking etc. Members of the audience could be invited to join on or form another caterpillar.

◎ Reinforce the butterfly life cycle by asking the audience to participate in a card game. Make a pack of cards with simple diagrams of eggs, caterpillars, chrysalises and butterflies. Ask one or two members of the audience to choose cards from the upturned pack, keeping them if they help complete a life cycle sequence and returning them to the bottom of the pack if they repeat cards already held. Display the cards which have been retained and encourage the audience to indicate when a correct sequence has been completed.

▣ Display paintings arising from the children's observations of butterflies. Discuss the pictures with the audience, emphasising the beauty of the different shapes, colours and patterns.

▣ Prepare a group of children to research into butterflies associated with a wide range of habitats such as woodland, hedgerows, heathland, coastal areas, marshlands and wild flower meadows. Suggest they choose one species of butterfly for each habitat and prepare a brief biography of it e.g. I am a Comma butterfly, I prefer to live in wooded areas, I feed on the nectar of flowers and fruits, my caterpillars eat nettles. Ask each child to present the biography of their butterfly during the assembly.

Emphasise that each butterfly depends upon a different habitat and discuss what would happen if that habitat were to be destroyed for building houses or motorways, etc. Explain that some butterflies are very rare and are in danger of becoming extinct because of habitat loss. For example, the swallowtail is now only found in one wet place in Cambridgeshire (Wicken Fen) and parts of the Norfolk Broads because the caterpillars only feed on a plant called milk parsley which, in turn, only grows in marshes. The royal fern butterfly is also a rarity because it prefers upland, acid bogs and these are rapidly vanishing due to land reclamation for forestry or agriculture.

▣ Develop a 'word round' with a group of children. Encourage them to suggest some interesting words and phrases to describe butterflies and caterpillars. Devise a sequence of words and phrases for each and recite in two groups as a 'round'. Use contrasts such as loud and soft, fast and slow, to vary the delivery. For example:

Butterflies	Caterpillars
Butterflies	Slow
Flickering flight	Stretch and crawl
Dart and dive	Caterpillars munching
High	Splitting their skins

The 'butterflies' words could be recited softly and quickly whilst the 'caterpillars' could be slow and louder.

▣ Breed some butterflies in the classroom. Prepare a group of children to explain the process to the assembly. Emphasise the importance of caring for the butterflies correctly and of returning them to an appropriate habitat once they are no longer needed. (See below for details.)

Breeding Butterflies

It is possible to breed butterflies successfully in the classroom provided adequate preparation is made to ensure as 'natural' conditions as possible. To witness the change from egg to adult butterfly is extremely exciting and very educational but obviously care must be taken to maximise the probability of a successful outcome. Dead caterpillars resulting from the wrong diet of leaves will be most unwelcome.

Eggs (and sometimes caterpillars) can be obtained from reputable companies e.g. Worldwide Butterflies Ltd., Compton, Sherborne, Dorset. However, it is wiser only to buy species which can be found locally as they are more likely to survive when released whereas less common species will die because they will be unable to find suitable conditions. Eggs can also be found locally, e.g. the Cabbage White butterfly eggs on cabbage leaves or

Tortoiseshell eggs on stinging nettles. However, it is obviously important to only take a small sample of eggs from each situation and to make sure they are not removed from the leaves where they were laid. Also, take note of the type of plant on which the eggs were found as supplies of this will be needed to feed the caterpillars later on.

Place the eggs in a transparent, escape proof container which can be easily observed by the children. It needs to be large enough to contain adequate supplies of food and to provide places for the caterpillars to pupate. The temperature needs to be cool and fairly even so avoid placing them in direct sunlight. Also ensure that the ventilation is good and that there is free circulation of air. The moisture content within the container is also important. If it is too dry, the development of the butterfly can be hindered but if it is too wet, mould and fungus diseases will develop and harm them.

Once the eggs have hatched into caterpillars, provide a regular fresh supply of their food plant, preferably in a container with water but with cardboard covering the top to prevent the caterpillars drowning. Care must also be taken when renewing foliage to ensure that spiders or wasps are not introduced into the container since both attack butterflies. Put a small amount of soil in the bottom of the container because although some caterpillars pupate on their food plant, some prefer crevices or soil. Droppings should also be removed occasionally although care must be taken not to disturb any caterpillars preparing to pupate. Once the butterflies have appeared, return them to a suitable habitat as soon as possible. Remind the children that careless handling of both caterpillars and butterflies can cause damage should be avoided.

At each stage, numerous questions can be posed to encourage the children to observe the eggs and caterpillars closely. Discuss the shape, colour and size of the eggs and whether any changes are noticed over a period of time. Study caterpillars under a microscope or with a hand lens to discover how they move, how they cling to a leaf, how often they shed their skins, whether they are well camouflaged, etc. Once the caterpillar is pupating, discuss the differences between the pupae and the larvae and the eventual adult. Before releasing the adult butterfly, place some appropriate flowers in the container which held the food plant for the caterpillars. This will enable the children to observe the butterfly using its proboscis to feed on the nectar. Is it possible to see the scales on the butterfly's wings?

Painting of a butterfly

Reasons for the Decline in Butterflies

The numbers of many species of butterflies have rapidly declined recently and several previously common species are now much more localised. According to the British Butterfly Conservation Society, there are now 55 species of butterfly in Britain. Whilst three species (the Wood White, White Admiral and Comma) are increasing in distribution, 11 species are 'holding their own' whilst the others are in various stages of decline.

Although butterflies are harmless to man and can be seen as beneficial because of their role in pollination, man can be held responsible for their decreasing numbers. The following are the major factors influencing their disappearance:

1 *Urban development.* Our need for houses, roads and industry results in the destruction of many species' natural habitat.

2 *Modern agricultural methods.* Many farmland habitats have been destroyed because of the increasing use of chemical spraying, hedge removal, drainage schemes and ploughing wild land.

3 *Collectors.* Although collecting is viewed as a less acceptable hobby in society, many still believe it is a contributing factor in the extinction of rare species.

4 *Acid rain.* Butterfly populations decrease whenever the countryside is adversely affected by pollution such as acid rain.

5 *Lack of knowledge.* The intricate and sometimes delicate balance of conditions required for some butterflies to breed successfully is still not completely understood for many species. Research is often not conducted until a species is seriously threatened and then knowledge often comes too late to prevent extinction. Unfortunately, this proved to be the case with the Large Blue butterfly which became extinct in the 1970s. It is possible that man's activities are inadvertently harming many species because of our ignorance about a species' life cycle.

For further information about butterfly conservation, please contact the British Butterfly Conservation Society, Tudor House, Quorn, Loughborough, Leicestershire LE12 8AD.

Caterpillar

by D. Evans in *Fingers, Feet and Fun* by D. Evans, Beaver Books

I can see a caterpillar
Wriggling on a leaf.
It wriggles on the top
And it wriggles underneath.
Then one day it's very still
I stand quietly watching till
It changes shape and falls asleep.
Every day I take a peep.
Then at last, it moves about.
I'm so surprised, I give a shout.
For now there's a butterfly
Sitting on the leaf.
It spreads its wings
And flies about.

Encourage the children to join in with appropriate actions to accompany the reading of the poem. What stages of the life cycle of the butterfly are mentioned in the poem? Which stage is not referred to in the poem?

RESOURCES

Poems

A Caterpillar Ask a Silly Question (Mammoth)
Message from a Caterpillar Rhyme Time 2 (Beaver Books)
The Butterfly The Squirrel in Town (Blackie)
The Caterpillar Young Puffin Book of Verse (Young Puffin)
Flutter By A Very First Poetry Book (OUP)
Caterpillar Walk Pudmuddle Jump In (Magnet)

Songs

Caterpillars Only Crawl Harlequin (A and C Black)
I went to the Cabbages Tinderbox Song Book (A and C Black)
Butterfly Flutterby Birds and Beasts (A and C Black)
3 White Butterflies Knock at the Door (Ward Lock Educational)
Flutter, Flutter Butterfly Jump into the Ring (Ward Lock Educational)
Arabella Miller This Little Puffin (Young Puffin)
9 Caterpillars Counting Songs (Early Learning Centre)

Stories

The Very Hungry Caterpillar E. Carle (Picture Puffin)
Grasshopper and Butterfly H. Piers and P. Baynes (Kestrel Books)
Two Green Butterflies (in Tell me Another Story) E. Colwell (Young Puffin)
The Butterfly Garden (in The Second Margaret Mahy Story Book) M. Mahy (Dent)
The Seed that Peter Found (in Story Time Two) W. Brown (Magnet)

A NIMALS (EXTINCT)

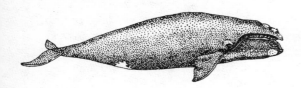

AIM

To introduce the idea that some animals are now extinct and the causes for this.
To encourage the children to think about the value of animals in our world.

Note   The two themes Animals (Extinct) and Animals (Endangered) are linked and many of the activities suggested are interchangeable. Also the causes for extinction are often the same as those responsible for endangering some species. To avoid repetition, these causes have been dealt with separately under one of the themes but not under both themes.

STARTING POINT

▣ Ask seven children to hold one letter each for the word 'extinct'. Each letter card could have a picture of an extinct animal or bird on the reverse side which the children could show to the audience, give its name and read a sentence or two about it.

The creatures could include the Texas Red Wolf from North America, the Mexican Silver Grizzly bear from Northern Mexico, the Javan tiger from Indonesia, the Blue Buck from South Africa, the North American passenger pidgeon, the Great Auk which formerly inhabited parts of Greenland, the Large Copper butterfly which can no longer be found in Great Britain, the Greenland whale, the Arabian ostrich which used to live in the Middle East, and the Laughing Owls of New Zealand.

Discuss   What does the word 'extinct' mean? Why do creatures become extinct? Sometimes there are natural causes as in the case of dinosaurs whose disappearance was due to climatic changes on the earth. However, sometimes man is responsible as in the case of the dodo which had no natural enemies and no fear of man who killed it for food and sport. Should we be concerned if more creatures become 'extinct'? What do animals add to our lives?

CORE ACTIVITIES

◎ Use the book *As Dead As A Dodo* (see page 52 for details) to introduce a variety of extinct animals. Discuss the reasons for their disappearance. What could have been done to prevent their extinction?

◎ Ask the audience to suggest a common animal and say what they would miss about it if it were to become extinct. For example, they might miss the wagging tail of a dog, the soft fur of a cat or the twitching nose of a rabbit.

◎ Read the story *The Hunter and His Dog* by Brian Wildsmith (see page 52 for details) which deals with a man who kills birds without really thinking about it and with no real purpose. Discuss the story and see if the audience can suggest why people hunt. Their reasons might include hunting for food, for sport, for skins and ivory to sell, to reduce the population of a creature which is a pest.

▣ Organise a small group of children to research one extinct creature each. They could draw a picture of it and give a brief description e.g. its size, colour, number of legs, what it used to eat, where it lived, when and why it became extinct. Ask them to read out their findings during the assembly.

CONCLUSION—WHAT CAN WE DO?

● Think carefully before killing anything.

● Remember that extinction is forever and cannot be undone.

● Stop buying goods which are a product of hunting. For example, the skins of crocodiles, turtles, lizards and snakes are used for manufacturing bags, belts and shoes. The skins of leopards and other big cats are made into clothes, hats and rugs. Elephant ivory is used for making jewellery and ornaments.

● Support organisations attempting to protect and care for animals. Write to them for information about the work they undertake. Probably the most well known example is the World Wide Fund for Nature – Panda House, Weyside Park, Catteshall Lane, Godalming, Surrey GU7 1WR.

Extinction

I've never seen a dodo.
I'm not sure what it's like.
Does it have four legs,
Big ears and a horn like a spike?

I've never seen a dodo
And now I never will.
The dodo is extinct because
Man thought it fun to kill.

My son's never seen a fox.
Will he find it a mystery
If all that remains is a photograph
To show it running free?

ALTERNATIVE ACTIVITIES

◎ Focus on one particular 'endangered' species such as the whale. Some whales are already extinct, as in the case of the Greenland whale, whilst others are endangered, such as the Bowhead whale. Even though some whales (such as Blue whales) are protected by international agreements, there are now so few and they are spread over such a wide area that it may not be possible for them to breed in large enough numbers to ensure their survival. It is obviously more difficult for young children to be concerned about a creature's future if they know nothing about it. Consequently, it is important to devise activities which will help the audience become familiar with whales. For example, whales can hold their breath longer than land mammals and some, such as the Sperm whale, can last for an hour. Use a one minute egg timer to see if the audience can hold their breath for one minute or longer.

Despite the fact that they have no vocal chords, whales can make a variety of noises. Listen to a recording of whale noises and encourage the audience to predict what they might be saying.

Whales are huge and some attempt can be made to convey this to the audience by using a metre stick to measure out the length of one species e.g. the Blue whale can be 30 metres long. Display a collection of whale based products such as candles, perfumes, brushes, fertilisers, jellies, cosmetics, pet foods, soups and wax crayons. Explain that for most of these products, alternatives do exist and it is no longer necessary to kill whales in order to have these.

◎ Read the following description of a dodo.

The dodo had a rather small, round head with two tiny orange eyes. Its beak was a sharply curved hook. It had a large, round fat body with two small useless wings. Drab feathers covered its body and three short feathers formed a tail. It had two short stubby yellow legs with four toes on each foot.

See if members of the audience can help draw a picture of a dodo based on the above description. Fold a large sheet of paper into three sections and let a different volunteer from the audience draw a part of a dodo in each section—the head, the body, the legs. If possible, have a picture of a real dodo to compare with once the drawing is completed. How are the children's efforts similar/different to the real thing? Remind the children how difficult it would be to draw a dog or cat if they had become extinct and we relied solely on verbal descriptions or drawings of them.

◎ Discuss the keeping of wild animals in zoos. Can the audience help compile a list of reasons for and against keeping animals in zoos.

For

● Educational reasons—To inform people about animals they would never normally be able to see and thus promote understanding and sympathy for them.

● Breeding—Some species such as gorillas which are rare can sometimes be bred in captivity and then reintroduced to the wild.

● Research undertaken by scientists—Sometimes it is easier to study certain species in captivity and these studies can result in the acquisition of important knowledge which can, in turn, be used to aid conservation.

● Environment—Good zoos attempt to simulate the natural conditions in the wild for each creature.

Against

● Environment—A zoo is not an animal's natural environment and it is cruel to remove them from their own habitat and place them in artificial conditions.

● Breeding—Some animals are kept in a very poor conditions and are, therefore, extremely unlikely to breed.

- **Boredom**—As the need to survive is removed because the zoo supplies food, water, etc., many animals become bored and display neurotic behaviour.

If possible, visit a local zoo and organise a small group of children to report back on the conditions in which the animals live, if any attempts are made to breed rare animals and whether they are successful.

▣ Read the poem *From Inside My Cage* (see page 52). The poem may prove more effective if different people assume the part of the guinea pig and the human being by reading alternate lines each. At the end of the poem, discuss the different viewpoints of the guinea pig and the human being with the audience. How would the children respond to being put into a cage?

Explain that some wild animals may become extinct because they are caught, put in cages and sold as pets. Although this is illegal in this country, the trade in wild animals is expanding in other parts of the world. If an animal is kept as a pet, what important points must be remembered when buying a cage?

Two Extinct Creatures

Brief details are given below of just two of the many hundreds of birds, reptiles, mammals, amphibians and fish which have become extinct. Unfortunately, in the majority of cases, the cause of their extinction has been due to the greed, cruelty, ignorance and sheer indifference of man. Despite current concern for endangered species, the rate of extinction continues to increase.

The Dodo

The dodo is a bird which once lived on the island of Mauritius (approximately 800 km west of Madagascar). It became extinct in 1680 despite the fact that it had no natural enemies.

The name dodo comes from a Portuguese word 'doudo' meaning stupid and it was certainly one of the strangest birds ever to have lived. The first explorers were fascinated by the appearance of this large ugly dove which was unable to fly. It had a round fat body with two small useless wings. Its beak was a sharply curved hook and two small beady eyes were to be found on a rather small head. Drab feathers covered its body and three small feathers formed a somewhat insignificant tail. Two short stubby legs supported the heavy body.

Although the island had been visited occasionally by Arab traders, no people lived there so the bird population flourished. As there were no mammals either, the dodo had no enemies. All kinds of birds such as parrots, sparrows, thrushes, owls, swallows, ducks and geese lived in harmony on the island. However, once the European explorers came (mainly Portuguese), this situation changed drastically. The crews of the ships killed the birds for sport and also to supplement their food even though the dodo was said to be tough and to taste rather greasy and bitter. As the birds had no experience of man, they were not afraid and often presented an easy target to their hunters.

Once the Dutch took possession of Mauritius in 1598, more and more ships stopped at the island and the crews killed hundreds of birds including the dodos. In fact, so many were destroyed that pigeons and grey parrots can no longer be found on the island.

However, it was not until the island became a Dutch colony in 1644 that the number of dodos decreased alarmingly. Although the dodo did not appear to be a nuisance or a danger to the people, they continued to hunt it. As the birds were almost tame and could not fly, they were easily caught and clubbed to death. Although the birds were no longer required for food, the slaughter continued.

Apart from being killed by men, the dodo also suffered because of the animals brought to the island by the settlers. Dogs killed the adult birds whilst cats, rats, monkeys and pigs destroyed the eggs and chicks. These creatures quickly adapted to the tropical island and multiplied so rapidly that they soon became a nuisance. As they roamed the island freely, they were able to kill the dodos even in the most remote and inaccessible places. By 1680, the island was so overrun by men and the animals they had brought with them, that the dodo became extinct.

The Barbary Lion

The barbary lion lived in North Africa and became extinct in 1922. It was one of the largest lions and had a particularly impressive shaggy mane which virtually covered half of its dusky yellow body. The male could weigh as much as 230 kg and measure up to 3 m from nose to tail. The female was smaller and also paler in colour.

The barbary lion used to live in the forests of North Africa but the spreading of the desert and the destruction of the forests by humans drastically reduced the area where it could survive. French and Arabian hunters also killed it for sport with guns which meant that the lions stood very little chance of evading them. Payment for the skins obviously helped to promote the sport. As more and more French settlers occupied the land where the lion lived, the forests were opened up and the herds, which had been the lion's main source of food, were carefully guarded thus preventing the lions from feeding on them. This combination of hunting and a change in its natural habitat proved too powerful for the lions.

By 1899 the lions were becoming increasingly rare and had been forced to live in the woodlands of the Middle and Great Atlas Mountains. As this was one of the wildest and least developed areas of North Africa, the barbary lions managed to survive into the twentieth century, albeit in limited numbers. However, civil wars and the increase in the number of bandits in Morocco contributed to the spread of guns which, as a consequence, resulted in more hunting. The last barbary lion was reported killed in the Atlas Mountains in 1922.

Don't Spray the Fly, Dad

by John Kitching in *A Second Poetry Book* by John Foster, OUP

Don't spray the fly, Dad.
I like to see its wings
Shuddering and shaking.
Busily it sings.

Busily and buzzily
It walks across the glass,
And bumps against the blind
Which will not let it pass.

Up and down it prances;
Up and down it dances.
It hops and it leaps
It never, never sleeps.

I like to see it caper
Don't whack it with the paper.
It isn't very kind, Dad,
It isn't very kind.

What was dad trying to do in the poem? What did his son or daughter enjoy about the fly? What words does the poet use to describe the fly's movements? Do the audience agree that it is not very kind to kill flies? What are the bad things about flies? They carry germs and diseases. Are there any good things about flies? Both the adult flies and their maggots feed on decomposing matter and thus they assume an important scavenging role in the process of decay. Are there any animals which the audience feel it is acceptable to kill? e.g. wasps, rats or foxes.

From Inside my Cage

by Lynne Burgess, in *Pets Project Pack*, Tressell Publications

'Look at the guinea pig, oh what a dear!'
'They've come to stare and interfere.'

'What a nice hutch with a little wire run.'
'It's far too small to have any fun.'

'See his food and water too.'
'I'm terribly bored with nothing to do.'

'He's sitting quite still, oh isn't he good?'
'I'd sneak out of the door, if I could!'

'Now, handle him carefully, don't let him go'
'Those clumsy fingers are squeezing me so!'

'I'm sure he knows how lucky he must be.'
'I'm lonely here, I wish I were free!'

See page 51 for suggestions on the use of this poem.

RESOURCES

Poems

The Little Hunter Over and Over Again (Beaver Books)
The Dodo Round about Six (Frederick Warne)
The Song of the Whale Hot Dog and Other Poems (Kestrel Books)
Whale Poetry Corner Summer 1982 (BBC)
Lion The Beaver Book of Animal Verse (Beaver Books)
So it Goes Dinosaurs and Beasts of Yore (Collins)
Our Hamster's Life Animals Like Us (Blackie)

Songs

The Whale Birds and Beasts (A and C Black)

Stories

As Dead as a Dodo P. Mayle and P. Rice (Methuen)
The Hunter and his Dog B. Wildsmith (OUP)
The Plum Tree Party G. Kaye (Hodder and Stoughton)
Basil and Boris in London E. and A. van der Meer (Dinosaur Publications)
The Hunter and the Animals T. de Paola (Arrow Books)
The Last Loneliest Dodo C. Bear and D. Frankland (Dinosaur Publications)
The Last Dodo A. and R. Cartwright (Century Hutchinson)
The Magic Finger R. Dahl (Young Puffin)
Trick a Tracker M. Foreman (Picturemac)
The Story of the Kakapo P. Temple (Hodder and Stoughton)
Odak Hunts the Seal Moore and Methold (Hulton)
The Grizzly Revenge R. Brown (Andersen Press)
The Deer in the Pasture D. Carrick (Worlds Work)
If I Were You B. Wildsmith (OUP)

Animals (Endangered)

AIM

To introduce the idea that some animals are endangered and the causes for this.

STARTING POINT

◎ Ask a child to pretend to be the postman or postwoman bringing a letter. With the aid of the audience, read the letter which could say 'Dear . . . . . . , Please help us. We are 'endangered' species and need to be protected. Love from . . . . . .' The letter could then open up, concertina style, with pictures of endangered species. These might include tiger, orangutan, polar bear, lapwing, barn owl, kingfisher, horshoe bat, otter, red squirrel, snow leopard, natterjack toad, panda, African elephant, gorilla and black rhino.

Discuss What does 'endangered' mean? What does 'protected' mean? Emphasise that not all endangered species live in exotic countries as many of our native animals are rapidly disappearing.

Can the audience say which of the animals pictured in the letter live in this country? Why are they becoming endangered? This is not only due to hunting but also to the changes man is making to the environment which result in habitat loss. According to Friends of the Earth, the world is losing one species every day.

CORE ACTIVITIES

◎ Some animals are endangered because their food chain has been affected. Illustrate this by:

1 drawing a simple diagram e.g.

2 a picture book with flaps

3 Prepare a small group of children to sing *The Farmer's in his Den* but with words which relate to a food chain e.g. The fox is in his den. The fox eats a frog, The frog eats a snail, The snail eats a plant, etc. Simple masks could be worn by the children representing the creatures or plant.

With all of the above suggestions, repeat the activity but interrupt the food chain by taking one of the creatures out and giving a reason for its disappearance. For example, it might be killed by weedkillers or insecticides, hunted by man or have its eggs destroyed. Can the audience predict what will happen to the remaining creatures in the food chain?

◎ Show how difficult it is for a species to survive and some of the dangers which exist for it, both natural and as a consequence of man's actions. For example, even though Barn owls are a protected species, their numbers are still in decline. Display a picture of a Barn owl plus a drawing of a ledge in the roof of a barn (Barn owls do not use nesting material) with five white eggs (stuck on with Blu-tack). Ask the audience what sort of owl it is, where it would live and count the number of eggs in the nest.

Explain that one of the eggs has been accidentally knocked off the ledge and must be removed. Ask a volunteer to remove one picture of an egg and count the number remaining. Continue removing the eggs, giving a reason for their disappearance each time. Some eggs could hatch into chicks (i.e. pictures could be stuck over the eggs or 'pop up' from behind) which could also be removed one by one, again giving a reason each time.

Reasons for removing the eggs could include:

● Stolen by a person collecting eggs.

● Nesting site destroyed when the old farm building being used is replaced by a modern metal one.

- Egg becomes cold because female leaves the nest in search of scarce food (the male Barn Owl usually feeds her when nesting but cannot manage to do so when food is scarce).

Reasons for removing the chicks could include:

- Chick eats a mouse poisoned by man.

- Chick eats food with a high concentration of insecticide.

- Chick deliberately killed by man.

- Food scarce and chick starves to death.

- Parent killed by car when hunting near a road, so chick starves.

- Parent killed by overhead cables, so chick starves.

All the eggs or chicks could be removed or one survivor could be allowed to remain to demonstrate the vulnerability of a species. Discuss how it is important for us to make it easier not more difficult for wildlife to thrive. For example, in the case of Barn owls, some schemes exist to reintroduce Barn owls into appropriate buildings with the consent of the farmer concerned.

▣ Help the audience to realise that they, too, are part of a food chain. For example, if there was no grass, would they be able to drink milk? This is superbly illustrated by the poem *The Chain* by Elizabeth Lindsay (see page 57 for details). Can the audience predict what or who is being described in each verse before the answer is given? Organise a small group of children to draw pictures to illustrate this poem. These could then be held up at the appropriate moment during the reading of the poem.

After the poem has been read, muddle the pictures up and ask members of the audience to help sequence them correctly. What would happen if one link in the chain were broken? Can the audience suggest similar food chains with human beings at the end e.g. flowers — bees — beekeeper — shopkeeper — honey; corn — farmer — miller — baker — bread.

CONCLUSION—WHAT CAN WE DO?

- Think about whether our actions may be affecting a food chain or destroying a habitat. If we use weedkillers to destroy wild flowers, we may be inadvertently taking away the food supply for a particular creature. Similarly, if we spray pesticides to kill insects, we may also be affecting those creatures who feed on the insects.

- Try to provide mini habitats at school and at home to compensate for those being lost. For example, plant wild flowers, build a pond or marshy area.

- Support organisations trying to preserve habitats and write to them for details about their work e.g. Nature Conservancy Council, Northminster House, Peterborough PE1 1UA.

Homeless creatures

'Don't take away my home', croaks the speckled toad,
'Don't fill in my pond to build a road.
I won't have anywhere to swim or feed.
I'll never find another place to breed.'

'Don't take away my home', the barn owl screeches,
'Don't pull down the barns and fell the beeches.
I won't have anywhere quiet to rest.
Where will be safe to build my nest?'

'Don't take away my home' whispers the butterfly,
'Don't build more houses, there's enough nearby.
My meadow's not full of nasty weeds
But plants which cater for my caterpillars' needs'.

'Don't take away my home', hums the dragonfly,
'Don't drain the marsh to make it dry.
I cannot lay my eggs elsewhere.
I need this place, so please take care!'

ALTERNATIVE ACTIVITIES

◎ Read a book which shows the creatures which live in a certain type of habitat. A good example of this is *In the Meadow* by H. Heyduck-Huth (see page 57 for details). Count how many different creatures live there. What would happen to those creatures if the meadow were replaced by houses? How many would be able to adapt and survive?

◎ Ask the audience to help complete a simple crossword of endangered animals. Pictures could provide the clues.

◎ Place pictures of endangered animals into separate large envelopes. Pull out the pictures a little at a time, asking the audience to raise their hands as soon as they can recognise the creature involved. Old calendars often prove a good source of large coloured photographs of wild animals. It could prove interesting to include one or two common animals such as horses or dogs to see if the children can spot the odd one out.

◎ Enlist the help of the audience in devising collective nouns to describe groups of endangered species. For example, a squirt of elephants, a flash of kingfishers, etc.

▣ Some animals are endangered because their habitat is being destroyed e.g. the orangutan is suffering because of the reduction of jungle habitat. Prepare a group of children to act out the destruction of a habitat. For example, in a river environment, otters eat fish, fish eat insects, insects eat water weed. If chemicals pollute the water, algae grow and use up all the oxygen causing the water weeds to die. Once these die, so do all the other creatures in the chain. Children could assume the role of the creatures, waterweed, chemicals and algae and demonstrate the contrast between the river habitat before and after pollution by chemicals.

▣ Prepare a small group of children to present a 'television' documentary programme about one or two endangered animals. Once they have researched the animal(s) in question, the children could decide on an appropriate brief commentary. They could then draw large, simple pictures to accompany the brief pieces of text. These could be mounted onto a continuous strip of paper which becomes the filmstrip. (See below for details.) Much discussion could be generated in attempting to decide which information to include and in what sequence to arrange it. However, the teacher will probably need to mount the work and assemble the television.

1 Cut a large rectangle in a large cardboard box and paint the outside. Add a control panel.

2 Cut two circular holes in each side of the box (one at the top and one at the bottom) for the cardboard tubes to slide through.

3 Mount the pictures and the text onto a long continuous strip of paper.

4 Staple the filmstrip onto the cardboard tubes.

5 Insert the tubes into the holes in the side of the box.

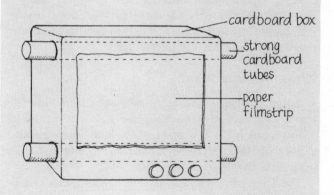

In the assembly, one child could wind on the filmstrip whilst one or two others read the text to the audience.

Rhino's Horn

by John Hare and Eva Gundersen, Hodder and Stoughton

Rhino had a horn which he could blow. He blew it when he was happy to call his friends. He blew it when he was sad to call his mother. One day, Rhino's mother said to Rhino, 'Don't blow your horn Rhino. If man hears it he will try to steal it. Man believes that every rhino's horn contains magic medicine. But Rhino would not listen to his mother. He loved to blow his horn and so he blew and blew and blew.

When the men heard Rhino's horn, they set a trap for Rhino and Rhino was caught in the trap. The men put Rhino in a horrid cage. They planned to send him to a country far away across the sea and to take his horn away from him. They took Rhino away in a truck. When Rhino's friends heard that he had been caught they cried and cried and cried, because there are not many rhinos left in the bush.

The tick bird has always been a friend of the rhinos. He sits on their backs and picks off insects which annoy them. A tick bird followed the truck which was carrying Rhino and found him crying in the cage. He unpicked the lock on the door with his long, pointed beak. Rhino escaped from his cage and the tick bird guided him back to his friends in the bush.

When Rhino returned home all his friends were so happy they held a party for him. And Rhino promised his mother that he would never ever blow his horn again. And he never has . . . . But man has not forgotten about Rhino's magic horn and he still tries to steal it. Unless you stop him there will be NO MORE RHINOS.

Rhino Rescue Trust

Although the black rhino has lived in Africa for 70 million years, it has recently come extremely close to extinction. Kenya is one of the few areas where it still survives but by the end of 1985, the rhino population in Kenya had fallen from 20 000 in 1970 to fewer than 500.

The cause of such a rapid decline in numbers is, not surprisingly, due to man. Highly organised bands of poachers shoot the rhinos with modern automatic weapons and then cut off their horns, leaving the dead carcase behind. The horns are considered to be extremely valuable and can be sold at a higher price than the same weight of gold. Some of the horn is sold in the Far East where the rhino horn is said to have magical powers which can be used to cure many illnesses. The remainder of the horn is made into handles on Djambia daggers which are prized by men in North Yemen because they indicate power and wealth. Thus, a great deal of money can be made from the sale of rhino horn and the bands of poachers will continue to kill as many of the black rhino as they can unless something can be done to prevent them.

The aim of the Rhino Rescue Trust is to protect, conserve and increase the numbers of the black rhino. In 1986 the Trust launched a successful appeal to raise money to help the Kenyan Government build a sanctuary at the Nakuru National Park. As the bands of poachers are extremely dangerous and would not hesitate to kill people in order to get to the rhinos, money has been spent on 74 kilometres of electric fencing to surround the National park and sanctuary. Regular manned guard posts and automatic alarms which are set off if anyone tampers with them, provide further security. As well as a long fire-break round the outside of the fence, roads have had to be built inside the sanctuary so that the fence can be checked and patrolled regularly.

In 1987, the sanctuary was ready to receive the first 19 black rhinos which were to form the basis of a successful breeding programme. It is hoped that their numbers will eventually increase to at least 60 which will probably be the maximum number the Nakuru sanctuary will be able to support.

Rhino Rescue has also helped to develop the water supply. Although three rivers feed Lake Nakuru, they only flow for three months of the year so artificial drinking troughs have to be provided. Natural water holes have been enlarged and new deep bore holes have been drilled. Rhino Rescue has also contributed to the building of two large dams to ensure that even in drought conditions, the rhinos still have water.

Education is another important aspect of the work of the Rhino Rescue Trust. If future generations do not learn to respect and care for the rhinos, then extinction will never be far away. As well as giving talks to visitors and tourists to the Nakuru sanctuary, Rhino Rescue is particularly concerned to inform local school children about the plight of the black rhino. School parties are encouraged to visit whilst a mobile education unit travels to schools in the area showing educational films, using a generator in areas where there is no electricity.

Money is still required both to maintain the Nakuru sanctuary and to develop others. For example, there is a pilot sanctuary at Tsavo and another being constructed at the Aberdare National Park. These projects need continued support because it will not be possible to return the rhinos to the wild until man values the whole of the black rhino and not just its horn.

For further information about the Rhino Rescue Trust, please contact

The Honorary Treasurer
Rhino Rescue
PO Box 1
Saxmundham
Suffolk
IP17 3JT

The Chain

by Elizabeth Lindsay from *Something to Think About*,
BBC Radio, Summer 1982

What grows in the spring
Lush fresh and green
All over the fields
And the banks by the stream?

Grass

Who eats the green grass
Chewing most of the day
And when it is winter
Munches the hay?

The cows

Who milks the soft cows
Both morning and night
Never missing a day
Never wishing he might?

The farmer

Who puts the cows' milk
In the bottles so clean
Makes all sorts of cheeses
Churns butter from cream?

The dairyman

Who delivers the milk
To our doorstep each day
Lining up the full bottles
Taking empties away?

The milkman

Who drinks the white milk
Poured into the cup
Or eats it with cornflakes
When they get up?

I do

See page 54 for follow up questions and suggestions
relating to this poem.

RESOURCES

Poems

Bat Poetry Plus—Creatures Real and Make Believe (Schofield and
    Sims)
Frog The First Lick of the Lolly (Macmillan)
Seal A First Poetry Book (OUP)
A Dragonfly A First Poetry Book (OUP)
Hurt No Living Thing Young Puffin Book of Verse (Young Puffin)
Circus Elephant A Very First Poetry Book (OUP)
Tigers Is a Caterpillar Ticklish? (Young Puffin)

Songs

The Farmer's in his Den The Funny Family (Ward Lock
    Educational)
Where Have the Seals Gone? Alleluya (A and C Black)
Do you Know the Fox? Birds and Beasts (A and C Black)
Rhino on the Run Birds and Beasts (A and C Black)
Panda Zmm! Zmm! (OUP)
The Sea Lions' Song Zmm! Zmm! (OUP)
Boris the Bat Ralph McTell's Alphabet Zoo Songbook (Ward Lock
    Educational)
Ollie the Otter Ralph McTell's Alphabet Zoo Songbook (Ward
    Lock Educational)
Orangutan Song Child Education Special 45 (Scholastic
    Publications)
Free to Roam Birds and Beasts (A and C Black)

Stories

When Dad Fills in the Garden Pond P. Ayres (Walker)
The Old Boot C. Baines (Frances Lincoln)
Operation Hedgehog M. Lane (Methuen)
Better Move on Frog R. Maris (Picture Lions)
In the Meadow H. Heyduck-Huth (Burke)
Grizzwold S. Hoff (Young Puffin)
Goanna J. Wagner (Viking Kestrel)
Bamboo Bamboo C. Barber (Macdonald)
Hare and Badger go to Town N. Lewis (Andersen Press)
The Otter who Wanted to Know J. Tomlinson (Methuen)
Over the Steamy Swamp P. Gerghty (Hutchinson)
Bush Vark's First Day Out C. Fuge (Macmillan)

BENEFICIAL BUGS

AIM

To develop an appreciation of the important role many apparently 'insignificant' creatures play in the environment.

STARTING POINT

◎ Have a container full of worms hidden inside a box labelled 'beneficial bug'. Discuss the meaning of the word 'beneficial' i.e. helpful. Bearing this in mind, can the audience guess what creature is inside the box? Give them clues and then show them. Ask volunteers from the audience to hold a worm and describe it in detail. (More specific questions are outlined in the Core Activities section.)

Discuss How are worms helpful to man? Why do some people kill them with chemicals? What other minibeasts perform important functions in the environment? The answers may include bees, ladybirds, hoverflies, lacewings, etc.

CORE ACTIVITIES

◎ Make a wormery to show during the assembly. (See page 61 for details.) If possible, prepare it a week or two before the assembly so that the effects of the worms on the various layers can be seen. Ask a member of the audience to describe what they can see. The following questions could prove helpful:

● What material is each layer made out of?

● Is each layer distinct?

● Can any tunnels be seen against the side of the tank?

● Can any worms be seen? How many?

● Are there any worm casts on the surface of the top layer?

If possible, have one or two worms in a separate container for a member of the audience to hold and examine closely. The following questions could prove helpful:

● What colour are the worms?

● Are they all the same colour?

● Is one worm the same colour all over?

● How many segments does one worm have?

● Do they all have the same number of segments?

● Can a head or tail end be distinguished?

● Do they have a top or bottom? Place one upside down to see what happens.

● Can the bristles on the underside of the worm be felt? Have a hand lens available to look at them.

● How do worms move?

Explain the positive contribution worms make to the environment. This could include the following:

1 As soil passes through a worm's body, organic matter, such as dead leaves, is broken down to form worm casts, thus accelerating the natural process of decay.

2 Worm casts provide food for plants.

3 As worms pass through the soil, burrows and tunnels are created which aerate the soil and help improve the drainage. Again, these are important factors in stimulating the growth of healthy plants.

4 When worms die, their bodies decay and are recycled to provide nitrogen which is a natural fertiliser.

Links could also be made with the important function worms perform in breaking down the organic matter in a compost heap (see page 20 for details.) A simple diagram might help convey the cycle of decay to the children:

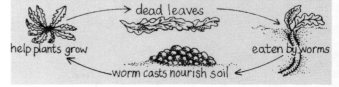

dead leaves

eaten by worms

worm casts nourish soil

help plants grow

After the assembly, leave the wormery in an easily accessible place for the children to observe when they have a free moment during the day. Also, emphasise the importance of returning the worms to an appropriate environment once they are no longer needed at school.

☒ Help a small group of children to devise a puppet play to show the number of beneficial bugs in the environment. One character, such as a farmer, gardener or child playing in a garden, could display a dislike for each creature he or she comes across. Each creature could then respond by explaining what they are doing and why it is important not to kill them. The following are examples of the kind of beneficial bugs which could be featured in the play.

Worms	Accelerate the breakdown of organic matter.
Hoverflies—larvae	Eat greenfly (sometimes as many as 50 a day).
adults	Eat caterpillars which feed on cabbages.
Lacewings	Eat greenfly.
Bees	Pollinate flowers, an important function in helping to produce fruit and seeds.
Ladybirds	Eat greenfly.
Beetles	Eat dead and diseased material. Ground beetles, in particular, eat the eggs and grubs of the cabbage root fly.
Wasps—larvae	Feed on cabbage white caterpillars.

☒ Exhibit 'beneficial bug' mobiles made by the children. A cardboard tube could be the basis for the design. These could be cut into small sections, painted brown and threaded to create worms. Alternatively, they could form a cylindrical body shape to which wings could be added for wasps, bees, hoverflies and lacewings. Ladybirds and beetles could also be made by sticking the appropriate body shape over the tube. Obviously, encourage the children to create their own designs, adding features gained from first hand observation of the real creatures. Can the audience identify each creature?

CONCLUSION—WHAT CAN WE DO?

● At home or at school, plant flowers to attract beneficial bugs. Try to provide a display of flowers for as long as possible. For example, for the spring, grow crocuses and wallflowers, for summer grow petunias and sunflowers, for autumn grow Michaelmas daisies, and for winter grow ivy.

● Leave some dead material, such as dead flowers, leaves and rotting logs, in the garden at home or in the grounds of the school. It is an important food source for many forms of wildlife.

● Don't automatically kill minibeasts, no matter how strange they may appear. Find out if they are helpful to the environment.

● Take care when choosing sprays because some chemicals will kill the beneficial insects as well as the pests. For example, some sprays intended to kill greenfly, also kill their natural predator the ladybird. In addition, some weedkillers destroy worms as well as weeds.

● Find out whether any chemical used will inadvertently kill other creatures in the food chain. For example, slug pellets can kill the hedgehogs who eat the dead slugs.

● Use natural predators to control pests instead of weedkillers. For example, the caterpillars of the cinnabar moth feed on ragwort which is poisonous to cattle. If the moth is deliberately introduced it may well reduce the amount of ragwort without the need to use weedkillers.

The Most Dangerous Creature on Earth

'Watch out! Watch out!' buzzed the bee angrily,
'Quickly, take cover, hurry, hurry!
That dangerous creature's stalking near.
Listen, footsteps, footsteps, I can hear!'

'What is the problem?' said worm calmly,
'Whatever it is, it cannot harm me.
Is it large and hairy, with sharp claws?
Does it sting or bite with snapping jaws?'

'Take no notice of its friendly ways
For it spits out poisonous, deadly sprays.
They kill me' cried bee 'with just one squirt.
The flowers I need are also hurt'.

'Beware,' warned ladybird 'The beast's about!
Whatever you do, worm, don't come out.
Even if I can survive the spray,
The greenfly I eat will die today.'

'I'm off,' said ground beetle, anxiously,
'That monster's coming to stamp on me.
He ignores the vital work I do.
He thinks I'm a pest which isn't true!'

'Well, I'm not afraid,' said worm with a grin.
But his smile faded, his head popped back in.
'Oh! I see what you mean—hide if you can!
It's the most dangerous creature on Earth—it's a
MAN!'

ALTERNATIVE ACTIVITIES

◎ Ask volunteers from the audience to complete pathways for 'beneficial bugs'. These are best drawn on a blackboard so that several children can have a turn. (See examples at top of next page.). The pathways can be made simple or complex depending upon the ability of the children involved. Each child is asked to draw a chalk line along the pathway from the 'bug' to the object it is trying to reach, without touching the two outside lines.

◎ Organise a simple quiz based on 'beneficial bugs'. Each class could be asked four or five questions about a variety of minibeasts. For each class, cover up a picture of a beneficial bug with four or five separate strips of paper, depending upon the number of questions asked. Each time a correct answer is given, the child could choose one strip of paper to remove. Obviously, once all the questions had been answered correctly, the picture would be revealed. Can each class identify their own particular 'bug'? The questions would have to be matched to the level of difficulty for each class in that a reception class might be asked to describe the colour of a ladybird whilst top infants might be asked how many legs it has.

◎ Display a jar of honey together with some bee keeping equipment. Explain how honey is produced, the organisation of a bee colony and the important role bees play in pollinating flowers, thus helping to produce fruits and seeds. (The information on page 61 may prove helpful.) Show examples of flowers which are especially designed to aid this process. For example, in antirrhinums, the stamens are positioned so that they brush against the bee whilst lilies have special markings, known as honey guides, to guide the bee to the nectar.

◎ Play classical music associated with minibeasts, such as *The Flight of the Bumble Bee* by Rimsky-Korsakov or *The Wasps* by Vaughan Williams. Can the audience identify the minibeasts involved? What instruments are used to represent the creatures?

▣ Prepare a group of children to make large pencil drawings of a variety of 'beneficial bugs'. Encourage them to draw from observation and use hand lenses to improve the quality of their 'looking'. Display these pictures and ask the audience if they can recognise each creature. Can they say what positive contribution each one makes?

▣ Invite a group of children to find out 10 facts about one particular beneficial bug such as the ladybird. Each fact could be written on a small piece of paper and mounted on a large ladybird shape. During the assembly, each child could read out the information and stick the ladybird onto a large frieze of flowers. The researchers could be asked to discover whether all ladybirds are the same colour, if they all have the same number of spots, how they move, what their breeding cycle is, how they are 'beneficial', etc.

▣ Arrange for a group of children to make a large frieze of flowers and vegetables growing in a garden. Encourage them to include 'pop up' 'beneficial bugs' drawn on thick card. Ask members of the audience to make each creature 'pop up', to name and describe it. How does each 'bug' help the gardener?

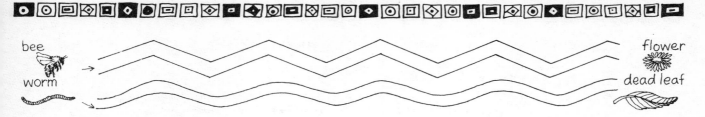

Making a Wormery

Apparatus required: A narrow glass tank or large plastic sweet jar, black paper, different types of soil—sand, peat, compost, garden soil, etc.

Method of construction: Place layers of different types of soil into the transparent tank or jar. Cover the outside of the container with black paper to encourage the worms to burrow against the outer edge. As they do not like the light, they will tend to stay in the middle of the container if the outside is not covered. The soil also needs to be kept cool and moist but not soaked or they will drown.

The children could be encouraged to collect their own worms to put in the wormery but they should be reminded to take care when handling and transporting them.

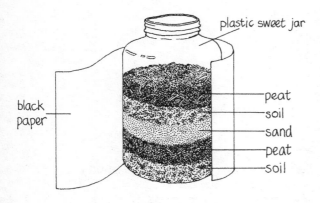

Honey Bees

Bees are extremely important both to the gardener and the farmer. As they move from flower to flower feeding on the nectar, the pollen from the stamens of the flower sticks onto the hairs on the bee's body and legs. In this way, the flowers are pollinated to produce seeds and fruit. Without bees, many food crops would fail and seeds for future generations of plants would not be produced.

Initially, the bees are attracted by the colours and scents of the flowers. Additional guidance is given by the bold markings (known as honey guides) on the petals e.g.

on the faces of pansies, inside the bells of foxgloves. Many flowers are also constructed so that the bee is forced to brush gainst the stigma and stamens, thus ensuring pollination.

Honey bees usually live in hives either in the hollows in trees or in special wooden bee hives supervised by a bee keeper. They live together in large colonies, sometimes as many as 60 000. Within the colony there are three different types of bee which each perform a different function. There is only one queen bee which stays in the colony as she cannot collect pollen. Her task is to lay eggs, one in each hexagonal cell inside the hive. She is the largest of the three bees and rules the colony. She is fed by the worker bees and never leaves the hive except to lead a swarm or to mate.

Most of the bees seen visiting the flowers in a garden will be worker bees who collect pollen in special sacs on their legs to store for food. They also collect nectar (which is sugar and water produced by the flowers) which they suck up with their tongues and store in honey sacs. They take this back to the hive either to feed to the other bees and larvae or to convert into honey which is stored in sealed cells. Special scout bees forage for nectar and if a good supply is discovered, directions are given to the other worker bees in the form of a dance which indicates the precise location of the new source. The worker bees also build the combs with hexagonal shaped cells. These are made from wax which is secreted in special glands on the worker bee's body. The cells are used to store honey or pollen or as breeding compartments for the queen to lay eggs in.

The third type of bees are called drones. These are the male bees who do not work but are fed and looked after by the worker bees. On warm sunny days, they fly around and mate with any new queen. They are not allowed to live in the hive in winter but are pushed out and left to die.

The queen lays specific eggs in certain cells. Unfertilized eggs are laid in drone cells but fertilized ones are mostly laid in worker cells with only a few laid in royal cells. The larvae hatch out of the eggs, pupate and then an adult honey bee chews through the sealed cell.

In a domestic bee hive, the bee keeper would harvest the honey and replace it with sugar so that the bees can survive. The honey varies in colour and flavour according to the flowers from which the nectar was collected.

Finding ladybirds

RESOURCES

Poems

Ladybird Stories and Rhymes, Spring 1975 (BBC)
Worm Rhyme Time 2 (Beaver Books)
Mister Worm Poetry Plus—Creatures Real and Make Believe (Schofield and Sims)
What do you Suppose? Fingers, Feet and Fun (Beaver Books)
Ladybird, Ladybird Over and Over Again (Beaver Books)
A Tiny Worm This Little Puffin (Young Puffin)
Here is the Beehive This Little Puffin (Young Puffin)
Under a Stone This Little Puffin (Young Puffin)

Ladybirds

by Stanley Cook, in *The Squirrel in Town*, Blackie

When the fields and wood are already bright
With the buttercup's yellow and daisy's white,
The orange ladybird dotted with black
Brings extra colour on its back.

It climbs up ladders of grass and flies to leaves
Hanging down low on bushes and trees;
It even makes beautiful
The hairy, rough, stinging nettle.

Ladybirds can often be seen
Colouring leaves that are only plain green
And, spreading their thin wings, they sometimes land
Upon my sleeve or decorate my hand.

Songs

Ladybird Tinderbox Song Book (A and C Black)
Ladybird, Ladybird Sing a Song 1 (Nelson)
Wiggley Woo Sing a Song 1 (Nelson)
Worm Song Zmm! Zmm! (OUP)
Says the Bee Birds and Beasts (A and C Black)
Lots of Worms Birds and Beasts (A and C Black)
The Worm Silly Things to Sing (E. J. Arnold)
Tiny Creatures Sing as you Grow (Ward Lock Educational)
I am a Worm Jump into the Ring (Ward Lock Educational)
Buzz a Buzz a Bumble Bee Jump into the Ring (Ward Lock Educational)
Eeny Meeny Minibeasts Child Education Infant Projects Number 65 (Scholastic Publications)

Stories

Zig-zag the Bee M. Cecil and C. Gascoigne (Methuen)
The Bad Tempered Ladybird E. Carle (Hodder and Stoughton)
The Giant Jam Sandwich J. Vernon Lord (Cape)
The Very Busy Spider E. Carle (Hamish Hamilton)
Ladybird, Ladybird R. Brown (Andersen Press)

Hedgerow

AIM
◻◻▣▣

To increase the children's awareness of the importance of hedgerows as a habitat for a diverse range of wildlife.

STARTING POINT

▣ Organise a group of children to draw/paint a long frieze of a typical hedgerow containing trees, bushes, flowers, animals, birds, insects, etc. The frieze could initially be rolled up and be slowly unrolled to reveal the hedgerow to the audience. As each section appears, ask the audience to name the creatures and plants which they recognise.

Discuss Which creatures live in the hedgerow? These might include fieldmice, shrews and hedgehogs. Which creatures visit the hedgerow and why? Birds use it for nesting, badgers search for food in them, insects visit flowers for nectar, some butterflies lay their eggs on hedgerow plants. Help the audience appreciate the valuable and diverse habitat provided by hedges.

Explain that many hedges have been, and continue to be, removed and that this can have far-reaching effects on wildlife. In fact, more species are disappearing through habitat loss, such as hedgerow destruction, than through direct killing because some plants and animals can only survive under a certain set of conditions.

CORE ACTIVITIES

◉ Make up riddles based on the wildlife/plants featured in the hedgerow frieze. For example, 'I am small and round, with two beady eyes and a prickly coat. What am I?' Ask members of the audience to point to the animal or plant being described.

▣ Prepare a group of children to present a role play in which opposing views are expressed over the removal of a hedgerow. One child could act as a television reporter or journalist interviewing all those involved in the conflict. The following points may arise in the debate:

For the removal of a hedgerow

- Larger fields are needed for larger farm machinery.

- Wire fences cheaper and more efficient for livestock.

- Wild flowers are potential weeds in crops.

- Hedgerows shade crops at the edge of a field and stunt the growth of the crops.

- Rain dripping from overhanging branches damages young corn.

- Hedgerows harbour potential pests on crops e.g. bullfinches on orchards

- Need regular maintaining, especially when close to roads.

Against the removal of a hedgerow

- Hedgerows help prevent soil erosion.

- They act as wind breaks for crops.

- They provide shelter for livestock.

- They provide a stockproof fence.

- They are an important habitat for wildlife offering food, shelter and breeding sites.

- They act as a roadway for wildlife to move along from one area to another.

- Sometimes they are a source of fuel for people.

- Occasionally they are a source of timber.

▣ Display a collection of badges designed and made by the children and based on a 'save the hedgerow' theme. In their design, they could be asked to invent a slogan, to consider the size and shape of the lettering, and whether an illustration would add impact to the message. The audience could then be asked to *assess* sensitively the designs by considering points such as how well the slogan encapsulates the message, whether it is easy to read or not, whether the illustration enhances the slogan.

▣ Organise a group of children to visit a local hedgerow regularly over a period of several weeks.

Autumn and spring are particularly good times to choose because of the many easily observed changes which are occurring in the hedgerow. The children could keep a diary of their observations and these could be read out during the assembly.

▣ Develop a drama situation to be performed during the assembly by a group of children arising from the question 'Whose hedgerow is it?' The teacher could pose the question and the children could respond in the role of the various creatures. In turn, each one could argue that the hedgerow belonged to them and support their case with a reason.

For example, a bird might argue that the hedgerow belongs to her because she builds her nest in it and feeds on the plants growing in it, whilst a hedgehog might be equally justified in saying it belongs to him as the dead leaves provide him with shelter, especially in the winter months. Thus, each creature could contradict the previous one. The teacher could ask the audience to decide who is right. Hopefully, the discussion arising from this would lead them to consider whether it is possible for them to share the hedgerow which, in fact, acts as a life support system for them all.

CONCLUSION—WHAT CAN WE DO?

● Make an opportunity to look more closely at the hedgerows around us.

● Plant more hedgerows using native plants to attract the maximum amount of wildlife.

● Preserve as many hedgerows as possible and don't dig them up without a considerable amount of thought.

● Avoid spraying the plants in a hedgerow with weed killers as it is possible to kill an important plant which acts as host to a multitude of wildlife.

● Never throw dangerous litter into hedges or ditches as it may harm the creatures living there. If any litter is spotted in a local hedge or ditch, ask for adult assistance to remove it.

The Hedgerow

This hedgerow seems empty,
Deserted and bare
But if I look carefully,
What will be there?

I can see hazel nuts,
In one there's a hole
Where the shell was emptied by
A hungry vole.

I can smell dampness
From a dead leaf heap.
A snug home for hedgehog when
It's time to sleep.

I can taste blackberries,
Juice runs down my chin.
The black shiny flesh hides the
Hard pips within.

I can touch lacey webs,
Delicate but strong.
Spider thinks he's trapped a fly
And scuttles along.

I can hear blackbirds
Fluttering their wings.
Squabbling over crimson haws
On twigs they cling.

This hedgerow's not empty
But teeming with life.
Let it always be home for
All this wildlife.

ALTERNATIVE ACTIVITIES

◎ Exhibit a poster showing poisonous berries and seeds which often grow in the hedgerow. These could include the berries of bryony, deadly nightshade, privet, cuckoo pint and holly, the nuts on beech trees, the whole of travellers' joy (also known as old man's beard) and the foxglove. Explain that whilst many of these look appetising, they could all be extremely harmful if eaten. Remind the children not to pick and eat any berries or seeds without adult supervision.

◎ Show a collection of dangerous litter which is often found in hedgerows and ditches. (See Litter section, page 18, for more details.) Can the audience say why it is dangerous to wildlife? For example, jagged tins and broken glass can cut animals' feet, deer can choke on polythene bags, hedgehogs can get their heads stuck in yoghurt pots, small mammals such as mice and voles become trapped in milk bottles.

◎ Focus on one particular hedgerow plant and show how it acts as host to a wide range of wildlife. The blackberry bramble is an extremely good example of this and a familiar plant to many children. Display a large diagram which illustrates this. For example, butterflies feed on the juice of blackberries, greenfly feed on the plant sap, spiders attach their webs to it to catch the flies visiting the blackberries, wasps feed on the sugar from berries, snails feed on the leaves, bees feed on the nectar from the flowers.

Explain to the audience that each part of the plant is important to a different form of wildlife. A similar approach could be used with the hawthorn which, apparently, acts as host to 143 different insects. What would happen to this diverse range of wildlife if the blackberry brambles or hawthorn bushes were destroyed in a hedgerow?

▣ Play a tape recording of children's observations during a visit to a hedgerow. Ask them to explain what they can see, hear, smell, taste and touch. Can the audience recall what was said on the tape recording? Have any of them had similar experiences when walking beside a hedgerow?

▣ Display a pictorial menu, representing the food available in a hedgerow. The pictures could be drawn by children, cut out of magazines or even the 'real' thing. Food items could include: nuts (e.g. beech, hazel, acorns); berries (e.g. haws, elderberries, sloes, blackberries); grain (e.g. rye grass, couch grass, meadow barley).

Individual name labels could be available for members of the audience to attach to the appropriate food picture. Display separate pictures of animals who would use the hedgerow as a food supply e.g. squirrels would eat nuts, birds would eat berries and grain, mice would eat grain and nuts, etc. Can the audience predict which creatures would eat each food item on the menu?

▣ Organise a group of children to conduct some research into one particular form of wildlife associated with the hedgerow. For example, more than 40 different species of bird are connected with the hedgerow, using it as a source of food, shelter and for providing nesting sites. However, only 6 species of bird can exist in open country without woods or hedgerows, indicating the importance of maintaining these vital habitats. The 40 species of birds vary greatly from seed eaters (sparrows, blackbirds), insect eaters (robins, thrushes) scavengers (magpies) to birds of prey (kestrels, owls). Each child could choose one bird to investigate and develop a profile to be presented during assembly. The profile could include: name; visual description; connection with hedgerow; feeding habits; nesting sites; and number of eggs laid.

The Harvest of the Hedgerow

Ryan was idly kicking a football against the wall when he stopped to listen to a strange noise. No, it was gone, nothing there. He carried on kicking the ball . . . bang . . . kick . . . bang . . . kick but there it was again. It seemed to be coming from the front garden. He decided to go and see what was going on.

Dad was rubbing the sweat from his forehead, holding a saw in his hand. 'Phew, I'm not used to such hot work,' gasped dad breathlessly.

'What are you doing dad?' asked Ryan with his eyes on the saw.

'Well, I thought it was time I took out this old hedge and replaced it with some decent wooden fencing,' replied dad 'But it's much harder work than I imagined!'

'But why are you doing that? You mustn't saw down this hedge. You'll spoil it for everyone!' said Ryan rather concerned.

'Be sensible, Ryan. Just take a good look at it. It's not a decent hedge but just a tangle of brambles and dog rose with nasty stinging nettles at the bottom. It's absolutely no use to anyone. I don't know why you're getting so upset.'

By now Ryan realised that dad was determined to pull up the hedge and he searched anxiously for the right words to convince dad to change his mind. 'But what about the harvest of the hedgerow?' he blurted out.

'What harvest?' dad asked, laughing in disbelief. But when he saw the earnest expression on Ryan's face, he stopped laughing and tried to take the problem more seriously. 'Alright. We could use some of the blackberries in an apple pie and I have heard people say you can eat stinging nettles but I'll only try them if you promise to have the first mouthful!' Dad was smiling patiently at Ryan.

'I don't mean a harvest for us. I mean the one for all the creatures,' explained Ryan.

'But there aren't any creatures—just a bare hedge,' exclaimed dad a little annoyed.

'Well, I can hear something. Listen and you'll hear it too,' said Ryan eagerly. They both stood statue still and listened intently.

'You're quite right Ryan. I can hear a bird singing. Why it's perching on a twig at the top of the branch. Can you see it? It's black with a yellow beak.'

'It's a blackbird,' said Ryan excitedly, 'and it's eating a shiny red haw from the top of the hedge. I found an old nest in the hedge near there.' Ryan searched amongst the mass of twigs and leaves. 'Yes. Look! It's a bit tatty now but it's still here. See, birds need our hedge for food and for nesting.'

'Alright but what about all these wretched nettles? Surely, they're only a nuisance?' asked dad.

'Why don't we have a look at this patch of nettles?' suggested Ryan, cautiously turning over a stinging nettle leaf. 'The back of this leaf is covered with wriggling caterpillars.'

'Don't they get stung?' asked dad in surprise.

'No, they can eat the leaves without any harm. They're probably the caterpillars of the Red Admiral butterfly. They won't lay their eggs on anything else but stinging nettles and when the eggs hatch, the caterpillars feed on the leaves. If you chop down these nettle leaves, there won't be any butterflies.'

'You seem to know an awful lot about this, Ryan,' said dad rather impressed.

'Yes. We've been finding out about the hedgerow at school. Mrs Black says . . .'

'Well, I'm very glad you've been listening so carefully to Mrs Black. But what about this hazel bush? It's sticking out in all directions and every time I mow the lawn, one of the twigs pokes me in the eye. Surely, I could trim this up?'

'But it's covered with hazel nuts.'

'I'm not very keen on nuts because they get stuck in my teeth,' answered dad.

'They're not for us,' said Ryan as he scrabbled amongst the leaves on the ground. 'If you look carefully at this nut, there's a small round hole where a vole has eaten the nut inside. And down here there's a hole in the soil—I bet that's where he lives.'

'You're probably right,' sighed dad, feeling he was losing the argument. 'But you can't tell me anyone needs these blackberry brambles. The blackberries are far too small to eat and it won't take a minute to cut them out.' Dad was brandishing his new lopping shears, eager to see how well they worked.

'Sorry but you're wrong again dad,' chuckled Ryan, enjoying dad's embarrassment. 'Look at those blackberries up there.'

Dad searched the cluster of gleaming blackberries which Ryan was pointing at. 'All I can see are two dead leaves stuck on top of a berry,' said dad rather puzzled.

'Those aren't leaves, they're wings. You wait till they open up.'

Dad watched silently until the two drab brown wings fluttered open. 'Why, it's the most amazing butterfly. The colours are incredibly bright. But what's it doing?'

'I think Mrs Black said that they feed on the blackberry juice. She said that lots of creatures need blackberry brambles. Wasps feed on the juice, bees feed on the nectar from the blackberry flowers, snails feed on the leaves . . .'

'Alright, alright! I give in,' groaned dad. 'You've persuaded me at last! Mrs Black and you are much too difficult to argue with. Anyway, it was going to be very tiring sawing the hedge down and then digging up the roots. And expensive, buying all that wooden fencing. You've just saved me a lot of money and hard work. I think you deserve some squash and a chocolate biscuit and I certainly need a cup of coffee after all that searching for wildlife. We'll leave the hedge just as it is so that all those creatures you mentioned can enjoy their harvest.'

Hedgehog

by Jean Kenward in *Poetry Plus—Creatures Real and Make Believe*, Schofield and Sims

Old Snuffler's in the grass
circling
his nightly track —
dark in the starlight
round and shy
with prickles on his back
sniffing and rustling
as he goes
on tiny, hurrying feet
with shifting eye
and eager nose
searching for food
to eat;
beetles, and berries
red or black,
worms,
secret wriggling things,
a bite of this . . .
a taste of that . . .
Sometimes
somebody brings
a saucerful
of milk and bread —
how sweet that is to sup!
Listen —
Old hedgehog's in the grass
Gobbling his supper up.

Read this poem without telling the audience the title. Ask them to listen carefully to the words and put their hands up as soon as they think they know which creature is being described. Can they guess correctly before the last two lines of the poem are read? What words or phrases are used to describe how the hedgehog looks? What is he hoping to find to eat? Can the audience name other nocturnal animals? Would any of them visit or live in a hedgerow? (**Important** – warn the children that it is dangerous to give hedgehogs cows' milk – only goats' milk should be given.)

Rabbit

Wanted

Wanted
URGENTLY
One hedgerow
In secluded setting
Older style if possible
Built with hawthorn, hazel and holly
Nettles and brambles highly desirable
Loft essential for squirrels and owls
Basement required for rabbits and voles
Dead leaves useful for hibernating hedgehogs
Running water within easy reach
Away from humans
NO dangerous litter.

Please contact these homeless creatures:
Squirrels, hedgehogs, rabbits and mice
Owls, sparrows and blackbirds
Butterflies, spiders and snails
Wasps and ladybirds.

RESOURCES

Poems

The Hedgehog Rhyme Time (Beaver Books)
Boot the Hedgehog Squirrel in Town (Blackie)
Curiosity Is a Caterpillar Ticklish? (Young Puffin)
The Hedgehog Seeing and Doing Poetry Anthology (Methuen)
The Fieldmouse Seeing and Doing Poetry Anthology (Methuen)
Blackberrying The First Lick of the Lolly (Macmillan)

Songs

Tiny Creatures Sing as you Grow (Ward Lock Educational)
Wild and Wary Mrs Macaroni (Macmillan Educational)
Which Animal? Birds and Beasts (A and C Black)
The Urban Hedgehog Birds and Beasts (A and C Black)
Holly the Hedgehog Ralph McTell's Alphabet Zoo Book (Ward Lock Educational)
The Squirrel The Music Box Song Book (BBC)

Stories

Smith and Matilda Althea (Dinosaur Publications)
Prickly Pig G. McClure (Andre Deutsch)
The Hedgehog Mirror E. Marder (Blackie)
Where Can I Sleep? (in Play School Stories) J. Watson (BBC)

GARDENS

AIM

To help children increase their awareness of the wildlife in a garden and to appreciate the conservation potential there.

STARTING POINT

◉ Read an appropriate poem about gardens. (An example is given on page 69 and sources for other suitable poems are listed on page 71.) Discuss the poem with the audience.

Discuss How many children have a garden? Do any of them have no garden at all? What gardening possibilities exist for those with a limited or no garden? What function does a garden have for humans? It provides somewhere safe for children to play, a place for all the family to relax, a place to grow plants, especially food such as fruit and vegetables, an enclosed area for pets.

Why are gardens becoming increasingly more important for wildlife? They provide homes, sources of food and sometimes water for a wide range of creatures, a place for plants and trees to grow relatively undisturbed.

CORE ACTIVITIES

◉ Show pictures of some common flowers and plants which encourage wildlife. Examples could include:

For birds	For butterflies	For bees
marigolds	aubretia	bluebells
sunflowers	primroses	forget-me-nots
teasels	honesty	pansies

Can the children identify the flower or plant? Where have they seen it growing? Can they guess which creature would particularly like it? Explain why each creature would be attracted to each plant. For example, birds eat the seeds from sunflowers and teasels, rain water is sometimes trapped in the leaf forks of teasels which birds then drink, butterflies and bees take nectar from honesty and aubretia, butterflies, such as the Orange Tip, also lay their eggs on honesty leaves which the caterpillars then eat.

◉ Play a recording of *Whose Garden Was This?* by

John Denver (RCA). Discuss the words of the song. For example, how would the audience feel if they had never smelt a flower but only seen pictures of one? Can they imagine only hearing records of breezes but never feeling one? What other things would they miss if there were no gardens? Where would they go as a substitute?

▣ Organise a display of gardens on a small scale, preferably made by some children. These could include window boxes, hanging baskets, bottle gardens, small tubs or containers. (See page 70 for details.) Ask each child to explain what plants they have used and which types of wildlife they hope it will attract.

▣ Ask a small number of children to make up a television commercial promoting gardens or gardening. Can they act out a short sketch and devise a 'catch phrase' or 'jingle'? How successful do the audience feel it is? If the equipment was available, the commercial could be recorded on video.

▣ Prepare one child to act the part of Mrs/Mr Sprayitall. The teacher organising the assembly could interview her/him about the progress of the plants in her/his vegetable garden. Together, they could look at various plants such as lettuces, cabbages, strawberries to see how they were growing. The interviewer could pretend to discover pests such as greenfly, caterpillars and slugs attacking the plants and Mrs/Mr Sprayitall could promptly produce a spray or pellets to deal with the problem.

The interviewer could then explain that some sprays kill beneficial minibeasts. For example, some chemicals which kill greenfly also kill ladybirds who are the natural predators of the greenfly. Other innocent predators may also be inadvertently harmed. Hedgehogs, for instance, eat dozens of slugs each day but slugs killed by some pellets could affect the hedgehogs adversely. Similarly, birds such as Blue Tits feed on caterpillars and, in killing the caterpillars, the birds can also be poisoned by mistake.

The interview could conclude with Mrs/Mr Sprayitall agreeing to use fewer sprays/chemicals and ensuring she/he always reads the labels to discover whether they are harmful to creatures other than the pest involved.

CONCLUSION—WHAT CAN WE DO?

• Encourage as much wildlife into our gardens as possible by choosing to plant trees, flowers or shrubs which will attract birds, bees, butterflies etc.

• Avoid tidying up the garden too much. For example, leave some fallen leaves, decaying logs and long grass as these provide some important habitats for creatures such as worms, beetles and hedgehogs.

• Grow wild flowers as well as cultivated ones. Many wild flowers, such as Lady's Smock, play an essential role in the life cycle of certain creatures.

• Use the minimum amount of sprays and chemicals for controlling pests. Take care to choose products which will not affect innocent animals or insects. Some sprays inadvertently kill creatures who are beneficial to the ecological balance in the garden.

Gardening for Wildlife

Gardens large or gardens small.
Size doesn't really matter at all.
A hanging basket or window box,
Tubs or a sink all covered in rocks;
All of these can provide a place
For growing plants in a small space.

With a little care and observation
We can play a part in conservation.
Choose the plants to attract the bees.
Feed the birds by letting plants seed.
Butterflies are drawn to purple flowers.
Minibeasts will scuttle for endless hours.

Why go to a museum or a zoo?
Encourage these creatures to come to you.
Spare a part of your home.
Allow them the freedom to roam.
Share your life with just a few.
Think what pleasure they'll give to you!

ALTERNATIVE ACTIVITIES

◎ Ask members of the audience to participate in planting some seeds which are particularly attractive to wildlife. Choose seeds that are relatively quick and easy to grow such as nasturtium, candytuft and sunflower. Discuss the various stages of growth and what conditions are essential for producing a healthy plant—water, warmth, nutrients. Where will these come from? How will the children be able to help the plants mature successfully? For example, they could water them if there has been little rain, prevent weeds from overpowering them, etc. Can the audience suggest whereabouts the seedlings could eventually be planted? Hopefully, a suitable space could be found in the school grounds.

◎ Discuss the advantages of making a compost heap (see page 20 for details). Briefly outline the construction of a simple compost heap.

▣ Children are often unaware of the diversity of wildlife living in a garden. With the aid of a small number of children, make a large picture of an ordinary garden but include flaps under which various creatures are hiding e.g. a stone with woodlice underneath, a toad hiding in a compost heap, a flower with a bee inside. Ask members of the audience to discover the flaps and predict what's hiding underneath.

▣ Cultivate a school garden or adopt the garden of a nearby resident who does not or cannot manage it themselves. Ask a small group of children to report back on the current stage of development such as plans, work undertaken so far and future ideas. Can they list the wildlife they have observed so far and indicate whereabouts in the garden it was found? The School Garden Company (PO Box 49, Spalding, Lincs. PE11 1N2) has an excellent catalogue giving details of equipment, seeds, books, charts, etc. which they can supply.

▣ Invite a small number of children to design a wildlife garden. When the design is completed, suggest they draw a large poster-sized version which will be visible in an assembly. Can they devise a simple key to show trees, water, flowers, etc? Allow them to explain to the audience which features are particularly good for encouraging wildlife. For instance, shrubs for birds/insects/hedgehogs, compost heap for worms/beetles/centipedes, logs and stones for woodlice, flowers for bees/butterflies, pond for frogs/newts/insects, and trees for birds/insects. If any of the designs are particularly clear, can one or two volunteers from the audience use the key to point to specific features such as the pond or the compost heap?

◼ Sing *We are going to plant a bean* (see page 71 for details). Encourage the audience to join in the accompanying actions. Devise extra verses using a gardening-for-wildlife policy. For example, we will plant a tree with berries, we will build a compost heap and we will leave a pile of dead leaves.

Small Gardens Project

The following guidelines may prove useful when planting a wide range of containers such as tubs, window boxes, etc. Similar principles will apply to the majority of containers, apart from hanging baskets and bottle gardens.

1 Make sure the container has enough holes in the bottom to allow water to drain out freely and air to circulate.

2 Prevent the holes at the bottom blocking with soil by covering them with large stones or broken flower pots.

3 Cover the bottom of the container with any coarse drainage material such as small stones or gravel.

4 Use a proper potting compost (or bulb fibre if planting spring bulbs) to fill the rest of the container. Ordinary garden soil is not so good because it often lacks the ability to retain water and nutrients and yet still be free draining.

5 Plant the flowers fairly closely together so as to eventually fill the container with blooms.

6 Once they are planted, water the plants well to settle the compost around their roots.

7 Check regularly to ensure that the plants do not dry out.

Discuss with the children the points to bear in mind when choosing plants to fill the containers. For example:

1 *Scale*—Obviously, choose small plants which will grow happily in small containers because trees or large flowers will soon look out of proportion.

2 *Easy maintenance*—Plants which demand a great deal of attention will also be inappropriate.

3 *Timing*—Consider the flowering times of the plants to be used. If they are likely to be in full bloom during the summer holiday, then they are obviously less desirable.

4 *Trailing plants*—Consider whether the container would benefit from having trailing plants in it or whether it is too small.

5 *Wildlife*—Choose plants which will be most attractive to a wide range of insects and minibeasts. For example, aubretia will attract bees, butterflies and many other insects.

Obviously, there is an endless range of suitable plants such as annuals (petunias, lobelia, trailing nasturtiums), small herbs (thymes) and even fruit or vegetables (small varieties of strawberries or radishes).

Throughout this project it is important to emphasise to the children that they should *not* dig up wild plants or flowers for any of their containers.

Gardener George Goes to Town

by Susan Moxley and Sara Sharpe, Hodder and Stoughton

Beneath the Blue Mountains, in the far-off countryside, Gardener George grew magical flowers. Because he had green fingers and thumbs, every seed he sowed grew and flourished. Every creature and tree in his garden was as brilliant as a rainbow. The countryside gave Gardener George all that he needed.

Still Gardener George dreamed about going to town. So one day, he put on his best suit, packed his bag full of fruit, stuffed his pockets full of seeds—and went to town. The streets were empty and drab. There wasn't a tree or bird in sight. The only flowers that Gardener George saw were in a shop window, looking sad and neglected. Poor George! There was no need for a gardener here. Instead of flowers there was only rubbish. Gardener George found work sweeping the streets.

That night, George sat in an empty yard to eat his supper, oranges from his country garden. As he caught the seeds in his handkerchief, George had an idea. 'I will plant a garden.' The next day he sowed the seeds he had saved from the oranges he had eaten and the seeds he had brought with him from the countryside.

Seeds sprouted. Magical plants began to grow. Birds and butterflies as bright as the rainbow appeared. People stopped to point and stare at the wonderful sight. And then George had his best idea of all. 'I will have a Garden Party,' he exclaimed, 'and invite everyone in town.'

Sewing machines hummed. Wonderful smells came from the bakery. Musicians tuned their instruments. And everyone tried to look their best for Gardener George's party.

At last it was time. Gardener George opened the gate and . . . never was there such a party. But, in the middle of it all, Gardener George slipped away, carrying his empty suitcase, a smile under his moustache. He was going home to the far-off countryside beneath the Blue Mountains. He left behind a special gift for each and every guest that day . . . and for the town.

In the Garden in Winter

by Stanley Cook from *The Squirrel in Town*, Blackie

In the garden in winter
One rose
Like a creamy ice-cream cornet
Still grows.

In the garden in winter
Two pears
That ripened all summer
Still hang there.

In the garden in winter
Three birds
Peck each other
And the bread.

In the garden in winter
Four trees
With leafless boughs
Comb the breeze.

In the garden in winter
Five cabbages grow
And wait to be eaten
In a row.

In the garden in winter
Six steps of stone
Are the only things
That don't feel cold.

In the garden in winter
Seven days of the week
Beneath the ground
The flower bulbs sleep.

At a casual glance, many gardens appear to be completely lifeless in winter. Can the children name any of the signs of the life still evident in the garden in the poem? Ask the audience to sequence the numbers from one to seven with the corresponding objects e.g. one rose, two pears, etc. Can they suggest which creatures might visit the rose, eat the pears or the cabbages? What other creatures might be sheltering in such a garden in winter? For example, snails could be hibernating under rocks or stones, and mice could be hiding under logs or piles of dead wood.

What creatures might be visiting the garden in search of food? For example, squirrels might be searching for nuts, and birds could be looking for berries. The poem refers to 'leafless boughs' but would all the trees be without leaves in winter? Can the children name two coniferous and two deciduous trees? Apart from food, what else would the birds need in winter?

RESOURCES

Poems

In the Garden in Winter The Squirrel in Town (Blackie)
A Spike of Green Young Puffin Book of Verse (Young Puffin)
Window Boxes Poetry Plus—Green Earth and Silver Stars (Schofield and Sims)
The Snail Poetry Allsorts 3 (Edward Arnold)
Slugs Seeing and Doing New Anthology (Thames/Methuen)

Songs

English Country Garden Harlequin (A and C Black)
Gardens Tinderbox Song Book (A and C Black)
In the Garden Every Colour Under the Sun (Ward Lock Educational)
Tiny Creatures Sing as You Grow (Ward Lock Educational)
One Potato, Two Potato Apusskidu (A and C Black)
Window Boxes Sing a Song 2 (Nelson)
My Garden Sing a New Song (Religious Education Press)
The Gardener's Song Action Songs (Early Learning Centre)
Gardens The Music Box Song Book (BBC)
We are Going to Plant a Bean This Little Puffin (Young Puffin)

Stories

Joseph's Yard C. Keeping (OUP)
Mr Plum's Paradise E. Trimby (Faber)
Meg's Veg H. Nicholl/J. Pienskowski (Heinemann)
In my Garden R. Maris (Julia MacRae)
Gregory's Garden W. Stobbs (OUP)
Planting a Rainbow L. Ehlert (Gollanz)
Growing Vegetable Soup L. Ehlert (Gollanz)
Our Garden (in The Julian Stories) A. Cameron (Fontana Young Lions)
Fred's Garden L. Jennings and M. Ursell (Hodder and Stoughton)
The Garden (in Anita Hewett's Animal Story Book) A. Hewett (Young Puffin)

AIM

To promote a concern for the built environment, past, present and future.

STARTING POINT

◎ Display pictures of various buildings e.g. old, new, with different architectural styles, serving a variety of purposes, using different building materials and techniques, etc. Ask the audience to describe each building in detail.

Discuss Why should old buildings be preserved? Responses might include: because of their architectural value, historical interest, as an illustration of a particular building technique, associations with well known characters or events, or because they add diversity to our environment. Why do we need new buildings?

CORE ACTIVITIES

◎ Show how buildings can be disfigured by unnecessary signs, ugly street furniture, etc. Display a large picture of one or two large buildings, covered with a transparent polythene overlay. Discuss the visual appearance of the building with the audience. For instance, are there any particularly interesting or pleasing features?

Ask volunteers from the audience to stick signs (logos and print taken from advertisements in magazines) onto the polythene covering the picture. Discuss the effects of lots of signs on the visual appeal of the building. Lift up the polythene to compare with the original building. Do the children prefer it with or without the signs? Would they find one or two signs more preferable to lots of them? Does the size of the sign concern them? If signs have to be put on the building, can they suggest the best place for them?

Ask the children to name any local buildings which they feel have too many signs on them. Perhaps they could look out for examples during the week and report back in another assembly.

▣ Prepare a small number of children to act out a television interview with two people representing opposing views to the building of a new housing estate. Their reasons might include:

For the building

● New homes are needed for homeless people.

● It is better to have one well designed estate than odd corners of infilling.

Against the building

● The estate may spoil a natural beauty spot.

● The development may destroy an important habitat for wildlife.

● More houses might put pressure on present facilities such as schools and doctors.

● More houses will result in more traffic.

Discuss the points raised in the interviews with the audience.

▣ Ask a small group of children to make pencil drawings of different buildings in the locality. Some could draw buildings which they consider worth preserving whilst others could draw those which they consider to be ugly. The children could then display their pictures and explain their feelings about each building.

▣ Invite a small group of children to develop a movement or mime sequence which represents building or demolition actions. For example, they could mime using hammers, machines, pneumatic drills, mixing cement and hauling pulleys. They could be accompanied by other children using home made musical instruments. (See page 74 for details.)

▣ Sing *Round and Round the Village* but change the words to fit in with a building or demolition theme. (See page 74 for details.)

▣ Arrange for a group of children to find out about one of the local public buildings such as the village hall, the community centre or the church. Can they discover anything about the history of the building, the times when the building is open to the public, what happens inside the building, how many different groups of people use it, how often they meet, etc.

CONCLUSION—WHAT CAN WE DO?

• Become more aware of the buildings surrounding us. Think about whether a building is a bad design because it does not fit in with the 'surroundings'. For example, does the scale, height, colour and type of decoration dwarf or overpower what already exists? Are there any unnecessary signs or ugly street furniture or telephone wires in the locality?

• Don't add more ugliness to buildings by spraying or writing graffiti or by vandalising empty properties.

• Visit buildings of historical interest so as to gain insight and appreciation of their importance in our culture.

They're Coming to Knock me Down

They're coming to knock me down.
With bulldozers and cranes,
Hammers and drills,
They'll batter me into the ground.

My windows are smashed.
My squeaky doors flapping.
Woodworm and damp
Scar what remains of my body.

For hundreds of years
I've stood happily here,
Watching and listening,
Soaking up secrets long forgotten.

The city web encircles me now.
Black tower blocks loom—
Poised—
Ready to pounce.
Will anyone notice I've gone?

ALTERNATIVE ACTIVITIES

◎ Ask the audience to help sort a set of pictures of buildings into old or new ones. What visual clues are they using to help decide whether a building is old or new? Which do they prefer and why?

◎ Show how objects from the past can tell us about how people lived. For example, borrow items of historical interest from a local museum (or Schools Museum Service) and explain how each item contributes to our knowledge about the everyday lives of people in the past. Emphasise that many old buildings also serve a similar purpose. The story *Lost and Found* by J. Paton Walsh (see page 75 for details) explores such a theme and, whilst it is too long to be read fully in an assembly situation, it could be summarised or used as a basis for developing a play.

▣ Arrange for a small number of children to draw features of particular houses in the locality such as chimneys, windows and doorways. During the assembly, invite them to hold up their pictures and describe them. Can they explain which features they find most pleasing and why?

▣ Organise one or two children to conduct a survey to discover how many different building materials are used locally. Does one particular material predominate and if so, why? Which other materials are used most or least often? Which do the audience like the appearance of best or least?

▣ Prepare a chart with a group or class of children to show how many different buildings they have used during one particular week. It would probably be simplest to start the chart at the beginning of one week and update it each day to discover if any new buildings had been used. The children could draw pictures of themselves on a square of paper which could then be stuck in the appropriate column. More able children could be encouraged to

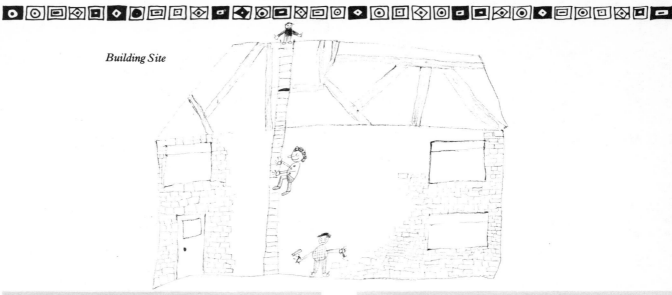

Building Site

devise their own means of recording such information. Discuss the completed chart with the audience. Can they determine which buildings were used by all the children? Which building was used least?

▣ Assign a group of children to compile a detailed report about the school buildings. This could include research into the history of the school, lists of materials used in its construction, plans or drawings of the current buildings and any proposals for future expansion. The children could be asked to consider the following questions:

● Whether the buildings are suitable for their purpose.

● Whether there are any problems in the design e.g. are the toilets a long distance from the classroom?

● Whether the outside of the buildings are pleasing to look at.

● If there are any parts inside the building which need improving e.g. is there a dark corridor which could be brightened up with a display of children's paintings?

● Any other suggestions they could make to improve the school environment.

The results of their research could be presented during the assembly.

▣ Read out a selection of stories which the children have written based on the following starting point: 'Your parents receive a letter saying that your house is going to be knocked down so that a new motorway can be built'. Encourage them

to reflect upon how they would respond to this. Would they be sad? What would they miss about their house? What would they do? Does the motorway go ahead or is their house saved?

▣ Use the music from the song *Round and Round the Village* (from *This Little Puffin*) but change the words to fit in with a building or demolition theme. Alternative words could include:

Round and round the village etc.
Pulling down the houses.

Knocking down the walls etc.
Until there are no more.

Tearing out the windows etc.
Until there are no more.

Digging up the floors etc.
Until there are no more.

Encourage the children to suggest their own verses together with accompanying actions.

Home-made Musical Instruments

The suggestions outlined below are for making simple musical instruments which could then be used by the children to accompany movement sequences arising from a building or demolition theme. Encourage the children to attempt to match the sound produced by the instrument to a particular action e.g. mixing cement. Where appropriate, paint or decorate the home-made instruments with coloured paper shapes.

Drums   These can be made out of cardboard boxes, biscuit tins, tins with plastic lids, upturned yoghurt pots or plastic ice cream containers. Beaters can include wooden or metal spoons, strong cardboard tubes or sticks.

Claves	Any object which produces a pleasant sound when tapped together can be used. Examples are sticks, metal and wooden spoons, strong cardboard tubes, stones, pencils, wooden bricks or long metal screws.
Stringed instruments	These can be produced by stretching rubber bands of different thicknesses across containers without lids. The strings can then be plucked on the open side of the container.
Scrapers	Again, any object which produces a pleasant sound when rubbed with a finger nail, spoon or stick can be used. Objects could include corrugated card, textured plastic bottles, sandpaper or a comb.
Jingle bells	Milk bottle tops, metal washers, buttons etc. can all be threaded on to fine string or cotton and shaken.

Demolition of a Crescent

by Marian Lines from *Poetry Plus—The World We Have Made*, Schofield and Sims

Families gone,
Boards in the windows,
Houses alone,
Waiting the end.
Ruin is near,
Street in its death-throes;
Leaving a scar
No one can mend.

Swing the hammer!
Fell the trees!
Bring the crescent to its knees!

See where they fall,
Lintel and staircase.
Batter them all
Flat to the ground!
Chimneystacks tumbled.
Skylight and fireplace,
Houses are humbled—
Crescent is down.

Swing the hammer!
Fell the trees!
Bring the crescent to its knees!

Houses

by Rachel Field from *Poetry Plus—The World We Have Made*, Schofield and Sims

I like old houses best, don't you?
They never go cluttering up a view
With roofs too red and paint too new,
With doors too green and blinds too blue!
The old ones look as if they grew,
Their bricks may be dingy, their clapboards askew
From sitting so many seasons through.
But they've learned in a hundred years or two
Not to go cluttering up a view!

Does the poet like old or new houses? What does she dislike about new houses? What makes her prefer old ones? Does the audience agree or disagree with her? Can they suggest other features of both old and new houses which could be detrimental in a landscape?

RESOURCES

Poems

House A First Poetry Book (OUP)
House Coming Down Young Puffin Book of Verse (Puffin Books)
Demolition of a Crescent (Poetry Plus—The World We Have Made (Schofield and Sims)

Songs

Round and Round the Village This Little Puffin (Young Puffin)
There are Houses and Houses Sing a Song 2 New Horizons (Nelson Stainer and Bell)

Stories

Lost and Found J. Paton Walsh (Andre Deutsch)
Isn't it a Beautiful Meadow? W. Opgenoorth (OUP)
Mole L. Murschetz (Methuen)
The Animals of Farthing Wood C. Dann (Heinemann)
The House that Moved D. Rees (Young Puffin)
Nowhere to Play Karusa (A and C Black)
Adam on Paradise Island C. Keeping (Oxford)
Cat's New House (in Play School Stories) M. Green (BBC)
The Old House and the New House (in Story Time Two) L. Smith (Magnet)

ANGER

AIM

To explore the reasons for feeling angry and consider the consequences.
To find ways of dealing with anger.

STARTING POINT

◉ Prepare a small group of children to devise an angry dance to be performed at the beginning of the assembly. (See page 77 for details.) Encourage them to accompany their movements with appropriate percussion sounds. Can the audience identify the emotion being conveyed through the dance?

Discuss   What sort of movements were the children using to communicate anger? Were any of the percussion sounds used particularly effective at conveying an angry mood?

Remind the audience that everyone gets angry at some time or another, adults as well as children. Point out that it can often be a very unpleasant experience and rather frightening, especially if the emotion seems uncontrollable.

CORE ACTIVITIES

◎ Read a poem which illustrates the powerful emotions being felt at a time of great anger. (See page 79 for suggestions.) Ask the audience to pick out the words and phrases which describe the feelings most aptly. Can they compile their own list of words and phrases? Would any of the audience's words or phrases make good substitutes for any of the words in the original poem?

◎ Encourage the audience to say what physical signs often indicate that someone is angry e.g. stamping their feet, punching, waving fists. Adapt an action rhyme to demonstrate these signs and teach it to the audience. For example, the song *Clap your hands* (see page 79 for details) is simple and repetitive and can be easily adapted for this purpose. The words could be changed to stamp your feet, shake your fists, punch the air, kick your foot, wag your finger, etc. Encourage the audience to add their own verses.

◎ Discuss ways of channelling angry feelings

harmlessly. Children often resort to retaliation of some kind by hitting out or destroying something treasured by the other person. Remind the audience that often we regret our hasty actions and end up apologising for our bad behaviour. Can they suggest ways of venting our anger without hurting a person or property? They might suggest punching a pillow, kicking a football, going for a long walk or shouting in private.

▣ Prepare a group of children to write similes about anger. For example, as angry as a spitting cat, as annoyed as a bubbling saucepan and as furious as a bursting balloon. Invite them to read out their similes during the assembly and discuss which ones the audience feel have the most impact.

▣ Arrange for a group of children to draw pictures of their own face when they are happy and, on the reverse side, pictures of their face when they are extremely angry. Ask the children to hold up their happy faces and then show their angry faces, giving an explanation as to why their happy face has disappeared. Their reasons might include the following: 'I get angry when . . . my brother teases me, my tower of bricks falls down, my mum won't let me watch television, my friends won't play with me'.

▣ Invite a group of children to think about some of the occasions when they make other people angry. What did they say or do to provoke this anger? How did the other person respond? Could the situation have been avoided? Ask the children to draw and write about these occasions and mount the results in a zigzag book.

▣ Organise a group of children to work in pairs with a different percussion instrument each. Encourage them to try to invent a dialogue or conversation between the instruments, during which anger is portrayed.

Discuss ways of making the instruments sound

angry by, for example, playing them faster and louder. The 'conversation' could begin with both instruments being played alternately in a gentle, rhythmic manner. They could gradually show signs of becoming angrier and reach a climax with both being played loudly and quickly simultaneously. The angry conversation could end abruptly or gradually subside.

Ask one or two pairs to perform their 'conversation' during the assembly. Can the audience correctly interpret the 'conversations'?

CONCLUSION—WHAT CAN WE DO?

- Try to avoid making anyone angry in the first place. Conflict can often be prevented with a little forethought.

- Try not to react angrily automatically. Learn to pause and consider whether the circumstances really merit an angry response.

- Think about the effects of our anger on other people and decide whether it is fair to inflict it on them.

- Find alternative ways of venting our anger to avoid hurting people or property.

Recipe for a Tantrum!

Cut a finger on a pencil sharpener.
Soak a sleeve with bright red paint.
Add some bricks which topple over
And a squabble with a friend.
Stir in a spoonful of messy writing,
A pinch of teacher's angry tongue
And simmer well.
Bring to the boil with a broken toy
And a missing satchel.
Whip up a clenched fist,
Sprinkle with tears
And chill quickly before home time!

ALTERNATIVE ACTIVITIES

◎ Discuss the effects of our angry behaviour on other people. Ask the audience to help compile a list of words to describe the feelings of the person receiving the angry behaviour. They might suggest hurt, sad, upset, worried or dismayed.

◎ Write a short description of someone becoming

angry because everything appears to be going 'wrong'. Try to incorporate 'sound effects' involving voice or body sounds which the audience can join in with. An example of such a description is outlined on page 78. Read the story during assembly and encourage the audience to participate where appropriate. Discuss the implications of the story with reference to anger. Has anyone in the audience ever experienced a day where nothing seemed to go 'right'? Can they describe how they felt at the end of it?

▣ Exhibit paintings or collage pictures of angry faces which have been produced by a group of children. Invite the audience to discuss the use of colours. Which 'angry' colours have been used? Do the colours convey anger just by themselves or do the shapes, lines or textures also support this emotion.

▣ Arrange for a group of children to try writing tongue-twisters arising from the theme of 'anger'. For example, 'Angry Arthur argues with anyone at all' or 'Furious Frank fell foaming to the floor'. Select two or three children to read their tongue-twisters during assembly and suggest that they teach them to the audience. How quickly can they all recite it without making mistakes?

Angry Dance

The following ideas are given as an example of how to develop an 'angry' dance from a fairly simple situation. Teachers will no doubt wish to adapt the suggestions to meet the needs of their own particular pupils. The starting point for the movement ideas below is that of a giant who is trying to sleep but is constantly disturbed by a whistling noise. Although other different starting points could be chosen, many of the movement suggestions would be applicable to any 'angry' dance.

Ideas	Movement suggestions
Giant preparing for bed.	Mime putting on night clothes, cleaning teeth, washing face, etc. Stretching and yawning movements on the spot. Climbing into bed, snuggling under covers and falling asleep.
Quiet whistling noise.	Restless movements in sleep, turning over, curling up.
Louder whistling noise and the giant awakes.	Stiff startled movements, rubbing sleep out of eyes, listening for source of noise.
Giant returns to sleep.	Rearranging bedding and pillows, settling down to sleep again.
Loud piercing whistle and giant leaps out of bed.	Angry jump out of bed, stamping interesting pathway, searching for source of noise, looking high and low, in front and behind.
Occasional peeps on whistle with giant becoming increasingly annoyed.	Stopping at whistle signal shaking fists, singly or simultaneously at noise.
Period of quiet lulls giant into believing noise has ceased.	Stamping and shaking of fists becoming less angry.
Giant about to get back into bed when piercing whistle is repeated.	Mime returning to bed, stiff startled movements followed by strong punching arms, high and low, on the spot and then travelling with heavy stamping feet. Fierce angry faces accompanied by angry noises.
Giant picks up pillow and jumps on it furiously.	Lifting and throwing strongly, jumping, feet together and then alternately stamping and jumping, arms high, fists punching the air.
Short blasts on whistle from different directions.	Running and jumping at source of noise, shaking fists, punching air, etc.
Whistle noises stop and giant gradually becomes less angry and sinks exhausted to the floor where he falls asleep.	Gradual slowing down of above movements, slow sinking to the floor, slumped still shape.

Mum's Busy Morning

The following is an example of a story which could be read during the assembly and it aims to encourage the audience to participate by making appropriate sound effects using their voices and body sounds. It might be more successful if one class had practised the story once or twice before the assembly so that they could lead the other children with the sound effects. Obviously, many other short descriptions would be appropriate and teachers will probably wish to adapt the following passage to their particular pupils. The proposed sound effects are shown in brackets.

Mum was rushing about trying to get all of the household chores finished as quickly as possible because Aunt Jane was coming to visit. So far, she had made good progress because the washing was swishing happily in the machine (*rub hands together*) and everywhere was beautifully polished. Also, she had just mixed up a chocolate cake and, as it was ready to go in the oven, she opened the door (*click teeth*) and carefully put it inside. When she had closed the door (*click teeth*), she went upstairs (*bang chest*) to wake Ben up again. He was still asleep (*snoring noises*) and wouldn't get up. 'Come on, Ben, it's very late!' nagged mum crossly. But Ben simply turned over and went back to sleep (*snoring noises*). Before mum had time to shake him, the dog barked (*woof, woof*) followed by a loud bang (*bang hands on floor*). Mum ran downstairs (*bang chest quickly*) to find that the dog had jumped up at the window and knocked over a plant. There was soil, crumpled leaves and broken pieces of flower pot all over the floor. Mum mumbled angrily (*mutter, mutter*) to herself. She had just found the dustpan when the telephone rang (*ring, ring*). When she returned from answering the phone, she could smell burning immediately. (*Sniff, sniff, sniff*) 'Not my cake!' moaned mum. But it was too late. Smoke swirled out from the oven as she rescued the charred cake. Suddenly, the swishing of the washing machine got faster and faster (*rub hands together quickly*) and there was a strange bumping noise (*rub hands together followed by clap*). Before mum could reach the switch to turn it off, water poured out of the machine (*glug, glug, glug, glug*), flooding the floor. 'Oh no!' shouted mum and stamped her feet in temper (*stamp feet*). She was so furious that she only just heard the doorbell ringing (*ding, dong*). Reluctantly, she opened the door. 'How lovely to see you, Aunt Jane,' she said, smiling with difficulty as she remembered the awful mess in the kitchen.

Untitled poem

in *A Kiss on the Nose* by Tony Bradman, Heinemann

When I'm feeling tired.
When things go wrong.
When mummy won't sing
My favourite song.

I'm naughty and nasty,
I'm not nice to know,
I scream and I shout
And a tantrum I throw.

When my stupid brother
Spoils all my games.
When he calls my teddy
Horrible names.

I'm naughty and nasty,
I'm not nice to know,
I scream and I shout
And a tantrum I throw.

But when I say sorry
And I suck my thumb.
I get a nice cuddle
From my favourite mum!

Sulk

by Felice Holman in *Pudmuddle Jump In*, Magnet

I scuff
    my feet along
And puff
    my lower lip
I sip my milk
    in slurps
And huff
And frown
And stamp around
And tip my chair
    back from the table
Nearly fall down
    But I don't care

I scuff
And puff
And frown
And huff
And stamp
And pout
Till I forget
What it's about.

What does the poet do to show that she is sulking? Do the members of the audience do similar things or do they have other ways of displaying their angry mood? What sort of things cause the children to sulk? Are they always important things or do they, like the poet, sometimes forget what had originally made them sulk?

RESOURCES

Poems
Anger Junior Voices 1 (Penguin)
A Skip to Beat Bad Temper Is a Caterpillar Ticklish? (Young Puffin)
The Quarrel A First Poetry Book (OUP)
Anger The Tinder Box Assembly Book (A and C Black)

Songs
Stamping Sing as you Grow (Ward Lock Educational)
Clap your Hands Sing a Song 1 (Nelson)
Getting Angry Every Colour Under the Sun (Ward Lock Educational)
Take the Time to Cogitate Every Colour Under the Sun (Ward Lock Educational)
The Angry Song Tinderbox Song Book (A and C Black)

Why Does it have to be Me? Tinderbox Song Book (A and C Black)

Stories
Peter gets Angry M. Macdonald (Dinosaur Publications)
Angry Arthur J. Oram and S. Kitamura (Puffin)
Let's be Friends Again H. Wilhelm (Picture Knight)
The Two Giants M. Foreman (Hodder and Stoughton)
I was so Mad I could have Split Book G. Frisen and P. Eckholm (A & C Black)
Cross Patch (in Tell Me Another Story) M. Baker (Young Puffin)
Two Monsters D. McKee (Andersen Press)
Would you be Angry? J. Oakley (Deutsch)
When Emily Woke Up Angry R. Duncan (Deutsch)
Mine's the Best C. Bonsall (Worlds Work)
The Fighting Sisters A. Harper (Macdonald)
The Temper Tantrum Book E. Preston (Picture Puffin)

Happiness

AIM

To consider what makes us happy and ways of making others happy.

STARTING POINT

◎ Sing a song with a happy theme, preferably one which is familiar to the audience so they can join in. *If you're happy and you know it* (see page 83 for details) is ideal because the audience can also participate in the actions.

Discuss Can the audience suggest further verses? For instance, If you're happy and you know it . . . jump for joy, shout 'Yipee!', give a grin. Are there other ways in which we show our happiness?

CORE ACTIVITIES

◎ Explain that different things make people feel happy. Demonstrate this by asking members of the audience to come to the front of the hall and name something which makes them happy. For example, they might suggest receiving presents, going to the seaside, playing games with a friend, painting, watching birds, talking to nanny on the telephone or building a snowman. Is it possible to find 10 different reasons for feeling happy?

◎ Sometimes children may get the impression that only momentous occasions or expensive presents can give rise to happiness. Ask the audience to help compile a list of simple, everyday things which can make us happy such as a hug from mum, praise from a teacher or biscuits shared with a friend. This activity links well with the poem suggested on page 81.

◎ Ask for two volunteers from the audience. Suggest that one of them tries to maintain a blank, expressionless face whilst the other one attempts to make them laugh by pulling funny faces, telling jokes, etc. Agree beforehand that no one is allowed to touch or tickle anyone else. Use an egg timer to limit the time available. Swap the two children for another pair of volunteers. Who is most successful at making people smile? Who is really good at keeping a straight face?

▣ Arrange for a group of children to paint clown faces. Encourage some of them to paint clowns with happy expressions and some with sad. Can they choose colours to reflect the mood being portrayed such as bright, sunny colours for the happy clowns and dark, sombre colours for the sad ones? Display these paintings in the assembly and ask the audience to count the number of happy and sad faces. Ask the children to offer reasons for the clowns' expressions.

▣ Organise a group of children to write a description of a particular 'happy' day which celebrated a special event. The occasions might include the birth of a sibling, a child's own birthday, a religious celebration such as Divali, Rosh Hashana or Christmas, a wedding or Guy Fawkes Night. Encourage the children to describe their feelings as well as the event. Ask two or three children to read their descriptions to the audience.

▣ Ask the children to look at the person sitting next to them. Study the shape of the mouth, the position of the eyebrows, look for any creases or lines. Then ask all the children to smile for a few seconds so they can observe the physical changes on each others' faces. Which parts of the face move? What muscles are being used? Where do lines and/or creases appear?

▣ Organise a Smile Day. Suggest that both staff and children try to remember to smile more often during the day. Explain how smiling can often be infectious and that if you smile at someone, they usually return the smile. Show the audience examples of a poster and a badge which advertise the Smile Day. Can the children design their own badges to wear for the day and make posters to display in their classrooms/corridors?

CONCLUSION—WHAT CAN WE DO?

• Be aware of whether our words or actions are affecting other people adversely and making them unhappy.

• Try to think of ways of making others happy.

• Remember that it is often small, apparently insignificant things that can make people happy.

What is Happiness?

Happiness is—

Biggest bike,
Pricey presents,
Sticky sweets,
Tons of toys,
Finishing first.

Or is it—

Blustery breezes,
Friendly faces,
Playful puddles,
Tatty teddy,
Giggling gleefully?

What is happiness?

ALTERNATIVE ACTIVITIES

◎ Arrange for two or three parents to attend the assembly to use face paints on some volunteers. Give the children different expressions. Whilst the children's faces are being painted, sing a song or read an appropriate story or poem. When the face painting is done, ask the audience to identify the different moods. How many happy faces are there?

◎ Enlist the help of the audience to sort words written on separate cards into two sets; those which describe happiness and those which relate to sadness. For example, the list of words could include cheerful, glad, delighted, merry, pleased, thrilled, unhappy, wretched, gloomy and miserable. Ask a member of the audience to mount each word onto a large happy or sad face as appropriate.

◎ Play a tape recording of several contrasting pieces of music and ask the audience to identify whether each section of music conveys a sense of happiness or sadness. Compare one happy and one sad piece of music—how did they differ? Which musical instruments were used? Did the 'happy' music make anyone want to clap, skip or dance?

◎ Often bizarre or unusual things make us laugh. Devise an activity to demonstrate this. For example, cut several pictures of animals in half. Mount them on a board incorrectly matched, trying to create strange creatures. Display the pictures during the assembly and encourage the audience to describe their reactions to them. Which creature do they think is the funniest? Would they laugh if they met that animal in the street? Conclude by inviting members of the audience to match the animal halves correctly.

◎ Read the poem *The Smile That Grew* by Lilian Murray (see page 83 for details). Discuss the poem with the audience. Can the children name any of the people affected by Sarah's smile? What words and phrases does the poet use to convey Sarah's happy mood? Can the audience suggest appropriate substitute words or phrases? Has anyone ever experienced a similar situation where their own or someone else's happiness proved contagious? Suggest that the audience make a conscious effort to smile more often during the day. What effect do they think it will have?

▣ Prepare a group of children to dress up as clowns and develop a funny clown act. They might decide to throw 'pretend' custard pies at each other, trip over objects, tip a bucket of water (shredded paper) over the audience etc. Ask the audience for their reactions to the act. What made them laugh most of all?

▣ Arrange for a small group of children to write an acrostic poem for the word Happiness. Write the word Happiness in large letters on a blackboard and point to the appropriate letter as each child reads his/her poem. Can the audience help devise an alternative poem to be written on the blackboard?

◻ Display three-dimensional funny faces which have been made by some of the children. Use cardboard boxes as a basis and add wool or curled paper for hair, paper teeth, parts of egg boxes for bulging eyes, etc. Can the children invent ways of making parts of the faces move? For example, can they make part of the hair stick up, the ears flap, and a tongue stick out. Ask some of the model makers to explain the construction of their funny face and to demonstrate any moving features. Which face do members of the audience think is the funniest and why?

When I am Happy

from *Sing as you grow*, Ward Lock Educational

1   When I am happy,
When I am glad,
I clap my hands above my head
   to show that I'm not sad;
When I am happy,
When I am glad,
I clap my hands above my head –
   CLAP – CLAP – CLAP!

2   When I am happy,
When I am glad,
I clap my hands down by my feet
   to show that I'm not sad;
When I am happy,
When I am glad,
I clap my hands down by my feet –
   CLAP – CLAP – CLAP!

3   . . . I clap my hands in front of me . . .
4   . . . I clap my hands behind my back . . .
5   . . . I clap my hands by the side of me . . .

Three claps should be made in the direction suggested in each verse, whilst the three claps are sung.

Special Things

by Tony Bradman in *Smile Please* by Tony Bradman, Young Puffin

These are my special things,
I keep them just here.
There's a badge, and a shell,
And a doll with one ear;

There's a necklace that's broken,
A ring with no stone,
A pen that won't write
And an old bit of bone.

There's a dried, withered flower
My dad gave to me,
A note from my granny
And a shiny 10p.

And each of my special things
Makes me want to smile;
Each one is a memory
I can hold for a while.

These are my special things,
They'll always be near;
I'll keep them for ever . . .
I'll keep them just here.

Can the audience name some of the special things listed in the poem? Why do they make the poet want to smile? Do any of the audience possess 'treasures' which some people might consider to be worthless but which give them great happiness? Do they have memories which make them feel happy?

RESOURCES

Poems

The Smile that Grew Child Education, March 1983 (Scholastic Publications)

The Friendly Cinnamon Bun Rhyme Time (Beaver Books)

Glad Things A Very First Poetry Book (OUP)

Biking Read a Poem, Write a Poem (Blackwell)

Happiness Singing in the Sun (Young Puffin)

Songs

Maja Pade—Let's All be Happy Tinderbox Song Book (A and C Black)

Stick on a Smile Every Colour Under the Sun (Ward Lock Educational)

When I am Happy Sing as You Grow (Ward Lock Educational)

If you're Happy and you know it Sing a Song 1 (Nelson)

O Lord Shout for Joy Someone's Singing, Lord (A and C Black)

I'd like to Teach the World to Sing Apusskidu (A and C Black)

The Clown Apusskidu (A and C Black)

I Whistle a Happy Tune Apusskidu (A and C Black)

One Finger, One Thumb Keep Moving Okki-tokki-unga (A and C Black)

Old King Cole Over and Over Again (Beaver Books)

Happiness is Alleluya (A and C Black)

When you're Smiling Ta ra ra boom de ay (A and C Black)

Make a Face Tinderbox Song Book (A and C Black)

Sing a Merry Song Zmm! Zmm! (OUP)

Come along, Sing a Song Zmm! Zmm! (OUP)

What Happiness Mrs Macaroni (Macmillan)

You're Smiling Child Education, March 1983 (Scholastic Publications)

What Would Make Me Happy? Kokoleoko (Macmillan)

Happiness Hullabaloo-Balay (Macmillan)

Stories

The Happy Owls C. Piatti (Benn)

Look what I've got A. Browne (Julia MacRae)

Pookins Gets Her Way H. Lester (Macmillan)

My Nightingale is Singing A. Lindgren (Methuen)

Chameleons Never Laugh (in The Anita Hewett Animal Story Book*)* A. Hewett (Young Puffin)

The Laughing Bird (in The Anita Hewett Animal Story Book*)* A. Hewett (Young Puffin)

The Happy Lion L. Fatio (Picture Puffin)

Feeling happy

SADNESS

AIM

To explore the causes of sadness and the various ways of dealing with it.

STARTING POINT

◎ Display a picture of a happy face and ask the audience to identify the emotion being expressed. Make some of the features detachable such as the mouth and eyebrows. Turn the happy mouth upside down, add tears and rearrange the eyebrows (using Blu-tack to refix them) to alter the expression. Can the audience identify the new emotion on the face?

Discuss   What causes people to be sad? Do the children always know why they are feeling sad? What actions do they take when they feel sad? Does crying make them feel better? Has anyone experienced an occasion when it was very difficult to stop crying or feeling sad?

CORE ACTIVITIES

◎ Ask the audience to help compile a list of words to describe feeling sad, such as unhappy, miserable, gloomy, wretched, tearful, or depressed. Write each one on a tear shaped piece of paper and ask a volunteer from the audience to stick the word on a large picture of a sad face.

◎ Invite volunteers from the audience to join in a singing game with a sad theme. Potential songs might include *Poor Jenny is a-weeping* or *If you clap* (see page 87 for details). Discuss with the audience the possible causes for the sadness suffered by the child in the song. What remedy is suggested in the song to make the child happier? What other ways can the audience suggest to make someone feel happier?

◎ Even at infant level, crying is sometimes regarded by some children as 'babyish'. Discuss the occasions when we cry with the audience, such as when we have been hurt both physically and emotionally. How does crying help? Do we feel better afterwards? Should adults cry? Is it acceptable for girls to cry but not boys? How do we respond when we find someone crying? Help the children to realise that crying can be an important emotional release for adults and children, boys and girls, and that it should not be regarded with disdain.

◎ Play a 'changing faces' game. Ask the children to practise changing their own expressions from happy to sad by passing a hand up and down over their face. Bang a cymbal to indicate the speed of change. For example, if the cymbal is banged softly and slowly, then their hands and expressions must move and change slowly. Conversely, if the cymbal is tapped sharply and quickly, their hands and expressions must alter rapidly.

▣ Prepare a small group of children to mime certain tasks in a sad manner. For example, sweeping the floor, washing up, planting a flower, playing with a toy could all be mimed with slow, heavy movements and glum expressions. Can the audience identify how the emotion is conveyed? Does the body language reflect the facial expression?

▣ Challenge two or three children to tell jokes to cheer up the audience. This will probably need to be arranged before the assembly so that the jokes can be 'vetted'! Here are two examples: What do sea monsters eat? *Fish and ships.* Why did the banana split? *It saw the apple turnover.* Is there anyone in the audience who has a joke which they would like to share?

▣ Organise a group of children to write about how they cheer themselves up when they are sad. For example, they might ask mum for a cuddle and a story, go and find a friend to play with, watch a funny television programme or go to a special place to be alone. Select one or two children to read their descriptions to the audience. How do members of the audience make themselves feel happier when they are sad?

CONCLUSION—WHAT CAN WE DO?

- Think carefully before we say or do anything to make someone sad.

- If we feel sad, do something enjoyable to help the sadness to go.

- Share the cause of the sadness with someone else such as our family or friends.

- Be sympathetic to someone who is feeling sad and help to cheer them up.

Sadness

Plants drooping,
Quietly dying
Through lack of care,
Make me sad.

Beautiful beaches,
Strewn with litter,
No one noticing
Makes me sad.

People's eyes
Glancing away,
Ignoring hungry faces
Make me sad.

Empty houses,
Derelict and dark,
No longer needed
Make me sad.

Butterflies trapped,
Pierced in glass cases,
Dazzling but dead,
Make me sad.

What makes you sad?

ALTERNATIVE ACTIVITIES

◎ Dress a child up as Mr Tickle with extremely long arms. Gloves could be fixed on the end of cardboard tubes which could be held by the child and covered with a large jumper or cardigan. Ask the child to choose someone in the audience to tickle. See if Mr Tickle can (carefully) make the member of the audience laugh. Follow up by reading the story about Mr Tickle by Roger Hargreaves. (See page 87 for details.)

◎ Hold up pictures of happy and sad faces (simple outlines drawn by an adult or pictures cut from magazines). Ask the audience to identify the emotion and for one child to place the picture into the correct sorting hoop (one for sad and one for happy). Alternatively, use the cards for making a happy family. Ask members of the audience to pick a card from the pack. If it has a happy face, the child remains at the front of the assembly whereas if a sad face is chosen, the child returns to his/her place. Agree beforehand with the children, how many members the happy family should have so that when that number is reached, the game stops.

◎ Read the story *The bird who couldn't fly* by Richard Buckley (see page 86 for details). If possible, prepare some children to play the parts of the animals so that they can reply to the bird's question 'Can you fly?' and also act out the squabbling behaviour towards the end. Discuss the story with the audience emphasising the fact that although the bird was very sad because she could no longer fly, she still possessed other, equally important, skills i.e. her singing. Try to relate this to the children's own experiences. For example, some children become very sad if they have suffered a disappointment—perhaps they have failed to swim a width of the pool or not progressed onto the next reading book as expected—and they may need help to restore their self-image by reminding themselves of the many other skills they possess.

▣ Prepare a group of children to act out three short scenes. One should be very obviously sad whilst the other two should reflect happy situations. Can the audience spot which one illustrates sadness? Are all the characters sad or only one? What is the cause of his/her sadness? What could he/she do to overcome this feeling?

▣ Letters can often bring both good and bad news. Enlist the help of three or four children to open envelopes during the assembly. Suggest the audience watch carefully to discover by the child's mimed response whether the letter contains good or bad news. Can the audience give examples for each type of letter? For instance, for 'bad' they might say the letter contains news of someone who has become ill or who has lost something. On the other hand, good news might be a letter which tells of an intended visit or the birth of a baby.

Deep down

by Michael Rosen in *The Hypnotiser* by Michael Rosen, Andre Deutsch

deep down
where I don't know
deep down
inside
there's a place
so sad
such a sad sad place

sometimes it fills up
and it fills up
and it fills up
and overflows in my eyes
and all of me is so sad
such a sad sad place

The Bird who Couldn't Fly

by R. Buckley, Hodder and Stoughton

Every morning the bird flew to the top of a tree to watch the sun rise. Every day the bird perched among the topmost branches and sang and sang and sang. It was a beautiful sound, and everyone who heard her felt happy.

One day there was a terrible storm. The sky was filled with dark and heavy clouds. The rain lashed. The lightning flashed. The thunder crashed. A bolt of lightning struck the tree where the bird was perched. With a loud crack, the branches splintered and the bird was thrown to the ground. She lay without moving for a long, long time.

Next morning the weather was calm again. When the bird felt the sun's warmth on her feathers, she tried to fly up to the treetops to sing as she had always done. But she could only flutter along the ground. Her wings were broken.

'I can't fly! I can't fly!' the bird sobbed. 'How can I sing, How can I live if I can't fly?' She sat on a log and wept bitterly.

A squirrel jumped down from a tree and tried to comfort the bird. 'I can't fly,' he said. 'Nor can I sing. But I get along very well.' But the bird just wept and wept.

Then an owl, who had seen and heard everything, added some more advice. 'You have cried for long enough, little bird. Now it is time to look around, listen and learn. You'll find there is more to life than flying.' So the bird set off to see what she could learn.

'Can you fly?' she asked the dog. 'No, but I can bark very loudly,' answered the dog. 'And I can wag my tail very fast.'

'Can you fly?' she asked the snake. But the snake only hissed and slid into the grass.

'Can you fly?' she asked the cricket. 'Not really,' chirped the cricket 'but I do have wings. And if I rub them together, I can make music.'

'Can you fly?' she asked the pig. 'That's a silly question,' grunted the pig. 'Whoever heard of a pig with wings?'

'Can you fly?' she asked the frog. 'No, but I can jump ten times my own length,' croaked the frog. 'That's as good as flying.'

'Can you fly?' she asked the mouse. 'Oh no, I'm much too timid for that sort of thing,' squeaked the mouse, and disappeared into a hole.

'Can you fly?' she asked the chicken. 'I can almost fly,' squawked the chicken proudly. 'And I can lay eggs by the dozen.'

'Can you fly?' she asked the cat. But when the cat miaowed and narrowed her eyes, the bird hurried away.

'Can you fly?' she asked the horse. 'No, but I can gallop like the wind,' replied the horse and neighed loudly, showing his teeth.

By this time, it was getting dark and the bird was very tired. She crept into a barn and went to sleep in the straw. The next morning the bird was woken by a loud and very strange noise. It was a chirping, hissing, croaking, barking, miaowing, squeaking, neighing, grunting, squawking sort of noise. 'Whatever is going on?' she wondered, peering out of the barn door.

It all began with one mistake. The cricket chirped too near the snake. The hissing snake woke up the frog who with a croak jumped on the dog. The dog then barked and chased the cat who miaowed and chased the mouse. At that, the squeaking mouse ran up the horse who neighed and kicked his legs, of course, and showered mud upon the pig who grunted and then danced a jig. The chicken, standing on one leg, squawked loudly and then laid an egg.

The bird laughed and laughed and laughed. It was the first time she had laughed since the storm, and it made her feel much better. Suddenly, without thinking, the bird opened her beak and began to sing. In the farmyard, the animals stopped their squabbling and turned to listen. It was the most beautiful sound they had ever heard. From that day onwards, the bird who couldn't fly sang from dawn to dusk. And everyone who heard her wondered at the beauty of her song.

Everything will be all right

by Tony Bradman, in Smile Please *by Tony Bradman, Young Puffin*

I'd had a really dreadful day,
Nothing would go right;
I failed a test and got told off,
Then got into a fight.

I fell down in the playground
Where I lost my special rubber,
And by the time that I got home
All I could do was blubber.

My little brother bit me
And I spilt my drink at tea . . .
Why, oh why I wondered,
Is this happening to me?

Later, dad came to my room,
And kissed me on my head.
He put his hand upon my hair,
And this is what he said:

'Life is sometimes difficult,
It's sometimes a real pain,
But something's bound to pop up, love,
To make you laugh again.

'So close your eyes now, and forget
That everything's gone wrong,
I promise you that in a while
You'll laugh both loud and long.'

And can you guess what happened next?
As dad went to the door,
He tripped and flew across the room
And crashed down on the floor.

I laughed, I giggled, and dad said;
'I hear you've changed your tune . . .
But when I said you'd cheer up,
I didn't mean so soon.'

Why had the poet had such a dreadful day? What did dad say to try to comfort him? How did dad cheer him up by mistake? Can anyone in the audience describe a similar 'dreadful day' which they had experienced? Has something funny ever happened to make any of the children change from feeling sad to happy?

RESOURCES

Poems

Sad . . . and Glad A First Poetry Book (OUP)
Sad Things A First Poetry Book (OUP)
At the Party Ask a Silly Question (Mammoth)
Squeezes Gargling with Jelly (Viking Kestrel)
At the Park Smile Please (Young Puffin)
Billy Batter Rhyme Time 2 (Beaver Books)
The Giggle of Wings Another First Poetry Book (OUP)
The Sad Bus The First Lick of the Lolly (Macmillan)
Sadness Poetry Allsorts 3 (Edward Arnold)

Songs

Poor Jenny Sits A-Weeping The Funny Family (Ward Lock Educational)
Sad Faces, Happy Faces New Horizons (Stainer and Bell)
If You Clap Flying A Round (A and C Black)
How Do You Feel Today? Songs from Playschool (BBC)
Frown The Music Fun Shop (Hamish Hamilton)
Goodbyes Every Colour Under the Sun (Ward Lock Educational)
Little Sally More Kokoleoko (Macmillan)
Water Come a Me Eye The Music Box Song Book (BBC)

Stories

Mr Tickle R. Hargreaves (Price Stern Sloan)
Miserable Aunt Bertha J. V. Lord and F. Maschler (Jonathan Cape)
Mr Grumpy R. Hargreaves (Thurman Publishing)
Desmond the Dinosaur Althea (Dinosaur Publications)
Jeannie and Jojo (in Playtime stories) J. Donoghue (Young Puffin)
Alpaca R. Billam (Picture Lions)
Munia and the Day Things Went Wrong A. Balzola (Cambridge)
The Bird Who Couldn't Fly R. Buckley (Hodder and Stoughton)
The Sad Story of Veronica Who Played the Violin D. McKee (Andersen Press)

AIM

To consider the causes of fear and to explore ways of coping with it.

STARTING POINT

◎ Place a rubber toy spider or snake into a small box with a lid. Tell the audience that you have a spider in the box but avoid admitting that it isn't a real one. Suggest that members of the audience put their hand in the box. Deliberately build up the tension so that the children are reluctant to put their hands in but without provoking any excessive fear. Coax those about to put their hand in the box to describe their fears and explain why they feel afraid. Eventually, allow a brave volunteer to put their hand in and discover the toy.

Discuss Why are some of us afraid of spiders and snakes? What other creatures are the audience fearful of? Are there any other people, places or objects which provoke fear? How does it feel to be afraid? How do our bodies react? Remind the audience that everyone feels afraid about something and that we should respect the fears that others have even if they seem insignificant to us.

CORE ACTIVITIES

◎ Read a story which illustrates the fact that it is often the unknown which we fear and that once we become familiar with the source of the fear, the frightening effect of it is diminished. *The Owl Who Was Afraid of the Dark* by Jill Tomlinson (see page 91 for details) is an excellent example of this. Plop, the barn owl, is afraid of the dark but by finding out about the many different aspects of the dark and discovering that it can be fun, exciting and kind, he eventually comes to terms with it. Have any children in the audience overcome their fear by finding out more about it e.g. by holding a spider which they had been afraid of?

◎ Read a poem which describes the way in which our body reacts physically to fear. There is an example of such a poem on page 89 and more listed on page 92. When they are afraid, do any of the audience experience similar responses such as dry lips, sweaty hands, heart beating faster etc? Explain that all these signs can be viewed positively in that they are warning signals, telling us to be alert and to take care. In some circumstances, such responses may prevent us from having accidents and are, therefore, quite healthy reactions. Make a list of all the physical signs of fear experienced by the audience.

▣ Prepare a group of children to undertake a mapping activity in which each child draws a picture of him/herself and uses a mapping arrow to indicate what frightens them most of all. For example:

For more able children:

John

Susan ⟶ the dark

Richard

Peter ⟶ spiders

Mark ⟶ ghosts

Kirsty

Display these mapping pictures and pose questions for the audience to solve. For example, how many children are afraid of ghosts? Are there more afraid of spiders or the dark?

▣ Arrange for a group of children to think up typical night time noises. One child could pretend to be asleep in bed whilst the others take turns to produce different sounds. After each sound, the child could wake up, pretending to be afraid and asking 'What's that noise?' The sounds could include a bicycle bell (a real one), a clock ticking (a two tone wood block), a fire engine (a voice shouting dee daa, dee daa), and a range of sounds which are open to interpretation such as strange rattling noises or voice sounds.

During the assembly performance, encourage the audience to say what the sound is and whether the child in bed needs to be frightened or not.

▣ Ask the audience to suggest times when they enjoy being frightened such as reading frightening stories, watching spooky films, playing scary games or going on rides at a funfair which involve an element of 'risk'. What do they enjoy about these activities? Invite members of the audience to come and sit in a Ghost Train which has been made by a group of children (see page 91 for details). Encourage them to describe their feelings. Are they really afraid or do they think it is funny?

▣ Bad dreams are often a cause of anxiety for young children and this is a good opportunity to share these feelings and show that many people have frightening dreams. Use stories which children have written about a bad dream, to initiate discussion with the audience. Do any of the audience identify with any of the fears expressed in the stories? What interesting words and phrases were used by the writers to describe their fear?

▣ Some fears are as a result of an over-active imagination. For example, in the dark, even quite ordinary objects can look like monsters, faces or spiders. *A Book of Ghosts* by P. Adams and C. Jones (see page 92 for details), cleverly explores this theme by giving glimpses, through cut out shapes, of what appear to be ghosts but which, when the page is turned, turn out to be everyday, harmless objects. The book could either be used directly with the audience or a group of children could be asked to invent their own pictures to show during the assembly.

CONCLUSION—WHAT CAN WE DO?

• Always respect other people's fears, however irrational they may seem.

• Remember that fear is a universal human experience and not something to be ashamed of.

• Sharing fears with someone else often eases the anxiety and puts the emotion into proportion.

• Never ignore the warning signals your body is giving you in case there is a good reason for feeling afraid and being alert to dangers.

Fear

Darkness
Envelopes my bed.
Nuzzling deep in my pillow,
I welcome sleep.

Shadows
Flicker on my wall.
I squeeze my scared eyes tight
So I won't see.

Tickles
Breathing on my cheek.
I shiver nervously
What could it be?

Wondering,
Dry lips, sweaty hands,
I grit my teeth bravely
To brush it away.

Frozen,
My arm motionless,
I hear my heart jumping,
Pounding loudly.

Slowly,
Timid fingers search,
I feel its soft, silky,
Slippery tongue!

Relief
Relaxes my body.
It's only the big bow
On my teddy!

ALTERNATIVE ACTIVITIES

◎ Write a brief description of several frightening situations on separate cards. Ask members of the audience to pick a card, read it out and then say what they would do if they found themselves faced with those circumstances. For example, the situations might include being bullied by someone in the playground, hearing a strange noise at night, being approached in the street by a stranger, or finding a strange beetle in your shoe. Encourage the audience to participate by making alternative suggestions for coping with these fears. Do the children realise that sharing a fear with someone else or finding out more about it, can often reduce anxiety?

◎ With the help of the audience, make a list of things which they are frightened of during the day and another list for things which frighten them at night. Does anything appear on both lists? Do some things frighten them at night but not during the day or vice versa?

▣ Display paintings of monsters prepared by a group of children. Encourage them to make some of the monsters look frightening and some friendly. Can the audience interpret whether each monster is frightening or friendly? What visual clues help them to decide which monster is frightening or friendly? For example, a smile, cuddly body shape or soft colours might make one monster appear friendly whilst sharp teeth, spiky body shape and bright, clashing colours might indicate an aggressive, terrifying monster.

▣ Sing the song *Who's Afraid of the Big Bad Wolf?* and add verses relating to other fears e.g. Who's afraid of the . . . dark at night, spiders in the bath, shadows on the wall, people with beards? Can the audience suggest ideas for other verses?

▣ Arrange for a group of children to dress up in 'scary' costumes. They could use the dressing up box as a basis but add masks, headdresses or face paints to turn themselves into witches, ghosts, monsters, etc. Ask them to make up frightening noises or actions to accompany their scary character. During the assembly, each one could appear from behind a screen and try to scare the audience. Obviously, it is important to ensure that no child is upset excessively. Can the audience guess who is underneath the costume? Suggest that the monsters take off their costumes to reveal the identity of the person underneath. This will also reinforce the idea that there were no real monsters but only children pretending. Compare this with television and films. Perhaps members of the audience would like to try on the costumes and invent scary noises or actions.

▣ Turn the play house into a cave by covering the roof/windows with a blanket to make it dark. Stick shiny pictures of scary faces (made by the children) onto the walls, suspend tickly mobiles from the ceiling and place strangely textured objects in the cave for the children to feel. Encourage volunteers to explore the cave and then write a description of their experiences. Ask one or two children to read their descriptions during the assembly. Invite members of the audience to come to the cave during playtime.

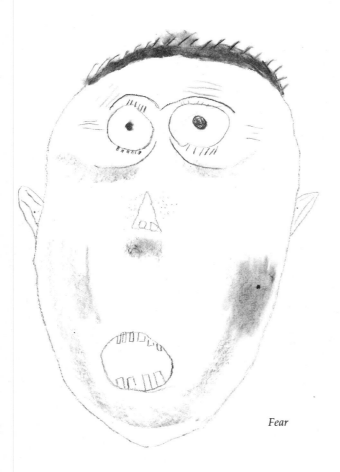

Fear

Ghost Train

The train could be made very simply from a series of cardboard boxes, some representing the engine and others the carriages for the passengers to sit in.

A screen is needed behind the train such as a playhouse, a clothes horse or table on its side with corrugated card fixed to it. The screen could have a frieze attached to it, depicting part of the journey of the train such as through woods or under the ground. Once the volunteers from the audience are sitting in the train, scary creatures could be dangled above them over the screen. These might include spiders, snakes and insects. Also, 'pop up' ghosts, witches, monsters and ugly faces could be pushed through or under the screen.

Encourage the constructors of the Ghost Train to think up their own ideas for creating a scary experience. They may wish to prepare a 'spooky' tape recording full of strange noises and voices to accompany the journey.

The Owl Who Was Afraid of the Dark

an extract of the story by J. Tomlinson, Young Puffin

Plop was a baby barn owl, and he lived with his mummy and daddy at the top of a very tall tree in a field. Plop was fat and fluffy. He had a beautiful heart-shaped ruff. He had enormous, round eyes. He had very knackety knees. In fact he was exactly the same as every baby barn owl that has ever been—except for one thing. Plop was afraid of the dark.

'You can't be afraid of the dark,' said his mummy. 'Owls are never afraid of the dark.'

'This one is,' Plop said.

'But owls are night birds,' she said. Plop looked down at his toes. 'I don't want to be a night bird,' he mumbled. 'I want to be a day bird.'

'You are what you are,' said Mrs Barn Owl firmly.

'Yes, I know,' agreed Plop, 'and what I are is afraid of the dark.'

'Oh dear,' said Mrs Barn Owl. It was clear that she was going to need a lot of patience. She shut her eyes and tried to think how best she could help Plop not to be afraid. Plop waited.

His mother opened her eyes again. 'Plop, you are only afraid of the dark because you don't know about it. What do you know about the dark?'

'It's black,' said Plop.

'Well, that's wrong for a start. It can be silver or blue or grey or lots of other colours, but almost never black. What else do you know about it?'

'I don't like it,' said Plop. 'I do not like it at all.'

'That's not knowing something,' said his mother. 'That's feeling something. I don't think you know anything about the dark at all.'

'Dark is nasty,' Plop said loudly.

'You don't know that. You have never had your beak outside the nest-hole after dusk. I think you had better go down into the world and find out a lot more about the dark before you make up your mind about it.'

'Now?' said Plop.

'Now,' said his mother.

Plop climbed out of the nest-hole and wobbled along the branch outside. He peeped over the edge. The world seemed to be a very long way down.

'I'm not a very good lander,' he said. 'I might spill myself.'

'Your landing will improve with practice,' said his mother. 'Look! There's a little boy down there on the edge of the wood collecting sticks. Go and talk to him about it.'

'Now?' said Plop.

'Now,' said his mother. So Plop shut his eyes, took a deep breath and fell off his branch.

His small white wings carried him down, but, as he said, he was not a good lander. He did seven very fast somersaults past the little boy.

'Ooh!' cried the little boy. 'A giant Catherine-wheel!'

'Actually,' said the Catherine-wheel, picking himself up, 'I'm a barn owl.'

'Oh yes—so you are,' said the little boy with obvious disappointment. 'Of course, you couldn't be a firework yet. Dad says we can't have the fireworks until it gets dark. Oh, I wish it would hurry up and get dark soon.'

'You want it to get dark?' said Plop in amazement.

'Oh, yes,' said the little boy. 'DARK IS

EXCITING. And tonight is specially exciting because we're going to have fireworks.'

'What are fireworks?' asked Plop. 'I don't think owls have them—not barn owls, anyway.'

'Don't you?' said the little boy. 'Oh, you poor thing. Well, there are rockets, and flying saucers, and volcanoes, and golden rain, and sparklers, and . . .'

'But what are they?' begged Plop. 'Do you eat them?'

'NO!' laughed the little boy. 'Daddy sets fire to their tails and they whoosh into the air and fill the sky with coloured stars—well, the rockets, that is. I'm allowed to hold the sparklers.'

'What about the volcanoes? And the golden rain? What do they do?'

'Oh, they sort of burst into showers of stars. The golden rain pours—well, like rain.'

'And the flying saucers?'

'Oh, they're super! They whizz round your head and make a sort of wheeee noise. I like them best.'

'I think I would like fireworks,' said Plop.

'I'm sure you would,' the little boy said. 'Look here, where do you live?'

'Up in that tree—in the top flat. There are squirrels farther down.'

'That big tree in the middle of the field? Well, you can watch our fireworks from there! That's our garden—the one with the swing. You look out as soon as it gets dark . . .'

'Does it have to be dark?' asked Plop.

'Of course it does! You can't see fireworks unless it's dark. Well, I must go. These sticks are for the bonfire.'

'Bonfire?' said Plop. 'What's that?'

'You'll see if you look out tonight. Good-bye!'

'Good-bye,' said Plop, bobbing up and down in a funny little bow.

Under the Stairs

by Daphne Lister, in *A Very First Poetry Book* by John Foster, OUP

I don't like the cupboard
Under the stairs,
It reminds me of caves
And dragon's lairs.

So I never look in
Once it is night,
In case I should get
A nasty fright.

I'm silly I know
'Cos it's only small
There wouldn't be room
For a dragon, at all.

But even in daytime
It gives me the scares
To go past the cupboard
Under the stairs.

What place in the house frightens the poet? What does she think might be hiding in there? Does she feel differently during the daytime? Do members of the audience have places in the house which scare them? Does it seem worse at night and why should this often be the case? Are there places outside the home which make them feel uneasy? E.g. in the garden, the park or even at school. Can the audience suggest how to overcome these fears?

RESOURCES

Poems

The Bad Dream Smile Please (Young Puffin)
It's Dark Outside Pudmuddle Jump In (Magnet)
Scary Things A Very First Poetry Book (OUP)
In the Dark A First Poetry Book (OUP)
Fear Rhyme Time 2 (Beaver Books)
The Ugstabble Rhyme Time (Beaver Books)
Bump Rhyme Time (Beaver Books)
The Longest Journey in the World A Second Poetry Book (OUP)
What is It? Another First Poetry Book (OUP)

Songs

The Owl who was Afraid of the Dark Sing a Story (A and C Black)
All Alone in the House Over and Over Again (Beaver Books)
Halloween is Coming Tinderbox Song Book (A and C Black)
I Whistle a Happy Tune Apusskidu (A and C Black)
Things that go Bump in the Night Flying A Round (A and C Black)
Helter Skelter Action Songs (Early Learning Centre)

Stories

A Book of Ghosts P. Adams and C. Jones (Child's Play Ltd)
Lights off Lights on A. Taylor (OUP)
Jeremy Mouse Althea (Dinosaur Publications)
The Owl who was Afraid of the Dark J. Tomlinson (Young Puffin)
Where the Wild Things Are M. Sendak (Bodley Head)
Michael in the Dark A. Coles (Hodder and Stoughton)
Who's Afraid of the Ghost Train? F. Rodgers (Viking Kestrel)
Can't you Sleep Little Little Bear? M. Waddell (Walker Books)
The Monster Bed S. Varley (Andersen Press)
Franklin in the Dark D. Bougeois (Hodder and Stoughton)
What are you Scared of? J. Larsen (A and C Black)
Be Brave Billy J. Ormerod (Picture Lions)
Longneck and Thunderfoot M. Foreman (Puffin)

LONELINESS

AIM

To develop an awareness of loneliness and to think about the need to spend time alone.

STARTING POINT

◉ Prepare four children to assume the role of elderly people. Simple paper plate masks could be made depicting elderly faces with grey hair, wrinkles, etc. Ask two of the children to make happy faces and two to make sad ones. During the assembly, interview the two sad old people first, asking them why they appear so miserable. Each child could give an appropriate reason such as 'No one comes to visit me, my neighbour never talks to me, I live on my own and I am lonely'.

Then interview the two happier elderly people, asking why they are smiling. Once again, each child could give appropriate reasons such as 'My grandson came to visit and we played snakes and ladders, my friend sent me a letter, my neighbour gave me a plant'.

Discuss Why were two of the elderly people happy and two sad? Help the audience to appreciate that elderly people often live on their own and loneliness can be a problem. Do any of the children's grandparents live on their own? Can any of them describe how it might feel to live by yourself? Do any of the audience know of elderly people living by themselves in their street?

CORE ACTIVITIES

◎ Explain that most people also like to have times when they are alone. Can the audience suggest circumstances in which they prefer to be alone? For example, when they wish to read a book undisturbed, paint a picture, watch birds feeding at a bird table, or build a model with Lego. Why is it important for people to be able to spend time on their own? Remind the children that it is unfair to interrupt people when they want to be on their own and quote some examples of when a parent, brother, teacher or friend might prefer to be alone.

◉ Develop a short play based on the story *Smith, the Lonely Hedgehog* by Althea (see page 96 for details). The story centres on a hedgehog's search for a friend in order to ease his loneliness. As the story is simple and straightforward, it would be fairly easy for even the youngest of infants to adapt into a play. An example of the play devised by middle infants is given on page 95. After the performance, discuss the play with the audience, focusing particularly upon Smith's loneliness and how this was solved.

◉ Prepare a group of children to write letters either to their grandparents or to an elderly person they know. Encourage them to give an account of their lives over the last couple of days, including details which they think might be of interest. Ask one or two of the children to read their letters during the assembly before posting them. Suggest that the children in the audience also write similar letters.

◉ Either prepare a group of children to sing *Streets of London* (see page 96 for details) or play a recording of the song by Ralph McTell (on an album of the same name, Pickwick Records). Discuss the meaning of the words of the song with the audience, concentrating on one verse at a time.

Can the audience describe any of the lonely people wandering the streets of London in the song? What sort of things might the old lady be carrying as her 'home' in two carrier bags? Which of their possessions would the audience choose if they had to carry all of their 'home' in two carrier bags? How would it feel to be lonely and homeless in the nearest large town or city? Would it feel worse on particular occasions such as a birthday? Are any of us really lonely compared to the people in the song?

CONCLUSION—WHAT CAN WE DO?

• Be more conscious of the lonely people around us and try to offer comfort to them.

• Respect other people's wish to be alone.

Lonely Times

You can be lonely
when everybody's out.
The silence soft and smothering,
it makes you want to shout.

You can be lonely
in a noisy playground.
Children swarm like furious bees,
humming and buzzing round.

You can be lonely
in a large crowded shop.
People rushing, blank eyes staring,
much too busy to stop.

You can be lonely
playing ball in a team.
Scowling faces scream 'You missed it!'
'How stupid!', 'Don't daydream!'

You can be lonely
when you are somewhere new.
Why does no one notice you shrink?
Surely, they've felt it too?

ALTERNATIVE ACTIVITIES

◎ It is quite possible to be lonely even though you are surrounded by people. Read the above poem to a group of children and ask them to write a story about someone who was lonely despite the presence of lots of people. How does that person feel and what do they do to overcome their loneliness? Ask one or two of the children to read out their stories.

◎ Invent a singing game using loneliness as a theme. For example, change the words of the traditional French song *Frère Jacques* to

> . . . . . . (name of child) is lonely,
> . . . . . . (name of child) is lonely,
> He (or she) needs a friend,
> He (or she) needs a friend,
> Close your eyes and choose one,
> You'll be glad you've got one,
> Dance and clap,
> Dance and clap.

Devise appropriate actions to accompany the song. For instance, in the song above, the 'lonely' child could sit in the middle of a circle with his/her hands over his/her eyes. The children in the circle could walk round holding hands whilst singing but stop when it is time to choose a friend. The 'lonely' child could point (still with eyes closed) to someone in the circle who then joins him/her in the circle. They could hold hands and skip round inside the circle for the last two lines, whilst the others clap. The child who has entered the circle then becomes the 'lonely' child. Either prepare a group of children to perform the singing game or enlist the help of volunteers from the audience.

▣ With a group of children, discuss the games or toys which they prefer to play with other people and those which they like to play with on their own. For each category, encourage the children to draw a picture and write the name of the game or toy beneath. Stick the pictures for each set onto a separate sheet. Display these sheets during the assembly and ask the audience if they agree with, or can add to the categories. Are there some games which cannot be played alone?

▣ Prepare a group of children to role play a family in which a young child is feeling lonely. After the performance, interview all the characters in turn in order to gain insight into their viewpoint. An outline for such a role play is given on page 96. Discuss each character's attitude with the audience and ask them if they think the character is behaving fairly or if they can offer suggestions to solve the problem.

Smith the Lonely Hedgehog

The example below is a play devised by a group of middle infants and based on the story *Smith, the Lonely Hedgehog* by Althea (see page 96 for details). If necessary, the teacher could read the part of the narrator whilst children assumed the other roles. Teachers will, no doubt, wish their pupils to create their own adaptation of the story.

Characters: Narrator
                Smith
                Mrs Rabbit
                Duck
                Hedgehog

Narrator   Once upon a time there was a hedgehog called Smith. He lived all by himself under a bush at the edge of the wood. He didn't know any of the other animals so he was rather sad and lonely. One day he went for a walk up the hill. Winter was coming so he needed to find somewhere safe and warm to sleep. He thought he wouldn't be quite so lonely if he could share with someone else. After a while he met Mrs Rabbit.

Smith   Hello. Can I come and stay with you for the winter. I'm lonely all by myself.

Mrs Rabbit   No. I'm sorry there's no room in my burrow. I've got lots of children.

Smith   But I don't take up much room. Look, I can curl up very small.

Narrator   Smith curled himself up to show her but when he uncurled Mrs Rabbit had disappeared. So Smith sadly plodded on, feeling more and more lonely. Soon he came to a pond and there standing beside it was a duck. He was cleaning and tidying his feathers. Smith said:

Smith   Hello. Can I come and stay with you for the winter? I'm lonely all by myself.

Duck   No. I'm sorry my nest is small and your prickles would dig in me. You'll have to find somewhere else.

Narrator   Smith felt very sad and lonely. Nobody wanted him. The wind started blowing and it was getting colder and colder. Smith shivered and sneezed.

Smith   I must be getting the 'flu.

Narrator   He said, as he shuffled through the dry leaves. Suddenly, he stumbled over a stick and fell head first into a hole. At the bottom he landed on a heap of prickles. Slowly, the prickles moved and a head poked out. What a surprise! It was another hedgehog. Smith said:

Smith   I'm sorry to drop in on you like this. Can I share your nest for the winter. I'm very lonely all by myself.

Hedgehog   Of course you can. I get a bit lonely on my own too. There's plenty of room in my nest for you.

Narrator   Smith said 'thank you' and hoped that now he would never be lonely again. Both the hedgehogs felt happy and rolled themselves up into a ball to go to sleep.

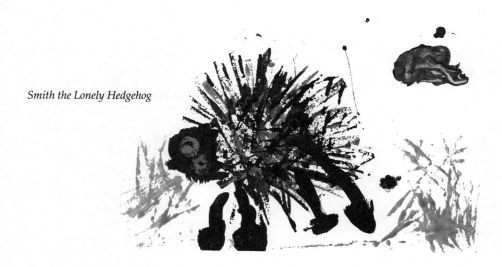

Smith the Lonely Hedgehog

Family Role Play

The following outline for a family role play is a suggestion only which teachers may wish to adapt or extend.

The scene—A family at home.

The characters—Mum, dad, brother, sister, young child.

The situation—Except for the young child, each member of the family is busy with an activity. For example, mum is digging the garden, dad is cooking the dinner, sister is playing a computer game, brother is cleaning out the rabbit hutch. The young child is lonely and approaches each member of the family in turn, asking them to play with him/her.

The outcome—Each member of the family refuses to play, making an excuse as to why they are too busy to help. The young child continues to be lonely.

Interview each character in turn:

Why haven't they got time to play? Could they have postponed what they were doing? Was it possible to promise to play with the child once the task was completed? Could they have tried to involve the child in the activity? Did they feel they were being fair to rebuff him/her or did they regret their actions?

Ask members of the audience for their opinion:

Which character(s) do they feel could most easily have found time to play with the child? Which activities could the child have most easily been involved in? Are there other solutions for the child's loneliness?

I'm Alone in the Evening

by Michael Rosen, in *Rhyme Time* by B. Ireson, Beaver Books

I'm alone in the evening
when the family sits
reading and sleeping,
and I watch the fire close in
to see flame goblins
wriggling out of their caves
for the evening.

Later I'm alone
when the bath has gone cold around me
and I have put my foot
beneath the cold tap
where it can dribble
through valleys between my toes
out across the white plain of my foot
and bibble bibble into the sea.

I'm alone
when mum's switched out the light
my head against the pillow
listening to ca thump ca thump
in the middle of my ears.
It's my heart.

Why is the poet alone even with his family nearby? Can the audience think of similar circumstances where they have felt alone even though people have been around? Do any of them identify with the poet's description of being alone in the bath or before falling asleep? How would they describe their feelings in these situations? Is being alone necessarily the same as feeling lonely?

RESOURCES

Poems

The Lonely Scarecrow Young Puffin Book of Verse (Young Puffin)
Loneliness Junior Voices 1 (Penguin)
Only the Lonely Smile Please (Young Puffin)

Songs

Kum by yah Someone's Singing, Lord (A and C Black)
Look out for Loneliness Someone's Singing, Lord (A and C Black)
All Alone in the House Tinderbox Song Book (A and C Black)
All Alone in my Quiet Head Tinderbox Song Book (A and C Black)
Streets of London Every Colour Under the Sun (Ward Lock Educational)
Oh, I am Playing all Alone Gently into Music (Longman)
It's not much Fun Something to Think About (BBC)
One Rag Doll Counting Songs (Early Learning Centre)

Stories

Smith the Lonely Hedgehog Althea (Dinosaur Publications)
We are Best Friends Aliki (Bodley Head)
Tariq Learns to Swim H. Khan (Bodley Head)
The Beetle Hunt H. Cresswell (Longman)
The Lonely Squirrel M. Stage (Burke Books)
Lizzie's Invitation H. Keller (Julia MacRae)
Millicent J. Baker (Andre Deutsch)
Mr Potter's Pigeon P. Kinmonth (Moonlight)
The Trip E. J. Keats (Hamish Hamilton)
The Lonely Prince M. Bolliger and J. Obrist (Methuen)
Ted Runs Away from Home J. Mogensen (Picture Corgi)
A Letter for Tiger Janosch (Hippo)
The Good Wizard of the Forest (in The Second Margaret Mahy Story Book) M. Mahy (Dent)

FAMILY

AIM
▣□◎▣

To develop insight into the various people who can constitute a 'family' and to promote an understanding of their point of view.

STARTING POINT

▣ Exhibit drawings made by a group of children which illustrate the various age ranges within a family. For example, the drawings could include a baby, a school child, a teenager, an adult and an elderly person. Muddle the pictures up and ask the audience to order them in the correct age sequence from young to old.

Discuss Can the audience help to arrange the pictures as a family tree? Do they understand terms such as son, daughter, grandfather?

CORE ACTIVITIES

◉ Discuss the numerous different compositions of a 'family'. Obviously, this needs to be approached with sensitivity because the stereotyped view of mum, dad and two children is unlikely to match the experiences of many children. Try to help the audience appreciate that a family may be defined in different yet equally valid ways, such as single parent families, extended families, foster homes, etc. Display a collection of pictures (from magazines or photographs of pupils' families) which depict family life and use them as a basis for discussion.

◉ Show the audience a picture of a very young baby. Prepare a list of simple tasks on separate cards, some of which can be achieved by a baby and some which obviously cannot. These might include smile, drink, sit, wave and run, draw, hop and use a knife. Ask the audience to help sort the cards into a set of tasks which the baby would be able to do and a set of cards which she/he would not be able to do.

◉ Display a range of baby equipment including clothes, toys, bottles, nappies, baby alarm, etc. Discuss each item—the colour, shape, purpose, material etc. Why is the babygrow made out of towelling and not denim? Why are bottles and feeding equipment usually made out of plastic and not glass? How are the toys designed to ensure the baby's safety? Emphasise the fact that babies are not able to control their own safety and need adults and older children to protect them. If they were left to look after a baby, can the audience suggest other important safety measures?

▣ Display a model of The Old Woman Who Lived in a Shoe. The giant shoe house could be made out of cardboard boxes whilst the old woman and the children could be made around washing up liquid or plastic lemonade bottles. Ask members of the audience to match the children to a giant counting strip to discover how many there are. Repeat this activity to find how many boys/girls there are.

How many children are there in the old woman's family? Does she look after them all on her own or does she have someone to help like a husband, other relative, someone outside the family? Does she look happy? What would be the difficulties in caring for such a large family? Which member of the audience has the largest family?

▣ Prepare a chart which shows the number of people in the family of each child in a class. Discuss the chart with the audience. Can they indicate how many children have 3 members in their family? How many children have more than 5 members in their family?

▣ Organise a group of children to compile a list of tasks performed for them by their dad, mum or other caring adult during a day. The tasks might include: prepare my lunch box, read me a story, give me a cuddle or drive me to school. After each child has read out his/her list, choose one to reread and ask the audience to put up their hands if they have a parent or carer who performs the same task for them. Can they add further examples to the lists? Why do they think parents or carers do these tasks for them?

■ Invite some elderly people to attend the assembly. Arrange for the children to sing songs, show pictures, dance or make cakes for the elderly people. If possible, encourage the elderly people to make a contribution to the assembly by, for example, showing photographs of themselves when they were young, describing their school days or talking about a favourite hobby or interest. Try to show that both children and the elderly have much to gain from each other and to stress the positive aspects of both youth and age.

■ Arrange for a group of children to write stories about an elderly person who is very lonely. Encourage them to describe what the elderly person looks like, what they do all day, how many people visit them, and whether they have any family or not. Does the story have a happy ending with the elderly person eventually finding a friend (a person or animal)? Or does he/she remain alone?

■ Read the poem *Emma Hacket's Newsbook* by Allan Ahlberg (see page 101 for details) to a group of children. Help them to prepare a mime to accompany the reading of the poem during assembly. The poem demonstrates the chain reaction which often occurs when one person's anger reverberates around the whole family. Can any of the audience identify with the poem and describe similar situations which they have experienced?

CONCLUSION—WHAT CAN WE DO?

● Try to be more sensitive towards the feelings of all the members of our family. Think about how we would feel in their position and bear this in mind in our responses to them.

● Show our appreciation of the many tasks performed for us by members of our family by offering them help when it is needed.

● Act responsibly with younger children, especially babies, who rely on others for their safety.

● Try to regard brothers and sisters positively by reminding ourselves of all the good things about them rather than allowing the bad things to predominate.

● Give special consideration to the elderly people in our family and think about what contribution we can make to enrich their lives.

Look at me!

'Dad — look at me!
I can do handstands now'.
With his head swimming in steam,
Dad grumbles,
'Not now, I'm cooking the dinner,
I'll look later on'.

'Mum — look at me!
I can do handstands now'.
With her head sprouting amongst the cabbages,
Mum sighs,
'Not now, I'm weeding the vegetables,
Show me tomorrow'.

'James — look at me!
I can do handstands now'.
With his head submerged in the Lego,
My brother mutters,
'So what, I can do cartwheels.
Go away, I'm busy'.

'Rover — look at me!
I can do handstands now'.
With his head panting in my face,
My dog licks my nose.
I wobble,
I topple with a crash!
My arm is broken.

They all look at me.
I can't do handstands now.
But. . .
Mum plays snap with me.
Dad reads me stories.
James draws on my plaster
Whilst Rover lets me pat him.
My family are not too busy
When I need them.

ALTERNATIVE ACTIVITIES

◉ Remind the audience of how they probably felt on their first day at school and ask them to pretend that their younger brother or sister is about to start school. Can they suggest ways in which they could help their brother or sister feel less apprehensive in this new situation? Perhaps they might show them the cloakroom, introduce them to their friends, play with them at playtime, help them to get their lunch or supervise them after school whilst waiting for a parent to collect them.

◙ Ask five or six children to bring in photographs of themselves when they were a baby. Display these during the assembly and ask the children to stand at the front of the hall. Can someone from the audience match the correct baby picture to each child? What are the similarities and differences between each child as a baby and as a child?

◙ Select a group of children to make a 'family' of puppets. Encourage them to add features to distinguish one member of the family from another such as a beard and glasses for daddy, a walking stick and white hair for grandad, a bib and rattle for the baby. Ask the group to use their puppets to devise a short play based around some kind of family celebration such as a birthday or a wedding. Encourage them to discuss what sort of character each member of the family will be. Perform the puppet play during assembly and ask the audience to describe each character.

◙ Prepare a group of children to work in pairs and role play being a brother and sister. Encourage the groups to show a variety of sibling relationships, from good to bad. Give each pair a pretend activity to do and help them decide whether they are going to do it co-operatively or with arguments. For example, they could be playing a board game, building a castle with bricks, preparing food, etc. Some pairs could show siblings sharing, caring for each other, enjoying each other's company whilst other pairs could show siblings arguing or deliberately annoying each other. During the assembly, the pairs could act out their role play and the audience could decide what kind of relationship each pair had. Can the audience suggest ways in which the 'poor' relationships could be improved? Do any of the audience strongly identify with any of the pairs?

◙ Organise a group of children to make a large 'Be careful baby' frieze showing a baby in a room with lots of hazards. Can the audience spot the dangers for the baby? These might include a fire without a guard, a sharp knife nearby or an unattended iron.

Another Kind of Family

Joe invited me to visit him at home one day. He lives in a children's home with Aunty Jane and Uncle Bob. His own mum and dad live in London and cannot manage to look after him. They visit sometimes but not as often as he would like. Joe didn't say a lot but I could tell from the gleam in his big brown eyes that he was keen for me to come to tea at the home. I decided to go.

It wasn't what I expected at all. It was an ordinary house in an ordinary street. It was larger than most houses but then that wasn't surprising when I remembered how many people lived there—Aunty Jane, Uncle Bob, their two children Julie and Sam, and the eight other children. The only difference from the outside was the blue mini van parked in the drive which Aunty Jane used to bring all the children to school.

Three excited faces wriggled in front of the net curtains and, before I could knock, the front door was flung open and I was dragged inside. Joe grabbed my hand, pulling me into the kitchen. 'Look at these cakes,' he bubbled, 'I made them. Uncle Bob helped me but I put the chocolate icing on top all by myself. That one's for you!' It was the most that Joe had ever said to me all at once. He was glowing with pride. The kitchen was just like mine at home but bigger and much tidier. I only had time for a quick glance round before Joe was tugging on my hand to follow him upstairs to his bedroom.

Joe ran and bounced on his bed. Then he pointed importantly to the two other beds in the room explaining who slept where. 'This is my cupboard where I keep my special things,' he said opening the door. 'No one's allowed to touch anything in here. It all belongs to me.' He showed me what was inside—a letter from his mum and dad, a seaside postcard from his nan, some toy cars, a clay pot which we had made at school, some shells and a small torch. 'Don't tell about the torch. I use it to read my books under the bedclothes at night when the lights are out,' confided Joe. I promised not to tell.

Next Joe took me to admire the large television in the lounge and the toys which all the children shared. There was a short argument about one particular favourite toy. Joe tussled with Leroy trying to grab a toy dog which he wanted to show me. He eventually managed to wrench it away from Leroy and demonstrated how to wind up the key to make the dog move. Joe and the other children giggled as the dog walked stiffly backwards and forwards, barking strangely, until finally it rolled over. 'Tea's ready,' shouted Uncle Bob but Joe insisted that I see the garden before we all sat down. 'Alright,' agreed Uncle Bob, 'but don't be too long!'

The garden was long and narrow with a group of old trees at the bottom. Joe, and two of the other children, immediately ran to the end of the garden shouting 'Come on, come and see the swings!' These were two large black tyres hung by a thick rope from one of the branches. A rope ladder also dangled limply from another branch. Leroy and Julie leapt onto the tyres and began to swing jerkily backwards and forwards. 'It's my turn now,' whined Joe. 'Use the rope ladder,' snapped Julie. Joe hesitated. It was clear that he didn't really like the rope ladder. 'Go on, baby,' chided Julie.

Joe was stung into action by these words and immediately began to climb up the rope ladder. I could sense Joe's fear. The ladder swung wildly. Each foot stabbed the air two or three times before finding the next rung. He was too scared to look down. I was just about to suggest we go into tea when the ladder twisted suddenly.

Joe's foot slipped and he tumbled to the ground with a sharp cry of pain. Leroy and Julie jumped off the swing and rushed to help him. Joe sobbed quietly, watching a trickle of blood slip slowly from a cut on his hand. Leroy put his arms round Joe's shoulders, reassuring him. 'It's alright Joe, it's only a small cut. Uncle Bob will put a plaster on it.' 'I'm sorry Joe. It was my fault,' said Julie, 'I should have let you have a turn on the swing. That rope ladder's too difficult for little ones like you.'

They both helped Joe back to the kitchen where Uncle Bob washed the cut and stuck on a plaster. Joe's tears quickly disappeared once we sat down for tea, especially when he remembered the cakes. 'Don't forget that's yours,' he said pointing to the one with an extra thick layer of chocolate icing.

On my way home, I couldn't help thinking that even though Joe's real mum and dad couldn't always be with him, he still had another kind of family.

Grandma

Be Nice to a New Baby

by Fay Maschler, in *The Mad Family* by Tony Bradman,
Young Puffin

Be nice to a new baby,
I know it's not much fun;
She doesn't joke, won't play games,
And cannot even run.

She occupies your mother,
Who could be doing things
Like cutting out, or sticking down,
or pushing you on swings.

Be kind to a new baby,
It might pay off in the end —
For that naggy little bundle
Could turn out to be a friend.

Why is a new baby 'not much fun'? What does the poet
suggest that a baby may eventually be? Does anyone in
the audience have a young baby in the family? What
difficulties does this cause? What pleasures do babies also
give?

RESOURCES

Poems

Dad Another First Poetry Book (OUP)
Grandpa is Very Old Another First Poetry Book (OUP)
Sisters Smile Please (Young Puffin)
My Little Sister Smile Please (Young Puffin)
Grandad Smile Please (Young Puffin)
Dads The Mad Family (Young Puffin)
Our Family The Mad Family (Young Puffin)
Daddy The Mad Family (Young Puffin)
Granny, Granny Please Comb my Hair The Mad Family (Young
   Puffin)
Thank you Dad for Everything The Mad Family (Young Puffin)
Daddy Fell into the Pond The Mad Family (Young Puffin)
My Mummy Over and Over Again (Beaver Books)

Brother Rhyme Time 2 (Beaver Books)
Father Says A First Poetry Book (OUP)
The Little Old Lady Tinderbox Assembly Book (A and C Black)
My Little Sister Child Education Infant Projects 61 (Scholastic
   Publications)
When I was Young Please Mrs Butler (Puffin)

Songs

There was an Old Woman who Lived in a Shoe Brown Bread and
   Butter (Ward Lock Educational)
Homes Mrs Macaroni (Macmillan Educational)
Supermum Tinderbox Song Book (A and C Black)
How many People Live in your House? Tinderbox Song Book (A
   and C Black)
Helping Grandma Jones Tinderbox Song Book (A and C Black)
I Have a Home Child Education Infant Projects 57 (Scholastic
   Publications)
No Two Families are the Same Child Education Infant Projects 61
   (Scholastic Publications)
She's the Best Mum in the World Sing a Song of Celebration
   (Holt, Rinehart, Winston)
Only one Mother for Me Sing a Song of Celebration (Holt,
   Rinehart, Winston)

Stories

Are we Nearly There? L. Baum (Methuen)
The Trouble with Jack S. Hughes (Bodley Head)
Grandfather J. Baker (Andre Deutsch)
My Grandson Lew C. Zolotow (World's Work)
A Baby Sister for Frances R. Hoban (Picture Puffin)
Peter's Chair E. J. Keats (Picture Puffin)
Amber's Other Grandparents P. Bonnici (Bodley Head)
My Family F. Sen (Bodley Head)
The House where Jack Lives M. Crompton (Bodley Head)
Jenny's Baby Brother P. Smith and B. Graham (Picture Lions)
The Not-So-Wicked Stepmother L. Boyd (Viking Kestrel)
George's Marvellous Medicine R. Dahl (Puffin)
The Visitors who Came to Stay A. McAfee (Hamish Hamilton)
Adelaide's Naughty Granny H. Sharpe (Methuen)
Jack's Basket A. Carley (Hutchinson)
My Old Grandad W. Harranth (Oxford)
My Baby Brother Ned Sumiko (Heinemann)
My Grandma has Black Hair M. Hoffman and J. Burroughes
   (Methuen)

FRIENDS

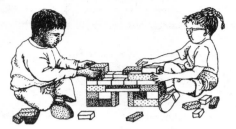

AIM

To examine relationships with friends; why we need them and how to behave towards them.

STARTING POINT

◎ Explain that you are going to try to make a 'chain' of friendship using children from the audience. Select one child to come to the front of the assembly hall. Ask that child to choose a friend from the audience to come and hold hands. Ask the first child to describe something which the two of them enjoy doing together such as skipping in the playground. Ask the second child to choose a friend from the audience, again describing an activity which they enjoy together. Repeat this until five or six children are holding hands.

Discuss   Point out that all the children are linked by friendship. Ask the audience to recall some of the activities which the friends enjoy sharing. How many children in the audience also share the same activity with a friend? What other activities do friends enjoy? Ask the six children at the front whether they have more than one friend? Is it possible to be friends with more than one child and yet all play happily together?

CORE ACTIVITIES

◎ Ask the audience to imagine that a new pupil has just joined their class. Can they suggest what they could do to show the new pupil that they were offering friendship? For example, they might suggest that they show the new pupil where to hang his coat, make an effort to talk to him, share the bricks with him, explain any classroom 'rules', invite him to join in the playtime games, supervise him at lunch time or agree to be his partner during the PE lesson etc. Why is it important to offer friendship to new pupils?

◎ What makes us decide not to be friends with someone? Are we influenced by their physical characteristics, their behaviour or their possessions? For example, if someone had a popular toy, would that alone prompt us to play with them? Read the extract from the story *Play With Me?* by Angela

Pickering (see page 105 for details). In this extract, two children decide not to play with someone because he cannot perform certain activities. Is this a sensible criteria to use when choosing a friend? Would members of the audience play with someone who was unable to do everything they could? What if they could not play football, draw pictures, or struggled with reading? Would these inabilities prevent them from being a good friend?

▣ Organise a small group of children to write a list of 'ingredients' which make a good friend. For example, they may wish to write as in a recipe:

> one large bag of fun
> 50 grams kindness
> one tablespoon of sharing
> a pinch of forgiveness

Choose one or two children to read out their list of 'ingredients' during assembly. Do the audience agree or would they add other qualities?

▣ Arrange for a group of children to make clay models of their friends faces (see details on page 104). Display these during the assembly. Ask one child to explain the various stages involved in making the models and two other children to describe what they like about the friend they have made. Invite members of the audience to say why they like one particular friend.

CONCLUSION—WHAT CAN WE DO?

● Be prepared to try to make friends with other children, especially those who are new to the school.

● Think about the qualities we value in a friend and try to make sure we, too, show those qualities in our relationships with friends.

● Be more aware of the influences which make us look upon someone as a friend or not. Are we choosing or rejecting a friend for the right reasons?

Five Good Friends

Five good friends went out to play
But very best friends they did not stay.

The first snatched the bike
and wouldn't share.
The second barred the way, shouting
'That's not fair!'
The third grabbed the bell
which broke in two.
The fourth kicked the first
just above his shoe.
The fifth gave one
tremendous push!
They all toppled over
into a prickly bush.
They landed in an angry heap on the ground.
The bike on top with its wheels spinning round!

Five good friends went out to play
But five foolish friends skulked home that day.

ALTERNATIVE ACTIVITIES

◉ Read a poem or story about an imaginary friend. The poem *John and Jim* by Barbara Ireson and the story *Oscar Got the Blame* by Tony Ross (see page 106 for details) are both good examples. Why do some people have imaginary friends? What are the advantages or disadvantages of this? Have any of the audience ever had an imaginary friend? What was he, she or it like?

◉ Friendship is a two-way process. Ask the audience to make suggestions to be written under the following two headings. Some examples are included.

What I do for my friend	What my friend does for me
I tie up his shoe laces.	He helps me read difficult words.
I let her play with my bike.	She holds my hand when I'm scared.
I give him one of my cakes.	He lets me be first in the line.

◉ Ask the audience to help make up a short story about a child who has no one to play with. Set the scene by supplying the first few sentences yourself. For example, 'One day John stood gazing miserably out of the window. He had no one to play with. He felt . . . . . .' Suggest that someone in the audience continues to describe how he felt. Continue in that manner with you helping to move the story forwards whilst the children supply the details. What does John see out of the window? What does he decide to do? Does he eventually find a friend? If so, what do they do together?

◉ Encourage some of the audience to make friends by joining in with some simple singing games. Two appropriate ones to use would be *Down in the valley* and *Good morning my friend*, both of which can be found in *The Funny Family* (see page 106 for details).

◉ Loyalty to a friend is an admirable quality but it can sometimes cause difficulties if taken too far. Invent some imaginary awkward situations involving friends and ask the audience to decide what would be the best course of action to take. For example, would they choose a friend to work with them on the computer knowing that he/she had already had a turn whilst several other children had not? What would they do if something important had been broken in the classroom and they knew their best friend had been responsible?

◼ Some children have a teddy, doll or toy animal which they regard as a 'best friend'. Invite a small group of children to bring their 'friend' to the assembly and to talk briefly about it. How long have they had it? Why do they like it? What do they do with it? Do they talk to it and does it talk to them? Ask members of the audience if they have a similar 'friend'.

▣ Prepare a group of children to write an advertisement for a friend. This could take the form of a 'wanted' advertisement, e.g.

Wanted

One good friend
Likes playing with sand
Kind and caring etc.

Alternatively, the advertisement could be promoting themselves as a friend, e.g.

For sale

One good friend
Enjoys swimming and painting,
Tells funny jokes etc.

Choose one or two children to read out their advertisement during the assembly. Does anyone in the audience think they fit the 'wanted' description? Does anyone like the sound of the friend 'for sale'?

▣ A friend does not always have to be of the same age and sex. Some children may have a friend who is elderly, an adult neighbour or an animal. Ask a group of children to write stories about an unusual friend, either real or imaginary, describing how they meet, what they do together and how they feel when that friend moves away to another part of the country. Make the stories into an anthology, perhaps asking the children to type them out using a word processor. Read one of the stories during the assembly and explain that the book is available for individual children or teachers to borrow. Have any children in the audience had a similar experience in losing a close friend? How did they feel? Do they remain in contact with the friend?

▣ Invite two or three children to each interview a child in another class whom they do not know. Challenge them to find out as much as they can about the unknown child such as age, physical characteristics, where they live and any hobbies they enjoy. Ask to them write a short report which could be read out during the assembly. How did they feel before they met the unknown child? Was it easy to talk to them? Did they share any common interests? Would the interview make it easier for them to become friends? Does finding out more about a person change our view of them?

Clay Models of Friends' Faces

The following guidelines may prove helpful for this particular activity. Encourage the children to make a model of a friend in the same class, thus enabling them to use direct observation to improve the quality of their work.

Real clay is obviously preferable for this activity but artificial clay, e.g. Cold Clay, New Clay, etc. can also be successful.

1 Give each child a lump of clay and encourage them to pat it into a sphere, smoothing any cracks with their fingers.

2 Push a thumb gently into the centre of the sphere and pinch the walls evenly, turning the sphere at the same time. Encourage the children to work with the sphere in their hand and not on the table, as they will tend to squash it flat against the table. Also suggest they try to keep the rim of the 'thumb pot' reasonably thick.

3 Turn the 'thumb pot' upside down and press/squeeze it into a head shape. Suggest the children look carefully at their friend's face before adding detailed features to the head. These can be achieved by pinching a nose/ears out of the body of the 'pot' if the clay is thick enough, sticking on hair/eyes with extra clay (using slip and sealing well to ensure adhesion), using implements (such as modelling tools) to incise a mouth/eyebrows.

4 If real clay has been used, leave the 'head' to dry out slowly away from direct heat and then fire in a kiln.

5 If artificial clay has been used, the 'heads' could be painted and varnished according to the manufacturer's instructions. If real clay has been used, the 'heads' could be glazed (not too thickly or the textures will be lost) or painted with iron oxide mixed with water. A variety of tones can be achieved by rubbing the oxide off with a damp sponge. If an oxide or a glaze is used, a second glost firing will be necessary.

Note: Care should be taken to ensure that children wash their hands thoroughly after using glazes or oxides to prevent contact with the mouth.

Friends playing in the playground

Play with me?

by Angela Pickering in *Story Time Two* by Dorothy
Edwards, Magnet

Alexander Brown is very sad because he doesn't
have anyone to play with. When he sees Nicholas
who lives next door, Alexander asks if he will play
with him . . . . . .

'Can you whistle?' asked Nicholas.

'I think so,' said Alexander Brown. He pushed
out his lips like Nicholas had done and made his
mouth into a little O. Nothing happened.

'You're not making a sound,' Nicholas laughed.
'I'm not going to play with you.'

And off he went down the street whistling
merrily. Alexander Brown looked sad again. Then
he saw Shemsha outside number seven. She was
hopping along the pavement without treading on
any lines.

'Will you play with me?' Alexander Brown asked
Shemsha. Shemsha stood still on one leg in the
middle of a paving stone. She didn't even wobble.

'Can you hop on one leg?' she asked.

'I think so,' said Alexander Brown. He stood on
one leg and jumped. He landed on a crack. He
stood on the other leg and jumped again. This time
he tripped and fell.

'You're lying on three cracks all at once,'
Shemsha said scornfully. 'I'm not going to play
with you.'

How do the audience think Alexander felt after both
children had refused to play with him because he couldn't
whistle or hop very well? What alternative course of
action could Nicholas and Shemsha have taken? They
could have tried to teach Alexander how to whistle or
hop, or suggested another activity which they knew
Alexander would have been able to play. Even if
Alexander could not whistle or hop, would this prevent
him from being a 'good' friend?

What are friends like?

from *Sing Say and Move*, Scripture Union

Friends are kind,
Friends are fun,
Friends can talk and listen, too.
Friends can help,
Friends can hug,
You like them and they like you.

Friends can share,
Friends can care,
Friends can play with you all day.
Friends say sorry,
Friends forgive,
Friends don't sulk or run away.

Friends are good,
Friends are great,
Friends can laugh and joke with you.
Friends are true,
Friends are fond,
Friends enjoy the things you do.

I like friends, don't you?

Do the audience agree with all the qualities mentioned above? Why would it be important for a friend to listen as well as talk? What sort of things would a good friend share? Are friends only important for 'laughing and joking' with or can they help when you feel sad? What qualities do the audience like in their friends?

RESOURCES

Poems

Small Quarrel Please Mrs Butler (Puffin)
Neighbours Round About Nine (Frederick Warne)
The New Neighbour Is a Caterpillar Ticklish? (Young Puffin)
Changing Places Ask a Silly Question (Mammoth)

John and Jim Over and Over Again (Beaver Books)
Jo Rhyme Time 2 (Beaver Books)
Friends . . . Enemies Another First Poetry Book (OUP)
Since Hannah Moved Away Another First Poetry Book (OUP)
Friends All Together Now (Viking Kestrel)
Various The Best of Friends (an anthology of poems about friends) (Blackie)

Songs

Down in the Valley The Funny Family (Ward Lock Educational)
Good Morning, my Friend The Funny Family (Ward Lock Educational)
Make Believe Friends Sing as you Grow (Ward Lock Educational)
Take Care of a Friend Every Colour Under the Sun (Ward Lock Educational)
When I Needed a Neighbour Someone's Singing, Lord (A and C Black)
Thank you for our Friends Sing a Song 1 (Nelson)
Make New Friends Flying A Round (A and C Black)
Old Friends Birds and Beasts (A and C Black)
With a Little Help from my Friends Alleluya (A and C Black)
Jesus the Best Friend Come and Sing (Scripture Union)

Stories

Elmer the Patchwork Elephant D. McKee (Dobson)
May I bring a Friend? B. Schenk de Regnier (Picture Puffin)
The two Windmills M. Resink (Oxford)
Frisk the Unfriendly Foal E. de Fossard (E. J. Arnold)
The Shy Little Girl P. Krasilovsky (World's Work)
Spud Comes to Play J. Solomon (Hamish Hamilton)
Alfie Gives a Hand S. Hughes (Fontana Lions)
Alex and Roy M. Dickinson (Deutsch)
Bill and Stanley H. Oxenbury (Benn)
Having Friends L. Berg and L. Kopper (Methuen)
Do you Want to be my Friend? E. Carle (Picture Puffin)
Best Friends for Frances R. Hoban (Hippo)
No Fighting, No Biting E. H. Minarik (World's Work)
A Playhouse for Monster V. Mueller (Picture Puffin)
Chester's Way K. Henkes (Viking Kestrel)
We are Best Friends A. Brandenberg (Piccolo)
Best Friends S. Kellog (Hutchinson)
Friends Althea (Dinosaur Publications)
Nice New Neighbours F. Brandenberg (Hippo)
That's what Friends are for F. P.Heide and S. W. van Clief (SBS)
Anna's Secret Friend Y. Tsatsui (Kestrel)

PEOPLE AT SCHOOL

AIM

To develop an understanding of the important role played by everyone in the school community and to value their contribution.

STARTING POINT

◎ Show photographs of all the different kinds of people who work in a school such as teachers, caretakers, lollipop ladies and men, kitchen staff, secretaries, and head teachers. Can the children identify them and say what jobs they perform?

Discuss Count the number of different kinds of people who all contribute to the efficient running of the school? Do the children consider that one person's job is more important than another's? Discuss what would happen if one of the non-teaching staff decided not to come to school. Could the school continue to function smoothly without the caretaker or the cooks? Help the children to realise that all the people working in a school have different yet important roles to play.

CORE ACTIVITIES

◎ Briefly tell the audience about the history of the school. Use the school log books, the library, parents' memories, etc. as reference material. Also, any old photographs would make excellent visual aids. Find out how the buildings have changed, the number of children and staff, whether a uniform was worn, what games were played in the playground, what type of lessons were given and what sort of equipment was used. If possible, after the assembly, arrange a display of photographs and documents for the children to look at. Remind the children that, in years to come, *they* will also form part of the school's history.

◎ Display a series of pictures of the people who help us at school. Ask the children to identify each person. Describe a variety of common occurrences during a school day and then ask 'Who do we need?' Encourage members of the audience to point to the picture of the appropriate person and explain how that particular person could help with the problem. For example, who do we need when a ball has been thrown on the roof, water has been spilt at lunch time, someone hurts themselves in the playground, a visitor arrives or money is found.

◼ Prepare a group of children to tape record an interview with one of the people who work in school. Encourage the group to plan their questions before they begin interviewing. They may wish to ask about the number of hours worked, any special clothing which needs to be worn, what tasks they do, what aspects of their job they like or dislike. Play the tape recording during the assembly and ask one or two members of the group to explain the preparations for and the organisation of the interview.

CONCLUSION—WHAT CAN WE DO?

● Find out more about the role each person plays in the school community so that we can understand and sympathize with their particular problems.

● Constantly think about whether our actions are making life difficult for someone else in the school.

● Remember to thank all the adults who make a valuable contribution to school life.

● A happy atmosphere in a school relies upon everyone being willing to admit to mistakes, apologize and make amends if possible.

Help!

What a terrible day I've had!
My class was full of disasters.
It began when I got to school
And found the floor covered in plaster!

Part of the ceiling had fallen
I stared at it in cold dismay.
Luckily, the caretaker came
And helped me clear all the mess away.

Then Jennifer wet her pants!
She hid her head and loudly wept.
At least the ancillary lady
Knew where the spare ones were kept.

Jonathan was upset as well.
He'd lost his toy frog, Hopperty.
I sent him to the secretary
As she deals with lost property.

I was glad when it was lunch time.
Guess what? Robert's flask sprang a leak!
The dinner lady rescued his food
And dried the tears on his cheek.

Finally, the hamster escaped!
It hid right behind the toilet.
But the Head displayed great skill
In catching the terrified pet!

What a terrible day I've had!
What would I have done on my own?
I'm glad I've plenty of helpers
I would hate to work all alone.

ALTERNATIVE ACTIVITIES

◎ Invite one of the people who work in the school to talk to the children during assembly. Ask them to explain in detail what their job entails and to focus particularly on problems which arise and which the children can help to alleviate.

◎ Write the name of each of the people who help at school on a blackboard or large piece of paper. Ask the audience to help compile a list of rules which would help to make each person's job easier. For example, the rules to assist the cleaner might include:

● Always mop up spills in the school or classroom when they happen.

● Always use the waste bin for rubbish.

● Wash the sink round after it has been used.

● Put all the chairs on the tables at the end of the day.

● Make sure the floors in the classroom and cloakroom are clear.

◎ Read the story *Anyone can make mistakes* by Margaret Joy (see page 109 for details). School is sometimes viewed by children (and even by adults too) as a place where it is important not to make mistakes and where you definitely don't admit to them. This story illustrates that everyone makes errors at sometime or another and, although it focuses on children's mistakes, it can also be applied to both teaching and non-teaching staff. After reading the story to the audience, explain that everyone including adults, makes mistakes and that it is better for all to admit freely to them rather than passing the blame on to someone else. Help the audience to understand that it is much better, for example, to say sorry to a dinner lady and to learn from that mistake for the future.

▣ Prepare a group of children to draw pictures for a time frieze which illustrates the main events of the day and highlights the adults involved in helping during that time. Large individual pictures of these adults could be placed underneath/round the outside of the frieze with pieces of string matching them to the pictures where they are helping. For example, the kitchen staff may be assisting with lunches and also supervising the playground. Display the frieze during assembly and ask members of the group to explain it to the audience. Can the audience add any more ideas to the frieze?

☒ Obtain permission to visit an area of the school which is usually out of bounds such as the school kitchen or the caretaker's store. Ask the children to draw and write about what they saw and select one or two of them to read these observations during the assembly.

☒ Arrange for a group of children to write letters to one of the people who help at school, thanking them for the particular tasks they perform. Before delivering the letters, ask one or two children to read their letters out during the assembly. Encourage the children in the audience to write similar letters or to thank those involved verbally.

☒ Focus on one particular person and examine their job in detail. For example, if the lollipop lady or man were chosen, ask to borrow the lollipop stick, the special clothing and the wand for operating the lights, and show these to the audience. Display pictures drawn of the lollipop lady or man which emphasize the luminous parts of her/his clothing. Wax resist is a useful technique, especially if used with a dark colour wash to contrast with the bright clothing. Discuss the safety aspects of crossing the road and use members of the audience to demonstrate the correct way to do so. What would happen if there were no lollipop lady or man to show them across the road?

☒ Arrange for a group of children to mime the activities of the various people who help at school such as a teacher taking the register, the lollipop lady or man supervising children crossing or the cooks serving the lunches. Can the audience identify the people involved? Are any of them willing to make up another mime?

Anyone Can Make Mistakes

by Margaret Joy, in *Allotment Lane School Again*, Young Puffin

Miss Mee was collecting the dinner money. Most people had given it to her already.

'Gary, have you brought yours?' she asked.

Gary felt in his pockets and searched in his tray, then looked in his jacket pockets. He shook his head slowly at Miss Mee.

'I think I've forgotten it,' he said.

'I'm glad I don't forget things,' said Paul.

'Anyone can make mistakes,' said Miss Mee.

Later, at playtime, most of the children had some sort of snack to take outside. Gary had an apple, Brenda had crisps, Nasreen had a little cake.

'You coming, Asif?' called Michael. 'We've got our footy cards.'

'I'm looking for my sweets,' said Asif. He was searching through all the pockets of his anorak. Then he lifted up all the other coats on the hooks, hunting underneath them for his sweets, but he couldn't see them.

'I think I've lost them,' he said crossly.

'I'm glad I don't lose things,' said Paul.

'Anyone can make mistakes,' said Miss Mee.

After play some people wrote in their diaries. Larry wanted to write about his lovely new bed, but he wasn't quite sure how to write 'bed'.

'Practise it on the blackboard,' said Miss Mee, 'and we'll see if you've got it right.'

Larry thought for a moment, then wrote 'deb' in big white letters on the blackboard.

'It's back-to-front,' said Mary.

'Try again,' said Miss Mee. 'Draw the back of the bed first, then the pillow, that makes b. Now put the e to sleep in the middle. Then draw a cushion for its feet and a tall end of the bed: that's d. Good boy—now you've written bed.'

'I think at first I was a bit muddled,' said Larry.

'I'm glad I don't get muddled,' said Paul.

After dinner, it was games afternoon, everybody's favourite. Miss Mee and the girls played rounders, while Mr Gill took the boys out to play football. They had already changed into their shirts and shorts when he arrived.

'Got your boots on?' he asked. 'Good—then, let's get out on the field.'

First they warmed up, running round the pitch and doing exercises to loosen them up. Then they practised dribbling the ball, first with the easy foot, then with the foot that didn't really want to. Then they practised different sorts of kicks—forwards, backwards and sideways. After that they chose partners and tried to get the ball away from one another by dodging and pretending and pulling at the ball with their feet. It was all very hard work, and when Mr Gill blew the whistle, they were glad to sink on to the grass for a few minutes' rest.

After that Mr Gill divided them into two teams and they had a really good game of football. In the end the team with the white vests won. Everyone streamed back indoors, breathless and sweating.

'Ten minutes until hometime,' said Mr Gill. 'I want you changed and back in your classroom with Miss Mee when the bell goes.'

They all changed as quickly as they could, talking non-stop as they did so. They packed their football kit into their games bags and went back to class, one by one.

'Come on, Paul,' said Mr Gill. 'You're going to be the last'.

'I am ready,' protested Paul. 'I just can't find my shorts. I've looked everywhere here in the cloakroom. They've just gone.'

'Then someone else must have put them with their games kit by mistake,' suggested Mr Gill. 'Go back and tell Miss Mee; she'll sort it out.'

Paul went back to class still looking puzzled. He explained why he'd taken so long.

'You'd better all empty out your games kit,' said Miss Mee.

They all groaned and emptied their bags on the tables. The bell rang and the girls went home, but Miss Mee and the boys were still searching for Paul's shorts. They weren't mixed up with anyone else's games kit. They seemed to have disappeared completely.

'Now think back,' said Miss Mee to Paul. 'You had them on for football—where did you put them after you'd changed?'

'I've forgotten,' said Paul.

'They must be somewhere,' said Miss Mee.

'I've lost them,' said Paul. He was beginning to look really upset. 'I took off my games shirt and put on my grey shirt, then I took off my football boots and socks and pulled on my trousers . . .' His face suddenly lit up and he undid the belt of his trousers. There, underneath, were his games shorts still on him! Everyone laughed and groaned

'I must have got muddled,' said Paul.

'Thought you never got muddled,' said Larry.

'Well—anyone can make mistakes,' said Paul.

My Mum's a Dinner Lady

by Tony Bradman, in *Smile Please* by Tony Bradman, Young Puffin

My mum's a dinner lady,
She helps out at my school;
My teacher says she's wonderful
And that she's no one's fool.

My mum's a dinner lady,
She helps us with our lunches,
She wipes the infants' noses
And she sorts out Sarah's bunches.

My mum's a dinner lady,
She wears an overall,
She picks us up and soothes us
If ever we should fall.

My mum's a dinner lady,
She makes me really proud;
But I must never call her mum
(That's simply not allowed!)

My mum's a dinner lady,
And when we're both at home,
I'm really lucky 'cos I've got . . .
A dinner lady of my own!

How does the dinner lady in the poem help the children at school? Have members of the audience ever needed the same sort of help from a dinner lady or man at their school? Can they suggest other ways in which dinner ladies and men help? What would happen if there were no dinner ladies or men at lunchtime? How can everyone help to make the kitchen staff's job easier?

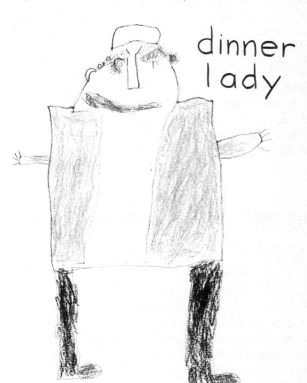

dinner lady

Lollipoplady

by John Agard, in *I Din Do Nuttin* by John Agard, Bodley
Head

Lollipop lady
lollipop lady
wave your magic stick
and make the traffic
stop a while
so we can cross the street.

Trucks and cars
rushing past
have no time for little feet.
They hate to wait
especially when late
but we'll be late too
except for you.

So lollipop lady
lollipop lady
in the middle of the street
wave your magic stick
and make the traffic
give way to little feet.

RESOURCES

Poems

First Day at School Strictly Private (Puffin)
The School Nurse (and many other poems about school life) Please
    Mrs Butler (Puffin)
The Lollipop Lady Another First Poetry Book (OUP)

Songs

God Made the People that I Meet Someone's Singing, Lord (A and
    C Black)
The Way we go to School Sing as you Grow (Ward Lock
    Educational)
Lollipop Man Flying a Round (A and C Black)
The Lollipop Man Granny's Yard (Bell and Hyman)

Stories

Desmond Starts School Althea (Dinosaur Publications)
Starting School F. Pragoff (Methuen)
My Brother Sean P. Breinburg and E. Lloyd (Bodley Head)
Lucy and Tom go to School S. Hughes (Gollancz)
Starting School J. and A. Ahlberg (Viking Kestrel)
Bill Buckets D. Webb (Hodder and Stoughton)
Allotment Lane School Again M. Joy (Young Puffin)
My School Sumiko (Heinemann)

$\mathcal{P}$EOPLE IN THE COMMUNITY

AIM

To show that there are many people in the community who play a vital role in our lives.

STARTING POINT

◎ Display special clothing or equipment which is associated with those people who help us in the community. Items might include a milk crate with bottles, a fireman's helmet, a doctor's stethoscope, a nurse's cape and a postman's sack. Obviously, real items may prove difficult to obtain but many similar items can be found in the playhouse and dressing up box.

Discuss Can the audience identify each piece of clothing or equipment and say who wears or uses it? Perhaps volunteers may like to try on the clothing or demonstrate the equipment. What do these people do for us in the community? Could we manage without them?

CORE ACTIVITIES

◎ Display a collection of toy vehicles used by various workers in the community such as a fire engine, a police car, a post van, and a dust cart. Can members of the audience identify each vehicle and say which group of workers uses it and what for? How should other road users respond when an ambulance, fire engine or police car is flashing its lights and sounding its siren? What hazards do parked dust carts present for children trying to cross the road? Would these workers be able to perform their jobs efficiently without these specialist vehicles?

◎ Invite a member of one of the groups working in the community to come and talk to the children during assembly. Ask them to bring along their clothing, any special equipment used in the course of their work, photographs of where they work, etc. Allow time at the end for the children to ask questions.

◎ Have a toy telephone available and ask for volunteers from the audience to demonstrate how to contact one of the emergency services. Can they name the three emergency services and describe circumstances in which their help might be required?

▣ Choose one group of workers in the community such as the police. Organise a group of children to make a picture number frieze depicting the police at work. For example, they may decide to draw: **1** policeman directing the traffic; **2** policewomen driving in a police car; **3** policewomen attending a motorway accident.

Number and label each picture and display them in the wrong order during the assembly. Ask the audience to help order the numbers correctly. Discuss the tasks being performed by the police in each picture, especially how they are helping people. Has anyone in the audience ever needed to ask a policeman or woman for help? Can they suggest other ways in which the police help the community?

▣ Organise one or two children to draw a large picture of one kind of community worker such as a nurse or fireman, wearing the appropriate clothing and equipment. Label each item of clothing and equipment, making the labels detachable. Display the picture during the assembly and ask volunteers to choose a label, read it and fix it in the appropriate place. Discuss the reasons for wearing particular items of clothing and the uses of the equipment. What other groups in the community wear a special uniform and why?

▣ Select one or two children to research into the job of an ambulance driver (or any other person who serves the community). Encourage them to record their findings in a book called 'A day in the life of an ambulance driver'. Ask them to read all or part of their book during the assembly. What would happen if we had no ambulance drivers?

▣ Prepare a group of children to sing *Did you ever see a lassie?* (see page 115 for details). Change the words or add more verses to give examples of people who help us in the community. Suggest that one or two of the children dress up in corresponding costumes and mime appropriate actions. Encourage the audience to join in with the singing and actions, where feasible.

CONCLUSION—WHAT CAN WE DO?

• Value the contribution made by these groups to the community and try not to take the service they provide for granted.

• Always try to make their jobs easier by being careful with matches or fireworks, by not vandalising telephone booths used to contact emergency services, by returning clean milk bottles, etc.

• NEVER contact an emergency service as a joke. Anything which delays one of the emergency services attending any real incident as quickly as possible, can result in loss of life.

The Fireman

this poem first appeared in the *Fire and Heat Project Pack* by Lynne Burgess, Tressell Publications

When the bells begin to ring
I know there is a fire.
I jump into my big black boots
And pull my leggings higher.

With my helmet on my head
And my sharp axe by my side,
I leap into the engine
To start the speedy ride.

The siren's shrieking loudly
And the lights are flashing blue
To tell all the people
We've an important job to do!

ALTERNATIVE ACTIVITIES

◎ Enlist the help of the audience in naming all the different people who help us and call at our houses each week. Display a large silhouette of a house and have pictures of these workers available (cut from magazines or drawn by pupils). Suggestions might include milkman, baker, postman or dustman. As each worker is named, ask a child to stick a picture of that person onto the house. Discuss the contribution which each person makes to our daily lives.

◎ Read out sentences about various people who help us and ask the audience to say whether they are true or false statements. Examples of sentences might include:

• A policeman drives sick and injured people to hospital.

• Sometimes a fireman has to wear breathing apparatus because there are poisonous fumes in a fire.

• A doctor drives a large red engine with a ladder and hose pipes on it.

• John was covered in spots so mummy phoned for the postman to come to see him.

• This morning the postman delivered a large loaf of bread.

◎ Display a selection of pictures of people who help us and play a 'Who am I?' game. Describe one of the people in the pictures without actually

Putting out the fire

naming him/her and ask the children in the audience to put up their hand as soon as they recognise who it is. For example, if a fireman were the subject, he could be described as follows: 'I wear a black uniform with a helmet. I need waterproof leggings and boots. My belt has an axe attached to it. . . . etc. Who am I?' Can members of the audience take turns to describe one of the people in the pictures?

▣ Prepare a group of children to act out situations in a street scene where assistance is required from one of the group of workers who help the community. For example, a child may get lost, an elderly person may be knocked over by a car or a shop might catch fire. Ask a group of children to dress up or wear labels for the appropriate person required. Repeat the role play and ask the audience to suggest whose help is needed and match the correct child to each situation. Can the audience describe alternative circumstances where each worker might be needed?

▣ Ask a group of children to work in pairs to develop a mime which shows one of the people who help us knocking at a door. For example, a postman could be delivering a heavy parcel, a milk man delivering milk and being paid, a doctor could be visiting a sick child, an ambulance driver could be calling to take someone to hospital for treatment etc. The children could perform their mime during the assembly and the audience could be asked to identify the person calling at the house. Do members of the audience know whether any of these people will be calling at their house this week?

▣ Arrange for a group of children to design a large, three-dimensional fire engine using cardboard boxes. If possible, encourage them to incorporate moving ladders, hoses, wheels and doors. Ask them to make five firemen, drawn on thick card and mounted on a stick. Use the fire engine and firemen to accompany the song *Five Little Firemen* (see page 115 for details). At the appropriate place in the song, each fireman could 'hop on the engine'. Use the song to reinforce numbers from 1 to 5 and to introduce the important work of firemen.

People we see

from *Sing as You Grow*, Ward Lock Educational

1   Listen, listen, what do I hear?
    Rat-ta-tat – rat-ta-tat, loud and clear,
    I'll look through the window to see who it can
       be,
    It is Mister Postman and he's waving to me.

2   Listen, listen, what do I hear?
    Jingle-jing – jingle-jing, loud and clear,
    I'll look through the window to see who it can
       be,
    It is Mister Milkman and he's waving to me.

3   Listen, listen, what do I hear?
    Clatter-clang – clatter-clang, loud and clear,
    I'll look through the window to see who it can
       be,
    It is Mister Dustman and he's waving to me.

4   Listen, listen, what do I hear?
    Chiming bells – chiming bells, loud and clear,
    I'll look through the window to see who it can
       be,
    It's Mister Ice-cream Man and he's waving to
       me.

5   Listen, listen, what do I hear?
    Clippety-clop – clippety-clop, loud and clear,
    I'll look through the window to see who it can
       be,
    It is a mounted Policeman and he's waving to
       me.

(See song score at the top of the next page.)

With expression

List-en, list-en, what do I hear? Rat-ta-tat-rat-ta-tat, loud and clear, I'll look through the win-dow to see who it can be, It(s) is Mis-ter Post-man and he's wav-ing to me.

(Verses 1, 2 + 3)

(Verse 4) Mis-ter Ice-cream man and he's wav-ing to me.

(Verse 5) is a mount-ed Police-man and he's wav-ing to me.

The Policeman

by Christopher Rowe in *Over and Over Again* by
B. Ireson and C. Rowe, Beaver Books

Watch the policeman in the street
Move his arms but not his feet;
He only has to raise his hand,
Cars and buses understand.
He can make them stop and go,
He can move them to and fro.
Watch the policeman in the street
Move his arms but not his feet.

What is the policeman doing? How does the traffic know
what to do? Mime some police traffic control hand signals
and see if the audience can guess what they should do.
What other tasks do the Police perform? In particular,
how can they help young children? Invite the local Police
Liaison Officer to visit the school to talk to the children
and explain the role of the Police.

RESOURCES

Poems

The Milkman Young Puffin Book of Verse (Young Puffin)
The Policeman Over and Over Again (Beaver Books)
The Dustbin Men A First Poetry Book (OUP)
Here Comes a Policeman This Little Puffin (Young Puffin)
The Policeman Walks This Little Puffin (Young Puffin)
Poor John Rhyme Time 2 (Beaver Books)
The Vet Seeing and Doing Anthology of Poems (Methuen)
The Dustman Seeing and Doing Anthology of Poems (Methuen)

Postman Seeing and Doing Anthology of Poems (Methuen)
In the Mornings Over and Over Again (Beaver Books)
Who's There? Over and Over Again (Beaver Books)
I'll be Doctor A Kiss on the Nose (Picture Corgi)

Songs

Doctor, Doctor Mrs Macaroni (Macmillan Educational)
Sing a Song of People Tinderbox Song Book (A and C Black)
People we see Sing as You Grow (Ward Lock Educational)
Somebody's Knocking at your Door Knock at the Door (Ward Lock Educational)
Mary is a Doctor Knock at the Door (Ward Lock Educational)
5 Little Firemen Sing a Song 1 (Nelson)
The Fireman Apusskidu (A and C Black)
In the Morning Over and Over Again (Beaver Books)
Miss Polly had a Dolly This Little Puffin (Young Puffin)
On a Work Day I Work New Horizons (Stainer and Bell)
Did You Ever See a Lassie Okki Tokki Unga (A and C Black)
Dial 999! Emergency New Horizons (Stainer and Bell)
Sitting in the Driver's Seat Songs from Playschool (BBC)
P.C. McGarry Sing a Song 2 (Nelson)
The Policeman Just Me (Kings Fund Publishing)
Mister Postman Just Me (Kings Fund Publishing)
Hello, Hello The Music Fun Shop (Hamish Hamilton)
The Postman Jump into the Ring (Ward Lock Educational)

Stories

Topsy and Tim at the Fire Station J. and G. Adamson (Blackie)
Fireman Sam Series D. Wilmer (and others) (Heinemann)
Jane's Policeman H. Cresswell (Ernest Benn)
The Mysterious Box (in Allotment Lane School Again) M. Joy (Young Puffin)
Postman Pat Series J. Cunliffe (Hippo Books)
Janine and the Carnival I. Thomas (Andre Deutsch)
My Naughty Little Sister at the Fair (in My Naughty Little Sister) D. Edwards (Penguin)

HELPING

AIM

To show how important it is to always be willing to offer help.

STARTING POINT

◼ Prepare three children to act out everyday situations where they need someone else's help. These might include lifting a heavy object, hurting themselves by falling from a bicycle, being stuck up a tree or losing a ball on a roof. After every role play, each child could hold up a card with 'help' written on it.

Another child could walk past each situation and make excuses to the audience as to why he/she is unable to help. Finally, a different child could stop and ask 'How can I help?' Ask the audience for practical suggestions which the child could pretend to mime. Once each situation has been satisfactorily resolved, collect up the help cards.

Discuss Ask the audience to think of other circumstances in which help is needed. Why do people refuse to help others? Can anyone describe an experience where they have needed help and been unable to find someone willing to do so?

CORE ACTIVITIES

◎ Invite representatives from organisations which help particular groups in the community to come and talk about their work. What sort of people do they help and how? What would happen to those people if the 'helping' agencies did not exist? Examples of 'helping' organisations might include Meals on Wheels workers or representatives from Help the Aged.

◎ Give a brief talk about the plight of a particular group of people in the Third World. Explain the problems which they experience, such as starvation, malnutrition, disease and poor access to clean water. Emphasize that we can help them despite the long distance between us and use the opportunity to introduce a fund raising activity, for example, to help dig a well or send agricultural tools and seeds. Why is it important for us to help people in these situations? What will happen to them if everyone refuses to help?

◼ Organise a group of children to list the 'helping' jobs in the classroom undertaken by pupils, such as washing up paint brushes, tidying bookshelves or doing up someone's shoe laces. Ask each child to choose one job and write instructions for that task on a giant hand shape. During the assembly, suggest each child reads out their task before sticking the hand shape on a large piece of paper. Can the audience add to the list of 'helping' jobs in the classroom?

◼ *The Little Red Hen* (see page 120 for details) is a popular children's story in which none of the animals wanted to help towards making the bread but they all wanted to eat it. Remind the audience of the story briefly and then ask them to watch a performance of a play by a group of children which translates the story into a more familiar situation. For example, instead of making bread, children could be asked to help make a bonfire for Guy Fawkes night or make preparations for painting pictures. A group of middle infants decided to focus their play on the preparations for a picnic. Their ideas are included as an example on page 118.

CONCLUSION—WHAT CAN WE DO?

● Think carefully before refusing to help someone whether at home or at school.

● Consider ways in which we can actively help people less fortunate than ourselves both locally and on a global scale.

● Be willing to participate in fund raising activities, even if in only a very small way. Every little bit of 'help' can make an important contribution.

Opposites

What would you like for dinner today?

I would like sausages,
green peas and chips,
with fried onion rings,
and lashings of sauce.
I would like strawberries,
with dairy ice cream.
I'm sure mum will get it
for dinner today.

What did you have for breakfast today?

I had crispy cornflakes,
floating in milk,
toast oozing red jam
washed down with juice.
But I didn't eat it all—
I threw some away.

What would you like for dinner today?

I would like rice,
fluffy and white,
an enormous bowl,
piled high to the top.
I would like fresh water
all sparkling and clear.
But my mum can't get it—
it's simply not there.

What did you have for breakfast today?

I had rice in my hand,
barely enough,
water with brown scum,
it tasted quite foul.
But I eat every small crumb—
It must last all day.

ALTERNATIVE ACTIVITIES

◎ Bring a school pet into the assembly and ask the audience to help compile a checklist of instructions on what care needs to be given to it. For example, with a guinea pig you would probably need to:

Daily checklist
Change the drinking water.
Feed it once or twice a day.
Remove any wet or dirty litter from the hutch.
Groom it if necessary (e.g. a long-haired breed).
Check to ensure it is active and healthy.

Weekly checklist
Clean the hutch completely.

Check there is an adequate supply of food, litter and bedding.

Who helps look after the school pet? Is there a rota so that everyone takes turns? What happens to the pet in the holidays? What would happen if nobody helped care for the pet? How many children in the audience have pets at home? How do they help to look after it or do they leave the daily care of it to someone else?

◎ Read a newspaper article which deals with a recent disaster. Discuss this with the audience. Consider ways in which the children can help.

▣ Prepare two children to help read the poems

Opposites shown on page 117. The teacher could ask the questions whilst the children could read the replies. Discuss the meaning of the poem with the audience. Why are the children 'opposites'? Which child needs our help? What could we do to help? Also encourage the audience to become more conscious of the amount of food we waste.

▣ Display a zigzag book designed by a group of children which contains illustrations of the various ways in which they help at home, such as making beds, tidying up and laying the table. Ask one or two of the children to explain each picture to the audience. Can other suggestions for helping at home be added?

▣ Arrange for several children to write to local or national charities asking how the school could help. If possible, use the replies as a basis for discussion during the assembly. Is it possible to carry out any of their suggestions?

▣ Sometimes our efforts to help do not always turn out as we intend. Ask a group of children to write a story in which someone's efforts to help always go wrong. Suggest that one or two of the children read their stories onto a cassette tape, adding sound effects if appropriate. Play the recording of the stories during the assembly. Have any of the audience tried to help someone unsuccessfully? Can they describe the circumstances? If our attempts to help do fail, should we stop trying to help?

▣ Scatter some bean bags at the front of the assembly hall. Pick them up by yourself, timing how long it takes to do so e.g. with a stop watch, sand clock, etc. Scatter the same number of bean bags again and ask five volunteers from the audience to help you pick them up. Again, time how long it takes. Compare the time taken to complete both tasks. Does it take less time with others helping? Compare this with situations in the classroom such as putting out the large apparatus or clearing away after an art activity. Point out that if everyone helps, there is more time available to spend on other activities.

The Picnic

The following play was devised by a group of middle infants as a result of reading the story *The Little Red Hen*. It is included as an example and teachers will obviously wish to encourage their pupils to devise their own play.

Characters   Mum
Dad
Boy
Girl
Dog

Mum Would you all like to go on a picnic this afternoon?

All Yes please. What a good idea!

Mum We'll have to start getting ready now. Let me think, what shall we take to eat?

Dad Beef sandwiches.

Boy A drink of orange.

Girl What about some crisps?

Dog Some chocolate buttons.

Mum Well, let's make the sandwiches first of all. Who will help me?

Dad Not me, I'm mending the car.

Boy Not me, I'm doing my homework.

Girl Not me, I'm playing with Lego.

Dog Not me, I'm playing ball.

Mum Then I'll just have to do it myself. (Mum gets sandwiches ready and puts them in the picnic basket.) Will somebody fill this flask with orange juice?

Dad Not me, I'm washing the car.

Boy Not me, I'm going to ride my horse.

Girl Not me, I'm going to lie down on my bed.

Dog Not me, I'm busy eating my bone.

Mum Oh well, I suppose I'll have to do it. (Mum fills the flask with juice and puts it in the basket.) Who will go and buy the crisps?

Dad Not me, I'm reading the newspaper.

Boy Not me, I'm listening to my tapes.

Girl Not me, I'm watching the television.

Dog Not me, I'm having a sleep.

Mum I'll have to do it myself. (Mum goes to shop and returns with crisps.) Who will fetch the chocolate buttons from the cupboard?

Dad Not me, I'm going to the pub.

Boy Not me, I'm flying my aeroplane.

Girl Not me, I'm sunbathing.

Dog Not me, I'm scratching my head.

Mum I'll get them myself. (Mum fetches chocolate buttons and puts them in the picnic basket.) Well, the picnic's all ready now. Who wants to come?

All Yes, I do.

Mum As not one of you helped me to get the picnic ready, I think I shall go by myself!

Helping a friend to cross the road

Richard Tries to Help

Richard's eyes lit up with excitement when mummy suggested that they should make a cake. 'Can I help too?' he asked eagerly. 'Yes, of course you can,' replied mummy. 'Come and stand up on this chair so that you can reach.'

'Let's wash our hands first,' suggested mummy, passing Richard the flannel. Richard rubbed his hands energetically and then dried them on the towel. Mummy collected all the ingredients and equipment together on the table. Richard watched as she carefully weighed out the margarine and the sugar and put them into the bowl. As she was beating them together with a wooden spoon, Richard said 'Can I help stir?' When mummy passed the bowl to him, he began to stir very quickly. In fact, he beat the ingredients so quickly that little pieces of sugar flew out of the bowl and all over the table.

'Careful,' said mummy. 'Here, let me crack the egg into the mixture now.' Mummy banged the egg on the side of the bowl but just as she was about to tip it in, Richard accidentally knocked the bowl with his elbow. The egg missed the bowl and dribbled down the outside, collecting in a pool on the table. 'Oh, Richard, you are so clumsy,' said mummy crossly. 'Why don't you look what you are doing?'

Fortunately, there was another egg in the fridge and whilst mummy was putting the second one into the bowl, Richard thought he would help open the new bag of flour. Although it was only a paper bag, the top was well sealed down and Richard's small chubby fingers tugged uselessly at it. He began to lose his temper and jerked the top of the bag angrily. The paper tore, the bag fell over and clouds of white flour puffed into the air. 'Oh, no!' groaned mummy loudly, as she watched the flour settle everywhere; all over the table, on the floor and the chair—even Richard was covered in a thin layer of dust! 'But I was only trying to help,' whimpered Richard. 'Just don't touch anything else,' ordered mummy before she hurried off for the dustpan and a cloth.

Richard stood silently with his lower lip pouting, whilst mummy cleared up the mess and rescued enough flour from the broken bag to put into the cake. 'Now let's see if we can put the cherries into the mixture without any more mishaps' sighed mummy. 'You can help me chop them up with your plastic knife.' Richard's smile returned as he carefully helped to chop all the cherries in two—one half he put into a neat little pile but the other half he popped slyly into his mouth when mummy wasn't looking. 'There don't seem to be many cherries,' said mummy looking suspiciously at Richard. But, before he could protest, the telephone rang and mummy hurried away to answer it. Richard got rather bored waiting for mummy to return and so he continued to pop the cherries into his mouth one by one until . . . . . they were all gone!

As soon as mummy returned, she could tell from Richard's guilty expression that something was wrong. The red stickiness around his mouth made her glance towards the plate where the pile of cherries should have been. 'Richard! You naughty boy! Now there won't be any cherries for the cake!' shouted mummy angrily. Richard ignored mummy's furious words and tried to please her by asking 'Shall I help you wash up?'

Helper

by Tony Bradman, in *Smile Please* by Tony Bradman, Young Puffin

I'm a little helper,
I like to tidy up,
I help dad do the dishes—
Whoops, there goes a cup.

I'm a little helper,
I like to dust and clean,
I help dad do the hoovering—
I've got my own machine!

I'm a little helper,
I like to dig and weed,
I help dad in the garden—
I'm the only help he needs!

I'm a little helper,
I like to do my room,
Dad says I should do it now—
I'll get around to it soon!

How does the poet help dad? What do members of the audience do to help their dad or mum? How can we help in the house and the garden? Who enjoys tidying up their own room? What sort of things usually need tidying in a bedroom? What would happen if we never tidied our bedrooms?

RESOURCES

Poems

Excuses Please Mrs Butler (Puffin)
Mummy Slept Late and Daddy Fixed the Breakfast Pudmuddle Jump In (Magnet)
The Mouse, the Frog and the Little Red Hen Rhyme Time 2 (Beaver Books)
What I like to do Over and Over Again (Beaver Books)
I wish I could Meet the Man that Knows Another First Poetry Book (OUP)

Songs

Why does it have to be me? The Music Box Song Book (BBC)
Cleaning Songs from Playschool (BBC)
We're the Ones Granny's Yard (Bell and Hyman)
Work Calypso Tinderbox Song Book (A and C Black)
The Little Red Hen Sing a Song 2 (Nelson)
Sing a Song of Work to do Over and Over Again (Beaver Books)
It's Good to Give a Meal New Horizons (Stainer and Bell)
We have Food to Eat New Horizons (Stainer and Bell)
Hands to Work and Feet to Run New Horizons (Stainer and Bell)
Cross over the Road Come and Praise (BBC)

Stories

The Little Red Hen P. Galdone (World's Work)
Everybody Said No! S. Lavelle (A and C Black)
Grandfather Gregory A. Wellington (Abelard)
Now one Foot, Now the Other T. de Paola (Methuen)
A Special Swap S. Wittman (Harper and Row)
I was only Trying to Help J. J. Strong (Bell and Hyman)
The Giant Alexander F. Herrmann (Methuen)
Alfie Gives a Hand S. Hughes (Picture Lions)
Little Miss Helpful R. Hargreaves (Thurman Publishing)
Helpers S. Hughes (Picture Lions)
Not so Fast Songololo N. Daly (Picture Puffin)
Kindhearted Jack (in Play School Stories) J. Watson (BBC)
The Kind Elephant (in Play School Stories) P. Gibson (BBC)
Can I help Dad? S. Grindley (Simon and Schuster)
Helpful Hattie J. Quin-Harkin (Methuen)
Jayne's Helping Day (in Story Time Two) P. Kremer (Magnet)

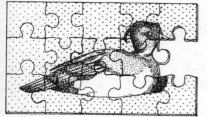

CO-OPERATION

AIM

To develop an understanding of the meaning of the word 'co-operation' and to show how it can be applied in daily life.

STARTING POINT

◎ Stick a large picture onto some stiff card and cut it up into four or five large pieces like a simple puzzle. Ask four or five members of the audience to each choose a piece of puzzle without looking beforehand. Suggest that each child adds his or her piece to the puzzle to make a complete picture. After each child has added one more piece, see if the audience can predict what the picture is going to be.

Discuss   Discuss the above activity with the audience, reminding them how difficult it was to recognise the picture with only one piece, that it became easier with several pieces but that it was only with all of the pieces in place that the complete picture could be fully appreciated.

Compare this to an aspect of the children's lives. For example, school is a place where lots of different people depend on each other with each representing an important piece of the puzzle. Could the head teacher work as efficiently without the secretary or the pupils work without food supplied by the cooks? Introduce the word 'co-operation' and explain that it means working together for everybody's benefit.

CORE ACTIVITIES

◎ Enlist a volunteer from the audience and show them an object which you intend hiding somewhere in the room. Suggest that the child waits outside whilst the audience helps you to find a suitable hiding place. Invite the child to return to look for the object. Ask another child in the audience to clap loudly when the first child is close to the object and softly when far away. Encourage the first child to listen to the clapping for guidance. This activity could be repeated two or three times with other volunteers and it could be extended by asking a whole class or even the whole school to clap together. Emphasise that the guidance provided by a child, a class or the whole school, involves co-operation.

◎ Singing 'rounds' successfully also demands tremendous co-operation on the part of those involved. Use one of the popular 'rounds' such as *London's Burning* and *Pease Pudding Hot* or teach a new one with words which reinforce the 'working together' theme. The song book *Flying A Round* (see page 125 for details) contains many examples of 'rounds', some of which are particularly appropriate e.g. *Let us endeavour, Sing sing together* and *Let us sing together*. What happens when someone forgets which part of the 'round' they are singing?

▣ Prepare a group of children to develop a sequence of mime or dance movements to accompany the reading of the story *The Great Big Enormous Turnip* by A. Tolstoy (see pages 123 and 125 for details). After the performance, discuss the story with the audience emphasizing that everybody needed to help in order to pull the turnip up. But what would have happened if they had all decided not to co-operate? Arrange for each character in the story to leave the line of people trying to pull up the turnip, making an excuse for not being able to continue. For example, the following reasons might be given:

Old man	(going to sit down) I'm tired and I need a rest.
Old woman	(moving to the opposite side of the turnip) I want to pull on the other side of the turnip.
Boy	I'm fed up with this, it's boring.
Girl	I want to go and watch the television now.
Cat and Dog	(arguing with each other) You keep pulling my tail. No, I don't. Yes you do. etc.
Mouse	Why should I bother to help? I don't even like turnip anyway!

Ask the audience whether they think the turnip would have been successfully pulled up under these circumstances? What would have happened if only one of them had decided not to help? Highlight the fact that the turnip could only be pulled up with every single character working together.

◉ Organise a small group to demonstrate some simple country dancing. The Pat-a-cake Polka is probably one of the easiest for infants.

Form a circle with your partner on your left. Skip 8 steps to the left then 8 steps to the right. Face your partner. Clap your hands 3 times quickly and then clap your partner's hands 3 times quickly. Hold hands and skip round to a count of 8, reform the circle and repeat.

Alternatively, make up your own dance to suit the abilities of your pupils. For example:

Form a circle with your partner on your left. Skip 8 steps to the left. Clap your hands 4 times. Skip 8 steps to the right. Clap your knees 4 times. Partner claps whilst you skip round her/him 8 steps.

After the dancing has finished, discuss the difficulties of performing even a simple dance and how it demands a high level of concentration from everybody. Ask the group to repeat part of the dance but with some deliberate and disastrous mistakes in it! Can the audience spot what mistakes were made and by whom? Emphasize the importance of everyone remembering to dance their part correctly.

◉ Many goods require several people to undertake different parts of the process e.g. bread making, car manufacture, postal service, etc. Explore one of these chains and explain how each person is dependent upon all the others in the chain to carry out their part of the process efficiently. If possible, organise a visit to a small local factory and prepare a group of children to draw pictures of the various stages of manufacture. Ask them to hold up their pictures in the assembly and briefly explain what is happening. What would be the result if one person in the process decided not to complete their particular task? (The poem *The Chain* by Elizabeth Lindsay on page 57 might prove a useful way of reinforcing or introducing this idea.)

CONCLUSION—WHAT CAN WE DO?

● Try to find more opportunities to co-operate with people in our daily lives.

● Try to be more concious of whether we are working *with* the people around us rather than *against* them.

Working Together

When two work together,
It's better than one,
Much more exciting,
Much more fun.

When one tries 'hide and seek' alone,
It's impossible to play.
Only two can really enjoy it;
One to search and one to hide away.

When one prepares a meal,
It's slow and seems a bore.
But with two cooking together,
It's no longer a chore.

When one lifts a heavy box,
You puff and strain your back.
But if two heave together,
It's no trouble to stack.

When one solves a problem,
Ideas don't always flow.
Two brains can spark each other,
So many answers grow.

When two work together,
It's better than one,
Much more exciting,
Much more fun.

ALTERNATIVE ACTIVITIES

◎ Keep a diary for a week noting down the occasions in the classroom where co-operation was occurring and those where self interest and conflict prevailed. Discuss these examples with the audience and ask them to say which ones involved co-operation and which ones did not. Encourage them to keep a similar diary over the next week and report back in another assembly.

◎ Playing musical instruments in a group can involve a tremendous amount of co-operation. Play a record of some music which involves several instruments. Can the audience name the instruments involved and indicate when more than one instrument was playing together? Devise an activity using percussion instruments which illustrates this. For example, volunteers from the audience could be given different percussion instruments which they have to play one after the other. Suggest each child plays three beats before the next child plays his/her instrument. Once the volunteers can manage this without problems, suggest a signal upon which they all have to play together. Repeat the above activity but include the signal at random. How easy is it to get everyone working together, taking turns and then playing altogether?

◎ Ask a member of the audience to try to move a large piece of PE apparatus. Can they suggest how to make moving the apparatus easier? Hopefully, they will realise that they need someone else to help. Ask for one or two more volunteers so that the piece of equipment can be moved easily.

▣ Play team games in a less competitive manner. Either prepare a group beforehand or select a small group of children from the audience. Instead of competing against each other, use a sand clock or stop watch to emphasize working together to improve their timing rather than 'beating' the other team. Attempt some co-operative games where the emphasis is on everyone helping each other. Either prepare a group beforehand or select a small group from the audience to teach. After the games, discuss how easy or difficult it was to co-operate in each game. Some examples of these games are given on page 125.

Sharing the Sticklebricks

The Great Big Enormous Turnip

The following suggestions are included as an example of how the above story can be accompanied by mime and movements. Teachers will obviously wish to adapt the story and movement suggestions to suit their own particular pupils. The story could be read by the teacher or a child.

Story

Once upon a time a little old man wanted to grow a turnip. Before he could plant the seed, he had to dig the soil . . .

and break up all the big lumps with a rake.

He took the tiny seed out of his pocket, pushed it into the soil and covered it over.

Movement suggestions

Strong digging movements with imaginary spade.

Strong pushing/pulling movements with rake.

Mime planting seed.

The rain fell gently all over the soil.

Quick running on tiptoe from space to space, fingers indicating the fall of rain, high to low.

The big round Sun shone.

Large round body shape, slowly spinning on spot.

Slowly, the tiny seed began to grow, putting out a little shoot which pushed upwards towards the sky. The root began to swell and swell until it was an enormous turnip.

Start in curled crouched position, slowly grow upwards, using fingers/hands to indicate upward movement of shoot/leaves. Use arms/body to indicate swelling of turnip. Hold shape.

The little old man tried to pull he turnip up. He pulled at the top . . . he pulled at the bottom . . . he pushed at the top . . . he pushed at the bottom . . . but the turnip was just too big!*

Push/pull high/low as appropriate.

(*This section could be repeated after each of the following characters.)

He called to the little old woman 'Come and help, little old woman!' and she hobbled stiffly towards him.

Encourge audience to join in call. Old woman with bent back, spiky fingers/elbows, knobbly knees. Slow, shuffling walk.

*

The little old man called to the boy 'Come and help, little boy' and the boy skipped happily over to the old man.

All call for boy. Boy skips over to join line.

*

Then the little old man called to the girl. 'Come and help, little girl.' So the girl skips happily over to help pull.

All call for girl. Girl skips over to join line.

*

Next the little old man called to the dog 'Come and help, naughty dog.' The dog was busy chewing a stick but when the old man called, he leapt up and bounded towards him, with his tail wagging.

All call dog. Long, low shape, using hands as paws to hold stick, leap up into dog shape, move on all fours, wagging tail, stopping to sniff ground, barking etc.

*

Then the little old man called to the cat 'Come and help, lazy cat!' The fat black cat was asleep and didn't really want to help. Slowly, she uncurled, stretched each paw and padded silently over to help.

All call cat. Start curled up on floor, slowly stretch each limb into cat shape on all fours. Move with slow, stretched steps.

*

Lastly, the little old man called the mouse 'Come and help, tiny mouse!' The furry mouse was eager to help and scurried quickly to help them all pull.

All call mouse. Hold hands high as paws, move with small, quick tiptoe steps, pausing to twitch whiskers.

Altogether they pulled and pulled as hard as they could when suddenly . . . POP! . . . up came the turnip!

All hold on to each other's waists, pretend to pull, clap hands for 'pop' and fall over.

(The above activity is based on ideas which were first published in *Child Education*, February 1990)

Co-operative Games

The following two books contain some splendid ideas for co-operative games and are highly recommended. Some of the ideas from each book have been briefly outlined below.

The Co-operative Sports and Games Book by T. Orlick, published by the Writers and Readers Publishing Co-operative.

Big snake game. The children work in pairs, stretched out on their stomachs to form a snake by holding on to the ankles of the partner. The snake then has to slither along, under or over obstacles, without breaking or letting go of each other. This activity could be extended by asking the children to repeat the activity in a four or eight person snake.

Co-operative musical hoops. Hoops are placed on the floor, one for each child. Whilst the music is played, the children skip round the hoops but when the music stops, they all have to stand in a hoop. Gradually, remove the hoops but instead of eliminating those without a hoop, encourage them to work together to get as many children into one hoop as possible.

Balloon game. The children work in pairs trying to hold a balloon between them without using their hands i.e. head to head, back to back, etc. Once they can manage to hold the balloon between them, ask them to walk along a set path, around obstacles or over a bench etc.

Games for all children by P. Heseltine, published by Basil Blackwell. This book contains some good ideas for team games where the emphasis is on fun and enjoyment rather than winning. Sand clocks or stop watches could be used to encourage an improvement in performance and to reduce the competitive element.

Over and under ball relay. The whole team stands in a line with legs apart. The first child passes a ball backwards over his or her head and this is then repeated to the end of the line. The last child crawls with the ball through the legs of the whole team to the front. The activity is repeated until the whole team return to their original positions.

Fancy dress game. The first child in the team runs to a box of dressing up clothes, puts them all on and runs back to the team. The first and second child then work co-operatively, taking the clothes off the first child and putting them onto the second. The second child then runs to the box and takes the clothes off. The activity is then repeated in pairs by the rest of the team. It is wise to restrict the number of clothes to, for example, a hat, coat, belt and gloves.

One finger can't catch flea

in *Say it Again Granny*, by John Agard, Bodley Head

One finger can wiggle
One finger can tickle
But have you ever seen
a one-finger snap?

One hand can wave
One hand can flap
But have you ever seen
a one-hand clap?

One finger can pat a cat
One finger can stroke a dog
But I'm sure you'll agree
with my Granny
that one finger can't ketch [sic] flea.

So let's work together, you and me,
like two hands from one body.

Re-read the poem, stopping after each verse and asking the audience to try out all the actions. Which ones can be achieved with one hand or finger and which ones cannot? Can the audience suggest other activities where only one hand or one finger is needed? Can they suggest activities where two hands or two fingers are essential? Which activities need two people to work together 'like two hands from one body'. For example, playing a board game, using a see saw or lifting a PE bench.

RESOURCES

Poems

The Runners Please Mrs Butler (Puffin)
Canoe Story Poetry World 2 (Bell and Hyman)

Songs

We must Learn Mrs Macaroni (Macmillan Educational)
All Work Together Granny's Yard (Bell and Hyman)
You'll Sing a Song and I'll Sing a Song Tinderbox Song Book (A and C Black)
The Enormous Turnip Sing a Song 1 (Nelson)
The Ink is Black Someone's Singing, Lord (A and C Black)
The Building Song Alleluya (A and C Black)

Stories

The Great Big Enormous Turnip A. Tolstoy (Picture Lions)
Grandfather J. Baker (Andre Deutsch)
Children of the Yangtze River O. S. Svend (Pelham Books)
Sharing, it's Mine A. G. de Lynam (Hutchinson)
Bet You Can't! P. Dale (Walker Books)

COMPROMISES

AIM

To increase awareness of compromise as a possible solution to conflict.
To develop a sense of 'fairness'.

STARTING POINT

◎ Read a story in which two characters are involved in a conflict where a compromise could have solved the problem. *The Owl and The Woodpecker* by Brian Wildsmith (see page 130 for details) illustrates such circumstances extremely well. The owl wants to sleep during the day but is prevented from doing so by the noise of the woodpecker working. Neither are willing to give in to the other.

Discuss What problem did the owl and the woodpecker have? What alternatives are suggested in the story to resolve the problem? Can the audience suggest any other solutions? How is their dispute eventually settled? With the help of the audience, define the word 'compromise', finding a solution which will suit all the parties concerned and which may involve both sides making concessions.

CORE ACTIVITIES

◎ Describe a series of common areas of conflict in which a third party proposes a solution. Ask the audience to judge whether the solution which is suggested is 'fair' or not? Examples of such circumstances are given on page 128.

◎ Sharing is often a good compromise to many arguments. Ask two volunteers from the audience to decide how to share a series of items. Such as 10 bricks, 5 cakes, 1 toy car and 1 bike. Encourage the audience to suggest ways of sharing the items fairly.

▣ At school, children quickly have to learn that they cannot always have exactly what they want and many compromises have to be made. Ask a small group of children to think of examples to demonstrate arguments which arise because children are determined to have their own way. Arrange for them to role play some of these situations during the assembly. The following examples might prove helpful.

1 Two children go out to play and find a skipping rope. They argue about who is going to play with the rope.

2 A group of children are queuing up to go to assembly. Two children are fighting at the front because they both want to be first.

3 Two children are playing with some bricks. The first child complains bitterly that the second child has most of the bricks.

Repeat all of the role plays but stop after each one and ask the audience to suggest a fair solution to the situation. Have any of them recently experienced a similar problem and how was it resolved?

▣ Organise a group of children to write stories which involve a conflict which is settled by a compromise. Relationships with neighbours sometimes give rise to conflict situations e.g. children playing too noisily, a dog digging up a neighbour's favourite plants. Encourage the children to write their story about a problem involving a neighbour. Select one or two children to read out their story during assembly. Can the audience remember how each conflict was resolved? What other solutions would they have suggested?

▣ Read the poem *But that's not fair* on page 127. If possible, arrange beforehand for two children to recite the parts of the children in each verse and mime appropriate actions. Discuss each verse with the audience and ask them to suggest a compromise for each argument. Have members of the audience experienced similar situations recently? How did they solve the disagreement?

CONCLUSION—WHAT CAN WE DO?

• When faced with a disagreement with someone, try to stop and think of a fair solution, acceptable to both parties.

• When a solution to an argument is imposed by a third party, try to be objective and see if their answer really is the best compromise.

But that's not fair

Emma grabbed the paints
frowning furiously at John.
'They're mine!
Go away!
I want them all to myself!'

'But that's not fair!
Surely we can share?'

Steven snatched the swing
glaring hotly at James.
'It's mine!
Go away!
I was here first!'

'But that's not fair!
Surely we can share?'

Susan clutched the cake
eyes smouldering at Ann.
'It's mine!
Go away!
It's the only one left!'

'But that's not fair!
Surely we can share?'

ALTERNATIVE ACTIVITIES

◎ Read the poem *Bedtime* by Eleanor Farjeon (see page 130 for details) which deals with a common area of conflict between parent and child. Initially, ask the audience to identify with the child. How do they react when they are in the middle of a game, halfway through reading a book or just about to finish building a castle when a parent declares it is bedtime? How do they feel if their parent insists on them stopping halfway through an activity? Then ask the audience to empathize with the parent. Why do they want the child to go to bed at that precise moment? How do they feel if the child makes a fuss? Can the audience suggest solutions to this common problem which would suit both parent and child?

◎ There are many occasions in school which involve choosing from a group of people. Children are often asked to choose a partner or a teacher has to choose one or two children from a class to take part in an enjoyable activity. It is important for everyone to feel the methods used for choosing are 'fair'. Discuss ways of making these choices and draw up two lists, one labelled 'fair' and one 'unfair'. Their suggestions might include:

It is *unfair* to choose:

• Your best friend

• The child who has finished his/her work first

• The child who gets all the answers to schoolwork correct

• The child who is outgoing and extrovert

• By gender, e.g. all the boys

• By age

It is *fair* to choose:

• By drawing up a rota

• By tossing a coin

• By drawing lots

• By using playground rhymes e.g. one potato, two potato . . .

▣ Organise a group of children to make a tape recording of common situations where disputes arise. These could occur at school, home, with friends, on the bus or in a shop. Suggest that a different person intervenes to settle the argument each time. For instance a dinner lady, the headteacher, an older brother, a parent, another adult, etc. Ask the audience to listen carefully to the recording, describe each situation and identify the person intervening. With the help of the children, compile a list of people who are called upon to resolve disputes. In each case, discuss whether it was really necessary for a third party to arbitrate. Help the audience realise that they are often quite capable of finding their own fair solutions to disputes.

▣ Conflict often escalates out of all proportion to the original problem because each party continues to retaliate, each trying to 'win' over the other. It is particularly difficult for young children to realise that this is happening and to make a conscious effort to stop it. However, it may be possible to raise their awareness through stories. For example, read *The Two Giants* by Michael Foreman (see page 130 for details) and then ask the audience to try to pinpoint exactly when the argument started to escalate. In the story, two giants called Boris and Sam find a small shell on the beach which they each want to have. Their disagreement escalates from hurling words, pebbles and then rocks at each other. Finally, they charge at each other with clubs whirling above their heads. Fortunately, before any harm can be done, they realise how ridiculously they are behaving and that they have even forgotten the original cause of their argument. Discuss when would have been the best moment for the giants to stop their argument and try to settle their dispute amicably. What solutions to their conflict were open to them? For instance, they could have thrown the shell back into the sea, taken turns to wear it, cut it in half or tried to find another similar one.

Is it fair?

The following descriptions are examples of familiar situations where a third party suggests a solution to a conflict. The audience should be encouraged to decide whether they feel the solution is a fair one or not. In each case, ask the audience to try to empathise with each of the characters involved. What would they suggest as a fair solution if they were the arbitrator? How would they feel if they thought the suggested solution was unfair? Obviously, the examples below may need to be modified or additional examples devised in order to make the situations relevant to the pupils in a particular school.

1 John has four apples and Sarah has eight plums. John would like some of the plums and Sarah would like some apples. They agree to swap but argue over how best to do it. Sarah wants to give one plum in exchange for one apple but John feels that is unfair because his apples are larger than the plums. Dad is fed up with them squabbling and takes all the apples and plums away, leaving them both with nothing. Is this fair? Is there a more acceptable solution?

2 A lot of food and empty crisp packets etc. have been dropped accidentally under the dinner table at school. Sam is the last one eating at the table and the dinner lady asks him to sweep up the mess with a dustpan and brush. He refuses saying that he didn't drop anything at all on the floor and that it was all done by someone else.

A teacher hears the argument and tells Sam to sweep up the mess as the dinner lady had requested. Is this fair? What other solutions are possible?

3 Mum is trying to watch the news on the television but her son, Daniel, wants her to stop watching and play a game with him straight away. Mum becomes angry because Daniel keeps pestering her constantly so that she cannot hear the television.

Daniel's brother, Dave, suggests that mum plays with Daniel as soon as the news is finished. Is this fair? Are there other solutions?

4 Paul and Emily are building a castle together in the sand. They are very pleased with it and have almost finished when baby sister Jane comes along and kicks it down. Paul and Emily are very upset and start to push baby Jane away.

Dad picks baby Jane up and takes her indoors, screaming and crying. Is this fair? Was there an alternative answer?

Anansi and the Plantains

The following story is about Anansi, a popular character found in many stories from the West Indies. Read the story and then ask the audience to judge whether Anansi had deliberately manipulated the situation so that he had more than his fair share of the plantains (a tropical plant like a banana). Can the pupils suggest a fair solution to the problem? It would probably be useful to have six separate pictures of plantains available to help the children decide on a fair way of sharing them.

Anansi was slightly worried. He had no money and, as he had not worked in his field at all lately, he had nothing to sell at the market. He was wondering how he was going to find food for his wife and children and, even more important, for himself.

His wife, Crooky begged him to find something for the family to eat because there was not a scrap of food left in the house. Anansi promised to go out to work for some food and told his wife not to worry.

As he was not keen to work, Anansi wandered lazily around until it became so hot that he fell asleep under the shade of a large mango tree. When he woke up, the Sun was beginning to go down and as it was cooler, he began to walk home. However, he was in no great hurry because he felt ashamed about not having found any food. His wife and family would certainly be very angry and disappointed with him.

On the way home, he met his old friend Rat who was carrying a large bunch of plantains on his head. 'Hello, Rat. And how are you, my good friend?' asked Anansi.

'I'm very well, thank you,' replied Rat. 'And how are you and your family?'

Anansi groaned and put on a gloomy expression. 'Not very well, I'm afraid, my dear friend,' he moaned. 'I just cannot find anything for my family to eat. I've searched and searched but there's not a yam or plantain in sight. My wife won't be happy when she hears we've only got water again tonight.'

Rat sighed and said, 'Yes, I'm sure it must be awful to have nothing to eat, especially for the poor children.'

Anansi stared hard at the plantains on top of Rat's head, saying nothing. Rat shuffled uncomfortably and then took the bunch from his head. Anansi continued to stare at the plantains on the ground and eventually said 'What a marvellous bunch of plantains, dear Rat. Where on earth did you find those?'

'They are the very last bunch from my field and I'm afraid they've got to last my family a very long time,' replied Rat with embarrassment.

'But couldn't you even spare one or two of the plantains just for the children?' pleaded Anansi. 'They won't live long on water alone.'

Sharing

'Oh, alright then,' replied Rat rather awkwardly and he gave Anansi the six smallest plantains in the bunch.

'Thank you very much, Rat. How very kind you are,' replied Anansi sweetly. 'But I think you have made a mistake, dear friend. There are not enough plantains for all of us here. How can I share six plantains when there are four people in my family—my wife, two children and myself? It will be very difficult. There will be a lot of arguments.'

But Rat ignored him, put the bunch of plantains back onto his head and walked away saying 'Good-bye, Anansi.'

When at last Anansi arrived home, he gave the six plantains to his wife and asked her to cook them. When they were ready, he gave two to his daughter, two to his son, and two to his wife. Then he sat down glumly with nothing on the plate in front of him. 'But don't you want a plantain?' asked his wife in surprise.

'No,' sighed Anansi. 'There's not enough for me too. You go ahead and enjoy them.'

'But aren't you hungry?' asked his daughter anxiously.

'Yes, very hungry, my dear,' replied Anansi. 'But I'd rather go hungry myself than let you starve.'

'That's not fair,' they all protested and they each gave Anansi one of their plantains. So, in the end, he had three plantains—one from his wife, one from his son and one from his daughter.

Adapted from a story in *Anansi and the Spiderman* by P. M. Sherlock, Macmillan

If you don't have horse, then ride cow

by John Agard, in *Say it Again, Granny*, Bodley Head

No biscuit!
No biscuit!

What to do?

Forget biscuit
and try some of Granny homemade bread.

No red paint!
No red paint!

What to do?

Forget red paint
and make do with blue.

Granny always telling you.

'Try the best with what you have right now,
If you don't have horse, then ride cow.'

What does Granny suggest the child does when there are no biscuits? What does she suggest when there is no red paint? Is this good advice? What does the last line of the poem mean? Has anyone in the audience recently had a similar experience? How did they respond?

RESOURCES

Poems

Bedtime Is a Caterpillar Ticklish? (Young Puffin)
You were Mother Last Time A Very First Poetry Book (OUP)
Groan Ups Gargling with Jelly (Puffin)
Swops Please Mrs Butler (Puffin)
Picking Teams Please Mrs Butler (Puffin)
Colin Please Mrs Butler (Puffin)
Sister Another First Poetry Book (OUP)
Grudges Another Second Poetry Book (OUP)

Songs

Points of View Every Colour Under the Sun (Ward Lock Educational)

Stories

The Owl and the Woodpecker B. Wildsmith (Oxford)
One Eighth of a Muffin R. Orbach (Jonathan Cape)
Waiting my Turn K. Erickson (Orchard Books)
Sharing: It's Mine A. Garcia de Lynam (Hutchinson)
It's Mine L. Leonni (Andersen Press)
The Sharing Story K. Erickson (Methuen)
The Two Giants M. Foreman (Hodder and Stoughton)
It's not Fair! A. Harper/S. Hellard (Picture Puffin)

LAZINESS

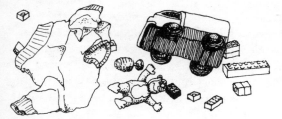

AIM
▫▢▢▣

To develop an awareness of the occasions when we are being lazy and to promote a more positive attitude.

STARTING POINT

◎ Use a dialogue with a glove puppet as a means of introducing an example of lazy behaviour. Introduce the glove puppet (which could be manipulated by yourself or a child) to the audience as someone who is going to help you complete a simple task e.g. tidy up toys, lay the table or make a pretend cup of coffee. Although you ask the glove puppet character to co-operate, by passing the table mats and pouring in the milk, the puppet avoids helping, giving weak excuses for his/her lazy behaviour such as 'I'm too tired', 'I can't reach', 'I want to go and play'.

Discuss Does the puppet help with the task at all? Who does all or most of the work? Are the puppet's excuses for not helping plausible or not? How could the audience describe the puppet's behaviour? Explain that everyone is lazy sometimes and give an example of your own lazy behaviour.

CORE ACTIVITIES

◎ Prepare a group of children to develop a short play based on the occasions when pupils are lazy at school. One child could assume the role of the teacher and the others could pretend to be the pupils. An example of a play devised by a group of top infants is included on page 133. After the performance, discuss the 'lazy' attitudes adopted by the pupils in the play.

Do the audience recognise any of these situations? Have they ever deliberately chosen the easiest or shortest piece of work or copied someone else? What are the disadvantages to adopting these strategies? Who does it eventually harm most? Is the teacher as lazy as the pupils when he/she passes all the pupils on to someone else? Can the audience suggest alternative courses of action which the teacher could have adopted?

◎ Display large pictures of Mr Lazy and Little Miss Helpful (see page 134 for details). Explain who these characters are and that their names reflect their behaviour. Have a selection of cards available with phrases written on them illustrating the different behaviour of each character. The phrases could include dropping litter, throwing a coat on the floor, tidying up the books or helping to carry something. Volunteers could be asked to choose a card, read it to the audience (with help, if necessary) and then pin it onto the picture of the appropriate character.

◎ Sometimes people regret their lazy behaviour later on in their lives but it is not always possible to reverse the harm caused. A good example of this can be found in Pam Ayres' poem *Oh, I wish I'd looked after me teeth* (see page 134 for details). Teeth cleaning is often regarded by children as a tiresome and rather unimportant task which they sometimes try to avoid with no thought to the long term consequences. Although some of the vocabulary in the poem may need explanation, the sentiments it conveys in a humourous style could be used to encourage the audience to consider the future effects of lazy actions. Can the children give other examples of lazy behaviour which could result in future regrets? For instance, what if they didn't bother to learn to read or write?

▣ Discuss the occasions when the children are lazy at home. Can members of the audience give examples to illustrate these occasions? Use these examples to make a collective poem entitled 'Laziness is . . .' The suggestions might include:

> Laziness is . . . leaving toys scattered all over the floor,
> making my sister fetch my coat,
> refusing to help mum carry the shopping, etc.

Write the poem on a blackboard or sheet of paper and display it as a reminder after the assembly.

CONCLUSION—WHAT CAN WE DO?

- Be more aware of the occasions when we are being lazy.

- Think about whether we will regret our laziness in the future.

- Always try to put as much effort as possible into our lives.

Mr Lazybones

Who leaves the top off the toothpaste?
Sticky fingermarks on the phone?
Who refuses to lend a hand?
Why—it's Mr Lazybones!

Who drops litter on the pavement
And pretends it was his friend, Ben?
Who treads carelessly on a book?
Mr Lazybones again!

Who won't help to tidy the toys
And ignores the sock on the floor?
Who is the last to volunteer?
Mr Lazybones, once more!

But—who needs help with his buttons?
Often pleads for someone to play?
Who wants a special birthday toy?
Mr Lazybones, did you say?

ALTERNATIVE ACTIVITIES

◎ Read the story *The Lazy Bear* by Brian Wildsmith (see page 133 for details). Enlist the help of a group of children to devise a suitable visual aid to support the telling of the story. Much of the story revolves around the trolley going up and down the hill. Can the children devise a picture in which the trolley can be moved up and down a hill?

▣ Arrange for a group of children to show the audience an example of a piece of work where they tried to produce their very best. The examples need not be absolutely perfect as the emphasis is more on effort than attainment. Also, the work need not only be of an academic nature but could include a painting, a model built with Lego, a sequence of beads on a thread, a box of equipment which had been tidied, etc. Encourage the children to express the satisfaction which they achieved from putting a great deal of effort into a task.

▣ Ask a group of children to write a story entitled 'The Laziest Child in the School'. Encourage them not only to describe the lazy behaviour of the child, but also to describe the reactions of other people and the consequences of his/her actions. Does something happen to make the lazy child amend his/her behaviour? Suggest that one or two children read out their stories during assembly and discuss them with the audience.

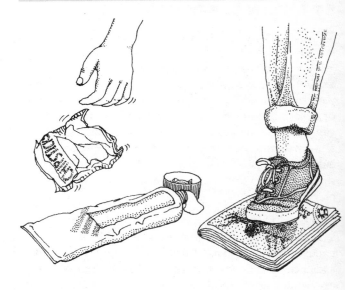

I'm Really Not Lazy

by Arnold Spilka, in *Pudmuddle Jump In*, Magnet

I'm really not lazy—
I'm not!
I'm not!
It's just that I'm thinking
And thinking
And thinking
A lot!
It's true I don't work
But I can't!
I just can't!
When I'm thinking
And thinking
And thinking
A lot!

Does the audience think the poet is really lazy or justified in denying it? Is it possible to work and think at the same time? Can the audience give examples of occasions where they need to think before working?

Laziness at School

The following play was devised by a group of top infants and is included as an example. Teachers will, no doubt, wish to help their pupils develop a play which reflects their own experiences.

Characters Teacher
Pupil 1
Pupil 2
Pupil 3
Pupil 4
Pupil 5
Pupil 6

Teacher (Blows whistle) Come in and sit down children. Carry on with your work please.

(Children file in and continue working at various activities)

Pupil 1 I'm fed up with this Lego. I think I'll go and do a puzzle. (Goes off and leaves Lego on floor)

Teacher Why have you left all this Lego on the floor? You can't expect other people to always tidy up after you! If you can't tidy up, then you can't play at all! Go and stand in the corner!

(Pupil 1 goes reluctantly to a corner)

Pupil 2 (Scribbling whilst colouring her picture) I'm going to colour this quickly so I can go and play with the sand.

Teacher What dreadful colouring! You had better go back to the reception class to learn how to colour properly.

(Pupil 2 leaves the room)

Pupil 3 I can't think of anything else to write in my story. I know, I'll make my writing huge so it fills up the page quickly. (Writing largely)

Teacher This story is very short and what's this large writing at the end? I know what you are doing. Go to the library and work on your own until you can write a better story.

(Pupil 3 leaves the room)

Pupil 4 (Sorting through workcards) I wonder where the shortest workcard is?

Teacher I heard you trying to find the workcard with not much work on it. Go and explain your behaviour to the headteacher.

(Pupil 4 leaves the room)

Pupil 5 (Copying the child next to him) I can't be bothered to do these maths questions so I'll copy Robert.

Teacher (Looking at both books) What's this? All the same questions wrong. Who's been copying?

(Pupils 5 and 6 both protest innocence)

Teacher Well, I think you had both better go to the headteacher straight away!

(Pupils 5 and 6 leave room)

Teacher (Looking around) That's good, no more children to teach. I think I'll sit down and have a rest!

The Lazy Bear

by Brian Wildsmith, Oxford University Press

Once upon a time, there was a bear who was so kind and thoughtful that all his neighbours were his friends. The bear liked to go for long walks, and one day, at the top of a hill, he found a trolley. It had been left there by the wood-cutter. The bear had never seen a trolley before, and he walked all round it, and sniffed it, and at last sat in it. To his surprise the trolley began to move. As it rolled downhill, the bear felt rather frightened. But, by the time it reached the bottom, he was enjoying the ride.

He liked it so much that he straightaway pushed the trolley back up the hill, and rode down again. Time after time he pushed the trolley up the hill and rode down at great speed.

'This is fun,' he thought. 'But I don't like having to push the trolley up the hill much.'

Every day he rode the trolley from morning till night, but the more he enjoyed the rides, the more he hated the hard work of pushing the trolley uphill.

Then he had an idea. He went to look for his friend the racoon. He told him all about the trolley, and the wonderful rides, and invited the racoon to come and see for himself.

The racoon was naturally curious, so he went along with the bear. On the way, they met the deer.

'Come with us,' said the bear, 'and have a ride in my trolley.'

The deer was naturally curious, so he went along with the bear and the racoon. On the way, they met the goat.

'Come with us,' said the bear, 'and have a ride in my trolley.'

The goat was naturally curious, so he went along with the bear, the racoon and the deer. In a short time they were all riding down the hill at a wonderful speed.

'This is lovely,' said the racoon.

'This is marvellous,' said the deer.

'Great, just great!' said the goat.

At the bottom, they all got out—except the bear, who sat tight.

'Hey! Come and help push,' cried the racoon, the deer and the goat.

'What, me?' said the bear. 'If I let you ride in my trolley, the least you can do is to push me back up the hill, don't you think?'

And he looked so fierce, that his friends were too frightened to argue. So they all went on riding downhill, and the racoon, the deer and the goat went on pushing the bear back to the top.

'What shall we do?' they whispered to each other. 'This is very tiring, but if we give up, the bear will get us. He's not his usual kind self at all.'

Then, when they were pushing the bear uphill for the hundredth time, the goat had an idea.

'Listen,' he whispered, urgently. 'I know what we'll do.' The others leant their heads towards him and listened to his plan. The bear was busy enjoying the scenery and noticed nothing—until they reached the top of the hill. Then—'Right!' shouted the goat. 'Over the top with him.' And the trolley, with the bear in it, went hurtling down the other side of the hill. Faster and faster sped the trolley, until it crashed at the bottom. The bear was flung out, head over heels, and landed right side up in a shallow pond.

But, worst of all, when he looked round, he saw all the other animals of the forest standing on the bank, and laughing at him. 'It serves you right,' they said. 'It was very unkind of you to bully your friends like that.'

But they helped him out of the pond, and set the trolley to rights for him. 'Now you must push the racoon, the deer and the goat uphill,' they said. 'Then you will know how they felt, having to push a great, heavy animal, like you.'

So the bear pushed his friends up the hill, not once, but many times, and each time he understood a little more how badly he had behaved. At last, he said, 'I am truly sorry for what I did, and I won't do it ever again.' At that, the racoon, the deer and the goat invited the bear to climb into the trolley, and they all rode downhill at a glorious pace. And at the bottom, they all got out and pushed the trolley back again, together.

RESOURCES

Poems

Oh, I Wish I'd Looked After me Teeth I Like This Poem (Puffin Books)
Lazy Lazy Rhyme Time 2 (Beaver Books)
Lazy Mary Over and Over Again (Beaver Books)
Juster and Waiter A Second Poetry Book (OUP)
Games are Never so Much Fun A Child's Book of Manners (Picture Puffin)
Lazy All together now (Viking Kestrel)

Songs

So Here Hath Been Dawning Another Blue Day With Cheerful Voice (A and C Black)
Try Again Tinderbox Song Book (A and C Black)
Lazy Katy will you get up The Funny Family (Ward Lock Educational)
On a work day I work Every Colour Under the Sun (Ward Lock Educational)
Such Hard Work Every Colour Under the Sun (Ward Lock Educational)
Do your Best Every Colour Under the Sun (Ward Lock Educational)
Work Calypso Tinderbox Song Book (A and C Black)
Try Again Tinderbox Song Book (A and C Black)
Lazy Coconut Tree Ta ra ra boom de ay (A and C Black)

Stories

The Lazy Rabbit (Children's Leisure Products Ltd)
The Lazy Bear B. Wildsmith (OUP)
Mr Lazy R. Hargreaves (Price Stern Sloan)
Little Miss Helpful R. Hargreaves (Price Stern Sloan)
Lazy Jack T. Ross (Penguin)
The Farmer and his Sons (in Fables of Aesop) V. Biro (Ginn)
Dragwag the Lazy Dragon C. Barber (Macdonald)
The Treeful of Pigs A. Lobel (Hippo)
Rabbit and Elephant (in Topsy Turvy Tales) L. Berg (Magnet)
The Tidying Up of Thomas (in Bad Boys) C. Hough (Young Puffin)
Rabbits Go Riding (in The Anita Hewett Animal Story Book) A. Hewett (Young Puffin)
The Silly Little Hen (in Story Time Two) I. Russell (Magnet)
Lazy Boy S. Hatherley (Macmillan)
The Ass and the Salt (in Aesop's Fables by J. Warrington) Aesop (Dent)

PREJUDICES

AIM

To show that in spite of superficial differences, people share many similarities.
To develop a respect for differences between people.

STARTING POINT

◎ Display three small boxes all the same size; two with bright and attractive wrappers and one covered with plain brown paper or newspaper. Ask individuals in the audience to say which one they would prefer to open and which they think is likely to have the best present in it. Try to determine whether they are being influenced by the attractive paper.

Select three members of the audience to unwrap the boxes. The two attractively wrapped boxes should contain something worthless such as an empty crisp packet or a screwed up newspaper. The box with the plain brown wrapper should contain something exciting such as a new toy or a box of chocolates.

Discuss Explain that appearances can be deceptive and something that looks appealing on the outside is not always as exciting on the inside. Judging the above boxes by their wrappers was not helpful. This is also true of people.

Use the opportunity to reinforce the 'stranger danger' idea. For example, a stranger who smiles, offers sweets and a ride in a car, may not be as nice as he/she appears. Conversely, people who are 'different' in some way should not be dismissed automatically without making any attempt to get to know them.

CORE ACTIVITIES

◎ Choose two children in the audience to stand up, explaining that they have been chosen because they are 'opposite' in some way e.g. tall/short, fair/dark skin, boy/girl, long/short hair, etc. Can the other children identify the 'opposites'? Repeat this for several pairs of children. Then look at each pair of children again, asking the audience to identify any similarities such as both have blue eyes, both wearing a green jumper or both the same age.

◎ Collect pictures of people who are 'different' in some way e.g. in ethnic origin, age, sex, etc. Display each of these pictures covered in a grey sugar paper silhouette. Ask the audience to imagine a world full of 'grey' people, like those on display. How would they respond to a world full of people who looked exactly the same? Remove the silhouettes from the pictures one by one, encouraging the audience to describe each person in turn. Can they highlight the 'differences' between them? Do they prefer a world full of 'grey' replicas or one where people are different? Do they think all the people in the pictures are capable of sharing the same emotions? Are they sometimes sad? Do they all get angry?

◎ Read a story which highlights sexual stereotyping. Both *Oliver Button is a Sissy* by T. de Paolo and *Herbie Dances* by C. van Ernst centre around male characters (a boy in the first example and a hippo in the second) who are teased because they enjoy dancing. Use the story to initiate a discussion about activities which are sometimes thought to be only appropriate for one of the sexes such as dressing up, playing with dolls or playing football. If possible, display toys and ask the audience if they think both boys and girls would want to play with them? Are there girls in the audience who enjoy playing football or boys who like dancing? Is there anything wrong with this? Try to encourage a more 'open' attitude.

CONCLUSION—WHAT CAN WE DO?

● Don't automatically dislike or be afraid of someone who is 'different' in some way but try to make an effort to get to know them.

● Remember that people share the same basic feelings inside however different they may appear on the outside.

● Try not to let our prejudices cloud our judgement so much that we make false assumptions about someone.

Just Like You

I'm not really different
though my eyes can't see.
I can read with my fingers
and listen to TV.

I'm not really different
though my skin is brown.
When my feelings get hurt
my face wears a frown.

I'm not really different
even though I'm a boy.
I like dancing and cooking.
and a doll as a toy.

I'm not really different
though I speak in a strange way.
At home, in my country,
I go to school every day.

We're not really different
We're just like you.
Please be our friend—
There's lots we could do.

ALTERNATIVE ACTIVITIES

◎ Read the fairy tale called *The Frog Prince* by the Brothers Grimm. A simplified and modernised version of the story is included on page 138. Despite his kind behaviour, the princess refuses to be friends with the frog because of his hideous physical appearance. Discuss this attitude with the audience. Should we place more importance on someone's appearance or on their behaviour?

◎ If possible, invite a local representative of a group which helps people with a disability such as the blind, deaf, wheelchair-bound or the mentally handicapped. Better still, find a disabled person who is willing to talk to the children. As well as asking them to describe their particular 'handicap' and how it affects them, ask them to focus on their achievements too. Perhaps they have a hobby or an interesting job which they are enthusiastic about. Also, encourage them to describe other people's responses to them, stressing the positive attitudes and behaviour which they prefer. Try to promote a positive image of handicapped people, accentuating the fact that many have demanding jobs, accomplish tremendous achievements and lead fulfilling lives.

◎ Prejudice can often stem from an illogical fear. Has anyone in the audience ever been afraid of someone because they were 'different' in some way? For example, they might be frightened by people with glasses or beards, people who wear unusual clothes, people who cannot speak English or people of different ethnic origin. Explain that the only way to dispel such fears is by taking time to get to know people.

▣ Help a group of children to prepare a play which illustrates prejudice. The most familiar context for them will probably be when choosing friends in the playground. How do they decide who they are going to play with at playtime? Why do they choose not to play with certain children? Can they devise a play about a child who no one will play with because she/he looks strange? An example devised by a group of top infants is given on page 137.

▣ Read the book *A Country Far Away* by Nigel Gray and Phillippe Dupasquier (see page 139 for details). This story shows that despite the fact that the two children live in different countries, their lives are remarkably similar; both enjoy playing football, both help their parents with chores, etc. Ask a group of children to draw pairs of pictures illustrating the activities which the children share— one picture of the child in the African village and one of the child in this country. During the assembly, the picture pairs could be held up and an explanation given as to how the children's lives are similar.

▣ Organise a group of children to use various mathematical charts to record the 'differences' between the children in one class. These 'differences' could focus on hair, skin or eye colour, height, sex, and favourite classroom activity.

◉ At some time or another, many of us are guilty of making false assumptions about people based on their appearance, sometimes totally misjudging them. Give a group of children the beginning of a story which explores this idea and ask them to continue it. Once again, try to choose a situation and circumstances with which they can relate. For example:

'John had brought his favourite book about dinosaurs to school to put on the class project table. Class 2 were finding out about dinosaurs and his book had some marvellous pictures in it. The next day, John discovered that the book had disappeared from the special project display. 'It's Duncan, Miss,' cried John tearfully. 'He's pinched it. I know it's him. He always pinches things!' The other children all agreed. 'Yes, it's him, Miss. He takes things and hides them!' . . . .

What happens next? Why do all the children pick on Duncan as the culprit? Does he look different in any way? Has he really stolen the book or was it someone else? Has the book just fallen down behind the table or been put on the bookshelf by mistake? Ask one or two of the children to read out their stories during assembly. Discuss the disadvantages of jumping to conclusions too quickly.

◉ Devise an activity which will foster empathy for a particular handicap. For example, to encourage an awareness of what it is like to be blind, ask for two volunteers from the audience. Blindfold the first child and ask the second child to make an unusual shape with their body e.g. crouching with arms extended behind them. Challenge the blindfolded child to make exactly the same body shape by using touch as a means of discovering the second child's body shape.

Alternatively, borrow a wheelchair and ask several children to work in pairs, one to use the wheelchair and one to record the difficulties experienced. Challenge each pair to visit a certain room in the school before the assembly and report back on the problems encountered. Were there awkward steps to negotiate? Did opening and closing doors present any problems? etc. Ask each pair to describe their experiences to the assembly. Can the audience suggest other difficulties which wheelchair-bound people might face when trying to carry out other everyday activities such as shopping or visiting the doctor? How can we help in such situations?

No One will Play with Me

The following play was devised by a group of top infants and is included as an example. Teachers will obviously wish their pupils to devise a play which reflects their own experience.

Characters   Narrator
Ugly child
Girl 1
Girl 2
Boy

Narrator   Once upon a time there was a little girl who was very very ugly. She had strange curly hair and she was nearly as fat as she was tall. Her nose was red and pointed and she had spots all over her face. Every day, she went into the playground to look for somebody to play with. She saw a little girl playing ball and went up to her and said

Ugly child   Please, can I come and play ball with you?

Girl 1   No you can't. I don't like you. You've got funny hair.

Narrator   This made the little girl very sad and she went to look for somebody else to play with. She saw another girl playing with a skipping rope and went up to her and said

Ugly child   Please, can I come and skip with you?

Girl 2   No. You're too fat to skip and anyway, you've got a horrid nose.

Narrator   Again, the little girl turned sadly away and went to look for someone else. She found a boy playing with a toy car. She said

Ugly child   Please, can I play with you and your toy car?

Boy   No. I don't like girls, especially spotty ones.

Narrator   So the little girl didn't have anybody to play with and she became more and more sad. A little while later she heard someone crying and went to see what was the matter.

Girl 1   I've lost my ball and I can't find it anywhere.

Ugly child   Don't worry. I'll help you look for it.

Narrator   Together they searched and found the lost toy. Then someone else started to cry loudly.

Girl 2   I've fallen over and hurt my knee.

Ugly child   Here, use my tissue to stop it bleeding.

Narrator   Then the boy started to cry too.

Boy   I've just remembered. I've left my sandwiches at home and I haven't got anything to eat for dinner.

Ugly child   Don't cry, you can share some of mine.

Narrator   So, one by one, the children realised that the little girl couldn't help being ugly and that it didn't matter anyway because she was kind and helpful. They decided to be friends with her and now they all play happily together.

The Frog Prince

Whilst some teachers may feel it appropriate to read the original story by the Brothers Grimm, others may prefer a more simplified version such as the one given below.

Long, long ago, there lived a king who had a beautiful daughter. Near the king's castle was a large dark forest and in that forest was a well under an old tree. When the day was very warm, the beautiful princess would go out into the forest and sit near the well where she could get a cool drink of water. Often, she would play with a golden ball because that was her favourite toy.

One day, when she was playing, the ball bounced away out of her reach and rolled straight into the well. The princess ran to have a look but the golden ball had disappeared and the well was so deep, she couldn't even see the bottom. She knew that she could never get the ball out and she began to cry.

After she had been crying for a few moments, someone called out to her. 'What's the matter princess? Why are you crying?' She looked round to see where the voice came from and she saw a frog poking its thick ugly head out of the water. 'I am crying for my golden toy which has dropped down the well' she sobbed to the frog. 'Stop crying', answered the frog, 'because I have a way of helping you. But what will you give me in return for bringing your toy up from the well?' 'Anything you wish to have,' she said. 'My best clothes, my pearls and diamonds, even the crown that I am wearing.'

'I do not care for your clothes, your jewellery or your crown but if you will be kind to me and let me be your friend, let me sit by you at your table, eat from your plate and drink from your cup—if you promise me all this, then I will go down and fetch your toy for you.'

'Oh, yes,' replied the princess, 'I promise all you wish if you can return my favourite toy'. But, even though she said this to the frog, she was really thinking that the frog was so horrid and ugly that she would never dream of having him for a friend.

As soon as the frog heard the princess promise, he dived under the water and after a short while, came swimming up again with the ball in his mouth and threw it onto the grass. The princess was so overjoyed when she saw her lovely golden toy again, she picked it up and ran happily away. 'Wait, wait!' shouted the frog. 'Take me with you. I can't run as fast as you'. But she didn't listen to him. She hurried home and promptly forgot all about the poor frog.

The next day, when the princess was seated at the dinner table with the king, someone knocked at the door and cried out 'Princess, open the door for me'. She ran to see who it was but when she saw the frog, she banged the door shut and went to sit down again. The king saw that she was upset and asked, 'What are you afraid of?' 'There's a great big ugly frog outside', she said, 'and he wants to come to see me.' 'But what does he want of you?' asked the king. The princess explained what had happened at the well and the foolish promise she had made. After she had finished the king said 'As you have made a promise, you must keep it. Go and open the door to the frog'.

She opened the door and the frog hopped in following her as far as her chair. There he stopped and said 'Lift me up to the table so that I may eat from your plate'. The princess hesitated, thinking how hideous the frog was but the king ordered her to do so saying angrily 'You should not despise someone who was good enough to help you!' Unwillingly, she gave the frog her plate. When he had finished eating, he said 'Now let me drink from your cup'. Again, the princess hesitated and again the king was angry. 'You should not judge by looks alone. The frog may not look beautiful on the outside but inside he is good and kind. Let him drink!' The princess passed her cup and the frog drank. Suddenly, as he drank the very last drop, he turned into a handsome prince. He told how he had been changed into a frog by a wicked witch and, as you can guess, he and the princess lived happily ever after.

Another version can be found in *Grimms' Fairy Tales* translated by V. Varecha, Cathay Books (Octopus Books Ltd)

Don't Judge by the Wrapper Alone

People are like chocolate bars.
We come in different wrappers.

Some of us are square,
Some of us are round,
Some of us are white,
Some of us are brown.

But—

We all feel happy,
We all feel sad,
We all get excited,
We all get mad!

We may look different on the outside
But we all feel the same within.

Some of us have wrinkles,
Some of us have spots,
Some of us are shiny,
Some of us are not.

But—

We all need friends
and family,
We all need care
and company.

We may look different on the outside
But we all feel the same within.

So—

Don't judge by the wrapper alone.
Peel it off to taste what's inside.

What does the poet think people are like? What words are used to describe us which could also be used to describe sweet wrappers? How are we different? In what ways are we similar? What do the last two lines mean?

RESOURCES

Poems

I'm Afraid of a Man who Looks Strange What are you Scared of? (A and C Black)
Lizzie Poetry Two: A Shooting Star (Blackwell)
The New Girl All Together Now (Viking Kestrel)
There's Nobody Quite Like Me All Together Now (Viking Kestrel)

Songs

Every Colour Under the Sun Every Colour Under the Sun (Ward Lock Educational)
Sing a Song of People Songs from Playschool (BBC)
The Ugly Duckling Seeing and Doing Antholoy of Poems (Methuen)
Use Your Eyes Every Colour Under the Sun (Ward Lock Educational)
Think of a World Without Any flowers (last verse) Someone's Singing, Lord (A and C Black)
The Ink is Black Someone's Singing, Lord (A and C Black)
The Family of Man Come and Praise (BBC)
Hair The Music Box Song Book (BBC)

Stories

A Country Far Away N. Gray and P. Dupasquier (Andersen Press)
The Trouble with Mr Harris D. Armitage (Deutsch)
Daniel Likes Dancing J. and C. Snape (Julia MacRae)
But Martin J. Counsel (Faber)
Some of Us L. Rylands (Dinosaur Publications)
Tusk Tusk D. McKee (Andersen-Hutchinson)
The Elephant with Rosy Coloured Ears B. Resch (A and C Black)
No Two Zebras are the Same Andersson (Lion Publications)
The Little Wood Duck B. Wildsmith (Oxford)
Onito's Hat P. Blakeley and K. Aman (Black)
Oliver Button is a Sissy T. de Paolo (Methuen Magnet)
Long Neck and Thunderfoot M. Foreman (Kestrel Books)
I have a Sister. My Sister is Deaf J. W. Peterson (Harper and Row)
Panda and the Odd Lion M. Foreman (Hamish Hamilton)
The Ugly Duckling S. and S. Corrin (Young Puffin)
The Rabbit with the Sky Blue Ears M. Bolliger (Canongate)
Stay Away from the Junk Yard T. Tusa (Macmillan)
Herbie Dances C. van Ernst (Hutchinson)
The Boy who Couldn't Hear F. Bloom (Bodley Head)
Rachel E. Fanshawe (Bodley Head)
Ben V. Shennan (Bodley Head)
Peter Pig Althea (Dinosaur Publications)
All kinds P. Adams (Childs Play International)
The Trouble with Mum B. Cole (Picture Lions)
Friska the Sheep that was too Small R. Lewis (Macdonald)
The Mice Next Door A. Knowles (Picturemac)
Martin is our Friend E. Hasler and D. Desmarowitz (Methuen)
Cromwell's Glasses H. Keller (Hippo)
Elmer D. McKee (Andersen Press)

Selfishness

AIM
◎◻◎▣

To make the children more conscious of selfish behaviour. To introduce the idea of making 'sacrifices'.

STARTING POINT

◎ Display two simple outlines of people, one with a smiling face and the other with a mean expression. Label the first one unselfish and the second selfish. Have a felt tip pen and sticky labels available. Ask the audience to think of as many words as they can to describe someone who is not selfish, such as kind, considerate or generous. Write each word on a label and ask a child to stick it onto the appropriate picture. Repeat this for a selfish character.

Discuss   Most of us are not totally selfish or totally unselfish but we tend to display characteristics of both in different situations. Can anyone in the audience remember a time recently when they had acted in an unselfish manner? Can anyone recall circumstances where they had been selfish? Which sort of character would most of us prefer to be?

CORE ACTIVITIES

◎ Outline the activities of a famous person whose unselfish attitude has benefited many people. For example, Mother Teresa has helped thousands of underprivileged people in India whilst Bob Geldof has been the catalyst for raising millions of pounds through Band Aid for people living in deprived regions of the world. Both characters have put helping others before their own personal needs.

◎ Use the opportunity to organise a fundraising event where the emphasis is more on the children making a sacrifice in order to help a particular charity. Either organise a whole school or class event such as donating a set period of pocket money or seek out a small number of children who could be sponsored by the others to give up sweets or watching television for a week.

◻ Prepare a group of children to devise sound effects to accompany the reading of the story *The Stamping Elephant* by Anita Hewett (see page 144 for details). One or two children (or the teacher) could read an abbreviated version of the story whilst other children used percussion instruments, their voices or junk materials, to add sound effects to the story.

◻ Read the story *Dogger* by Shirley Hughes (see page 144 for details). Bella willingly sacrifices a newly acquired teddy bear in order to get back her brother's toy dog, Dogger. Organise a group of children to draw several large pictures to illustrate the story and to explain what is happening in each picture. Would anyone in the audience have been able to make the same sacrifice as Bella?

◻ Select a small group of children to write about their most treasured possession—what does it look like, where did they get it from, why do they like it, how would they feel if they had to give it away? Ask one or two of them to read their descriptions during the assembly. Do any of the audience have similar possessions which they would be reluctant to give up even for a very good cause?

CONCLUSION—WHAT CAN WE DO?

● Try to be more aware of the occasions when we are acting in a selfish way.

● Be prepared more often to give something up for someone else.

Is This You?

I want an ice cream from the van!
I want a new toy car!
I want a jumper just like Jim's!
I want! I want! I want!

Give me that red book on the floor!
Give me lots more biscuits!
Give me a bike all of my own!
Give me! Give me! Give me!

Get my tea ready straight away!
Fetch my trousers downstairs!
I will not wait a minute more!
Do it now! Do it now!

You can't have my helicopter!
Leave my teddy alone!
Don't touch my bucket or my spade!
No, it's mine! No, it's mine!

Do you behave in this manner?
Do you say things like this?
Is your head nodding sheepishly?
Is this you? Is this you?

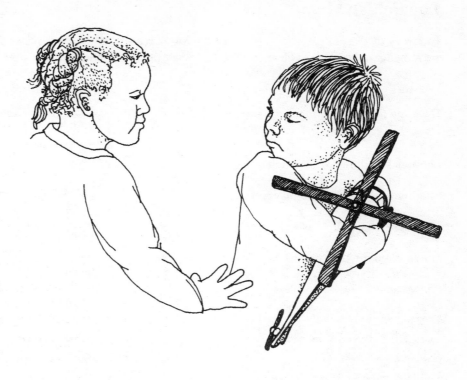

ALTERNATIVE ACTIVITIES

◉ Find a newspaper article (preferably from a local paper) which deals with the unselfish behaviour of one person. For example, a fireman may have rescued someone from a particularly dangerous situation or a child may have been fundraising for a charity. Read or summarise the article to the children, trying to relate the situation to them. How would they feel if someone had saved their lives? Would they be prepared to fundraise for someone else by walking or doing extra household chores?

▣ Read *The Selfish Giant* by Oscar Wilde (see page 144 for details) to a group of children. Develop a series of movements related to the story; suggestions are given on page 142. Can the audience retell the story from the movements performed by the group? Why does the giant not allow the children into his garden? How would the children feel about this? Why does the giant change his mind?

▣ Prepare a group of children to act out the story *The Gift of the Magi* by O. Henry (see page 144 for details). In this story, a husband and wife each make a great sacrifice so as to be able to buy a Christmas present for each other. After the performance, discuss the sarifices made by the couple with the audience. Would they be able to make a similar sacrifice for someone they loved? Can they suggest any sacrifices which their parents make for them? A simplified version of the story, performed by top infants, can be found on page 143.

▣ Arrange for a small group of children to write a story about a person or animal who is very greedy. Read a selection of stories on a similar theme (see page 144 for details) to inspire the children. Why is the character greedy? What effect does his/her greediness have on the other creatures or people around them? Does something happen to make him/her decide to change? Ask one or two children to read out their stories during the assembly. Encourage the audience to think of examples of greediness within their own experience, either at school or at home.

The Selfish Giant

The story of *The Selfish Giant* is very suitable for interpretation through dance. The following are only suggestions for movements and teachers will, no doubt, wish their pupils to generate their own ideas and movements.

The story	Movement suggestions
Trees and flowers growing in the garden.	Start in low curled up position, slowly moving upwards into interesting tree/flower shape.
Sun is shining.	Large round body shape, turning slowly on spot.
Children searching for hole in the wall.	Creeping on tiptoe, follow my leader style, pausing occasionally to search for hole, high and low.
Children enter garden and play games.	Skipping and clapping round in circle. Mime throwing ball across circle.
Giant rushes out and chases children away.	Fast, stamping movements, waving fists, angry faces, in and out of children.
The children run back to the hole in the wall and jump through.	One by one, children run quickly and jump through imaginary wall.
Winter comes. The snow falls . . .	Twisting, swirling snowflake movements, travelling and on spot, high to low.
The cold winds blow . . .	Running on tiptoe, arms indicating force of winds.
Giant sad because spring never returns.	Slow, plodding movements, head and shoulders drooping.
Giant goes to sleep.	Stretching and yawning, slowly curling up to sleep.
Children creep back into garden to play.	Soft creeping on tiptoe, pausing to look for giant, one by one begin to skip happily.
Giant wakes to find spring has returned when the children come to play.	Jumping up suddenly, rubbing eyes.
Giant knocks down wall with children.	Mime using hammer, strong swinging arms, pushing/pulling firmly.
All play happily together.	Skipping and clapping happily, on the spot and travelling.

The Gift of the Magi

Characters   Narrator
Jim
Della
Hairdresser

Narrator   Many years ago, when it was very nearly Christmas, a young man and his wife sat at the breakfast table. Even though Christmas is usually a happy time of the year, they were both feeling very miserable.

Jim   I wish I had enough money to buy you a Christmas present. I've seen some lovely combs that would look very pretty in your long hair.

Della   And I would like to buy you a golden chain for your pocket watch so you could hang it on your waistcoat.

Narrator   They both sighed because they knew their dreams could never come true without any money.

Jim   I'm off to work now, dear. Goodbye.

Narrator   When the husband had gone to work, the wife sat and thought about how she could buy him a present. Suddenly she had a brilliant idea. She put on her her coat and hat and went to the hairdressers.

Della   Please will you cut off my hair and buy it for making wigs?

Hairdresser   Certainly, madam. Please come this way.

The Selfish Giant

Narrator   When she came out of the shop a little while later, her beautiful long hair was gone and she was wearing her hat to hide her short stubbly hair. But now she had enough money so she hurried along to the jewellers and bought the golden chain for her husband's pocket watch.

Della   How pleased Jim will be when he sees this.

Narrator   When her husband came home from work, he stood staring at her strange appearance. He soon realised why she had kept her hat on. Without a word, she gave him his present. He opened the bag and looked inside.

Della   Come on, let's put it on your watch.

Jim   We can't do that. I sold my watch to buy you a present.

Narrator   He gave her the bag and inside were two beautiful combs for her hair.

Della   Oh, no! I have sold my hair to buy you a chain for your watch and you have sold your watch to buy me some combs.

Narrator   Although Della had the combs and no long hair and Jim had a chain but no watch, it was still the happiest Christmas they had ever had. They knew that each had given up something very precious to make the other happy.

Untitled Poem

by Fay Maschler in *A Child's Book of Manners* by Helen Oxenbury and Fay Maschler, Picture Puffin

Little Arty at the party
Ate up every single Smartie.
After that I saw him take
The hugest slice of chocolate cake.

His glass he filled with something fizzy;
Then, keeping Jenny's mother busy,
Asked if he could please take back
That jelly just refused by Jack.

In bed that night his tight pyjamas
Let him know, too much can harm us.
And after all, when some are needy,
Isn't it dreadful to be greedy?

What was Arty doing which demonstrates greedy behaviour? Why is this kind of behaviour being selfish? How can too much harm us? What does the phrase 'some are needy' mean? Can the audience name any groups of 'needy' people? Encourage them to consider others apart from those who are hungry such as the homeless, lonely people, the sick and children without families. If we all behaved like Arty, what sort of world would we live in?

RESOURCES

Poems

Betsy Pud A Very First Poetry Book (OUP)
Sometimes Multi-Poems (Nelson)

Songs

The Selfish Giant Sing a Story (A and C Black)
Don't Bother Me Tinderbox Song Book (A and C Black)
Jesus' Hands Were Kind Hands Come and Sing (Scripture Union)
Poor Child Come and Sing (Scripture Union)

Stories

The Gift of the Magi (in 101 School Assembly Stories) O. Henry (W. Foulsham and Company)
The Selfish Giant O. Wilde (Picture Puffin)
The Stamping Elephant (in Tell me another story) A. Hewett (Young Puffin)
Dogger S. Hughes (Picture Lions)
The Legend of the Blue Bonnet T. de Paola (Methuen)
The Christmas Train I. Gantschev (Viking Kestrel)
My Naughty Little Sister at the Party (in My naughty Little Sister) D. Edwards (Young Puffin)
The Golden Touch (in Stories for 7 Year Olds) S. and S. Corrin (Young Puffin)

Herbert and Harry P. Allen (Hamish Hamilton)
The Bad Tempered Ladybird E. Carle (Hamish Hamilton)
The Turtle and the Monkey P. Galdone (Worlds Work)
John Brown, Rose and the Midnight Cat J. Wagner (Picture Puffin)
Greedy Zebra M. Hadithi (Hodder and Stoughton)
The Miser who Wanted the Sun J. Obrist (Methuen)
The Greedy Python and the Foolish Tortoise E. Carle and R. Buckley (Hodder and Stoughton)
Piggybook A. Browne (Magnet)
Stop Copying Me A. G. de Lynam (Hutchinson)
The Pudding like a Night on the Sea (in The Julian Stories) A. Cameron (Fontana Young Lions)
Bad Boris and the New Kitten S. Jenkin-Pearce (Hutchinson)